Elementary Spanish:

AN AUDIO-LINGUAL APPROACH

By Alan M. Gordon

Of the four language skills—understanding, speaking, reading, and writing—Dr. Gordon believes that understanding and speaking are the most essential in a first-year course. Consequently, the main purpose of this text is to develop the student's ability to give rapid, correct oral responses to aural stimuli—to understand and speak Spanish.

Elementary Spanish has 25 lessons. Each consists of lucid grammatical explanations and intercalated Pattern Drills, and is supplemented by recorded Lab Drills. All the material is carefully coordinated, and can be covered in 25 classroom hours and either 25 or 50 lab hours.

The Pattern Drills in the text provide immediate application of each new grammatical point. The Lab Drills (recorded by *madrileños*) are based exclusively on material already presented in the classroom. These self-correcting drills give the student intensive practice in understanding and speaking Span-

(Continued on Back Flap)

Elementary Spanish

ELEMENTARY SPANISH

An audio-lingual approach

ALAN M. GORDON
University of Toronto

THE MACMILLAN COMPANY, NEW YORK
COLLIER-MACMILLAN LIMITED, LONDON

To the Teacher

This textbook, with its accompanying package of Lab Drills, has one purpose: to develop, through frequent and systematic drill, the student's ability to give rapid, correct responses to aural stimuli. The more fluent the student is in spoken Spanish, the greater the carryover to reading and, eventually, to writing. Since the converse is not true, there are no *lecturas* and no written exercises. Everything is to be done orally. Drill, drill, and drill again, until the responses become automatic. Only by "overlearning" can the student acquire real, lasting fluency.

The 25 lessons in this book can be taught in 25 classroom hours (or in more, of course, if a slower pace is deemed desirable), with an additional one, or preferably two, laboratory periods per lesson, depending on the time available in your own language laboratory. Such flexibility is possible because the Lab Drills for each lesson, printed on loose-leaf sheets and recorded on magnetic tape, are divided into two 15-minute parts, and the second part can be assigned as oral homework if your laboratory time is limited. Ideally, each laboratory period should allow a "working time" of 45 minutes; a working time shorter than 30 minutes is of little use for the purposes of this approach. Thus, each set of Lab Drills can be performed either two or three times. The brief Appendix can be mastered by the student on his own, outside the laboratory.

The package of Lab Drills accompanying this book is to be delivered to you, unopened, by the student. The reason for this somewhat unusual procedure will soon be obvious.

Each lesson in this course consists of three sections:

A. Grammatical Explanations and Intercalated Pattern Drills,
    which appear in the textbook itself.
B. Lab Drills, Part I
C. Lab Drills, Part II

Both Parts I and II are contained in the accompanying package and are recorded on the tapes.

v

SECTION A. GRAMMATICAL EXPLANATIONS AND INTERCALATED PATTERN DRILLS

This first section is designed for the classroom and is the only written Spanish seen by the student before he goes to the laboratory. You should present the new grammar and lead the students' choral performance of the Pattern Drills found after the explanation of each new point. The importance of these drills—of doing them orally and in order—cannot be over-emphasized. The Pattern Drills provide the student with an opportunity to practice and master each point while it is still fresh in his mind. In addition, they are the major source of new vocabulary. After this material has been covered, the remainder of the classroom period can be used to begin the corresponding Lab Drills. You will provide the aural stimuli, and the whole class will give the oral responses.

The student should be told to review the textbook material of each lesson *before* going to the laboratory. This review should be active rather than passive, with the student doing each Pattern Drill *aloud* before proceeding to the explanation of the next point.

SECTION B. LAB DRILLS, PART I

The Lab Drills, Part I, require between 14 and 15 minutes. Except for the instructions, the drills are entirely in Spanish. They are of the self-correcting type, with the format "Stimulus—Student Response—Correct Response—Student Repetition." This section of Lessons 11–23 will end with a brief passage for aural comprehension.

Ideally, the student should *not* see the drills before he has heard and recorded them once. Thus, he will be required to depend on, and develop, his ear. After the student has performed the drills once, the laboratory assistant can distribute the drills in their printed form. With the printed drills in front of him, the student is to perform Part I again. If the laboratory period permits 45 minutes of working time, the student is to record the same drills a third time, with the printed version still available to him.

The student is expected to review Part I *aloud* as "laboratory homework" before returning to the laboratory to perform Part II.

SECTION C. LAB DRILLS, PART II

The Lab Drills, Part II, also require 14–15 minutes and are self-correcting. Again, the student ideally should not receive the drills in printed form before he has heard and recorded them once. A "Pronunciation Review Drill," lasting no more than five minutes, begins Part II of Lessons 1–13.

If a second laboratory period is unavailable, this set of drills can be assigned as oral homework. Or, a portion of Part II, such as the "Pronuncia-tion Review Drill," can be done in the laboratory after the student has recorded Part I for the second or third time. It is not advisable to have the student perform Part I and all of Part II during the same laboratory period.

Although the Lab Drills are primarily a learning device, they are also a convenient method of testing the student's progress. You can grade as many responses as you choose, using the revolution counter on the tape recorder for prompt location of any portion of the tape. Since the student has no way of knowing which responses of his final recording will be marked, he obviously must strive to give every response perfectly.

A simple, rapid grading system that has proved to be an effective teaching device uses only two marks: 100 or 0, Perfection or Failure. When more than one response is graded, the student must earn 100 for each, or else he fails everything. Whenever a student fails a tape (or is absent), he is required to remove the 0 by re-recording the entire tape as often as neces-sary until his performance deserves 100. This system offers every student ample opportunity to reach the level of achievement set by the teacher, and, equally important, rewards him for getting there. (A "fringe benefit" for the teacher is the simplified record keeping, requiring no long columns of marks to be averaged.)

This book does not have the Spanish-English and English-Spanish vocabularies traditionally found at the end of textbooks. A glance at any lesson will show why such lists are unnecessary. Each new word is intro-duced, along with its English equivalent, in an appropriate context in either an illustrative sentence or a Pattern Drill. Then the word is used as often as possible in subsequent drills and model sentences. In this way, the student's active vocabulary is gradually increased to some 700 high-frequency words.

In the later lessons you will notice that not every Spanish illustrative sentence has a corresponding English gloss. These omissions are intentional.

The only valid way to test the student's grasp of the lessons is with an oral examination. It need be no longer than 15 or 20 minutes. A sample final oral examination follows the Appendix.

When a student has mastered the material in this book, he is ready for the first-year reader of your choice.

This book definitely does not propose to make the student of elementary Spanish a "grammatical hairsplitter" or a master of "exceptions to the rule." The initial explanation of every point is deliberately kept as simple as possible, and the more difficult points are postponed. After the student has had a chance to attain fluency with material that "obeys" the so-called rules, the explanations will be expanded. What purpose is served by distracting the student with the odd exception before he masters the general rule? Consequently, I beg the teacher who uses this book not to complicate my explanations by adding exceptions to them. This is neither a course in stylistics nor an attempt to show off my knowledge (or ignorance) of the finer points of Spanish grammar. I want the student to speak acceptable Spanish as soon as possible, not to talk in English about Spanish! Every complication delays his progress.

In this manual I have tried to follow the recommendations made by Edward M. Stack in *The Language Laboratory and Modern Language Teaching*, New York, Oxford University Press, 1960; by Nelson Brooks in *Language and Language Learning*, New York, Harcourt, Brace and World, Inc., 1960; and by Robert L. Politzer and Charles N. Staubach in *Teaching Spanish: A Linguistic Orientation*, Boston, Ginn and Company, 1961. I have freely adopted or adapted many of their ideas, and I am very grateful to them.

I am indebted to many people for advice and encouragement. My colleagues in Toronto have been most generous with their time, patience, and wisdom. Professors M. L. Kay and C. D. Ellis contributed much to the lessons on phonology. I am particularly obligated to Mr. P. B. Bell for his careful reading of the manuscript, and to Mrs. B. A. Barclay for her painstaking preparation of the original stencils. Many valuable suggestions were made by Professor W. Burghardt, who used the mimeographed version for three semesters at the University of Western Ontario, and by Professor Donald G. Reiff, of the University of Rochester. The help that I received from my wife, like my gratitude, cannot be put into words.

A. M. G.

Note: The term *transformation* is used in the taped Lab Drills in a way that I hope will be self-explanatory. No reference is intended to Noam Chomsky and generative grammar.

To the Student

Learning to speak a foreign language is analogous to learning to play a musical instrument. Before you can hope to perform the great concerti, you must first master the individual notes and then the scales. The drills that you will do in the classroom, in the language laboratory, and at home can be considered your Spanish "scales." You may find them tedious at times. But until you know certain basic material so well that you can produce it automatically and instantaneously, you will never be able to converse intelligibly or intelligently with a native speaker of Spanish.

The language lab plays a major role in the learning process. Used correctly, the lab will serve you as an indefatigable tutor, pointing out your mistakes and providing you with corrections. The key to success is listening critically to your tapes. The format of the lab drills is "Stimulus—Your Response—Correct Response—Your Repetition of the Correct Response." Constantly compare your response and your repetition to the correct response; unless all three are identical in every respect, you are wrong.

Each lesson has three sections. The first, containing grammatical explanations and intercalated Pattern Drills, constitutes this textbook and is the only material that you will see before going to the lab. Your teacher will go over the explanations in class, and, equally important, conduct the class in choral performances of the Pattern Drills. Thus, you will have a chance to practice and master each point as it is presented. Before you go to the lab, review this material step by step and do each Pattern Drill aloud before proceeding to the next explanation.

The package that you will deliver to your teacher contains the Lab Drills for each lesson. In the lab you will hear and record Part I of the Lab Drills before you receive the corresponding printed material. With the printed drills in front of you, you will record the same drills again, striving to better your initial performance. If your lab period is longer than 30 minutes, you will have time to perform the drills a third time, with the printed material still available for consultation.

You are expected to review Part I of the Lab Drills aloud before returning to the lab to record Part II. The procedure with Part II is the same as was just outlined: you record the drills once, receive the corresponding printed materials, and record again, once or twice, with the materials before you. After the second lab period, you should review Part II *aloud* as lab homework. You might keep the printed Lab Drills in a notebook or loose-leaf binder in the order in which you receive them, so that they can be used for review and reference.

Perhaps the most important thing for you to remember is that the absence of the traditional written homework should *not* be interpreted as an absence of *all* homework. You must take the responsibility for drilling ORALLY until your responses become completely automatic.

Your success in learning to speak Spanish is practically guaranteed as long as you consistently do two things: always strive for perfect imitation of the native models on the tapes, and remember to drill *aloud* what you have learned in class and in the lab.

Contents

Lesson 25 249

PERFECT INFINITIVE · «DEBER» · POSITION OF DESCRIPTIVE ADJECTIVES · APOCOPATION · ADJECTIVES USED AS NOUNS AND PRONOUNS · NEUTER ARTICLE · OBJECT PRONOUNS · RECIPROCITY · NOUNS · EUPHONY · IDIOMS

Appendix 261

PRETERITE PERFECT · POSITION OF OBJECT PRONOUNS: «LEÍSMO»

Sample Oral Examination 265

Index 271

Lesson 1

1.1 THE SOUNDS OF SPANISH

A language is a system of arbitrary vocal symbols employed by the members of a speech community to communicate with each other. These arbitrary vocal symbols consist of various sequences of speech-sounds. The speech-sounds of the Spanish language may be classified into 24 units of differentiation. Each unit is called a **phoneme.** For practical purposes, many phonemes of Spanish may be regarded as single distinctive "sounds." The arbitrary graphic symbols used to represent phonemes are conventionally placed between slant lines: /a/, /θ/, etc.

Some phonemes of Spanish will appear to a learner of this language to be represented by different "sounds" in different contexts. These positional variants of phonemes are called **allophones.** The arbitrary graphic symbols used to represent allophones are conventionally enclosed in square brackets: [đ], [ɛ], etc. In order to pronounce Spanish acceptably, you must be able to produce in the proper contexts the correct variant sounds that represent each phoneme. Consequently, although Spanish has only 24 phonemes, you will have to learn to produce a minimum of 33 different Spanish speech-sounds.

Some Spanish speech-sounds are practically identical to sounds that you already produce when speaking English. Your major problem with these sounds will be learning to produce them in unfamiliar contexts. A number of Spanish sounds will be new to you, and you may need considerable practice to produce them correctly. Some other Spanish sounds will seem to you identical to English sounds, but, in fact, will be produced somewhat differently from the way they are produced in English. Until you master these differences, you will have a "foreign accent" when you speak Spanish.

The concept of the phoneme is useful to the learner of Spanish because Spanish orthography is in many respects a phonemic writing system. That is, its symbols often represent not the precise variant sound to be used in a given context, but rather the phoneme to which this sound belongs. Thus, once you know (a) what phoneme or phonemes each Spanish letter or

2

sequence of letters represents, and (b) which variant sound of a given Spanish phoneme to produce in a given context, you can automatically produce acceptable, comprehensible Spanish speech-sounds from written Spanish.

1.2   STRESS AND INTONATION IN SPANISH

The term **stress** refers to the relative prominence of certain syllables as compared to other syllables in the same word. Stress has phonemic value in Spanish because it differentiates between words that are otherwise identical. Stress is phonemic in English, too. For example, stress distinguishes the noun "*per*vert" from the verb "per*vert*." Stress follows certain simple patterns in Spanish. For the time being, you need not worry about these patterns—merely stress the phonemes that are in **boldface type** on the following pages.

Intonation (or **pitch**) refers to the raising and lowering of the voice within a word or an utterance. Spanish intonation patterns are unlike those of English, and eventually you will be expected to master them. For the present, intonation need not concern you, for you will be producing vocal symbols in isolation, not in meaningful utterances.

1.3   SOME SPANISH-ENGLISH "EQUIVALENTS"

The most logical way to learn Spanish phonology is to start with those Spanish sounds that are practically identical to sounds used in English. Such sounds presumably do not require detailed description or extensive drill:

/m/: For all practical purposes, the Spanish sound represented by /m/ may be considered almost identical to the initial English sound in the English word *mat*.

/f/: For all practical purposes, the Spanish sound represented by /f/ may be considered almost identical to the initial English sound in the English word *fat*.

/ch/: For all practical purposes, the Spanish sound represented by /ch/ may be considered almost identical to the initial English sound in the English word *chop*. Spanish /ch/ never resembles the initial English [sh] of *chauffeur*.

Before you can use the Spanish phonemes /m/, /f/, and /ch/ to form Spanish vocal symbols, you must learn to produce the Spanish vowel phonemes. The difference between consonant phonemes (such as /m/, /f/, and /ch/) and vowel phonemes is that in the production of vowel phonemes the air stream is not interrupted or impeded as it passes through the speech organs. In the production of consonant phonemes, on the other hand, the air stream is impeded or momentarily stopped by an obstacle.

1.4 SPANISH VOWEL PHONEMES

The sounds of Spanish vowel phonemes may be more or less familiar to you, depending on how you speak English. Because of the wide variety of English dialects represented in the average North American classroom, and because of the wide variation of vowels among English dialects, it is practically impossible to give meaningful English approximations of the Spanish vowel sounds. Therefore, it is imperative to watch your teacher closely, noting the position of his lips and the distance between them. Try to imitate these positions and to mimic exactly the sounds that you hear. Remember, you are not speaking English, and consequently the Spanish vowels will probably sound strange to you at first. Be careful not to fall into the common error of replacing "strange" Spanish vowel phonemes with the closest English vowel sounds that you know. Remember to stress the phonemes in **boldface type** in the drills.

/**a**/: To produce the sound that represents the Spanish phoneme /a/, the mouth is opened wide, the tongue is kept lying flat, and the corners of the mouth are pulled back slightly. Listen to your teacher produce /a/, and strive to imitate him exactly. After you successfully produce /a/ in isolation, then produce /a/ before and after the other Spanish phonemes that you already know: /ma, ama, acha, fama, facha/.

/**i**/: To produce the sound that represents the Spanish phoneme /i/, the mouth is opened slightly, the lips are spread, the front of the tongue is raised as high as possible, and at the same time it is pushed as far forward in the mouth as possible. Listen to your teacher produce /i/, and try to imitate him exactly. When you master /i/, contrast it with /a/: /i/–/a/, /a/–/i/. Then imitate your teacher's production of the following: /mi, fi, chi, chicha, ficha, mima, mimi/.

/**u**/: To produce the sound that represents the Spanish phoneme /u/, the mouth is opened slightly, the lips are rounded, the back of the tongue is raised as high as possible, and at the same time it is pushed as far back in the mouth as possible. When you have successfully imitated your teacher's /u/, contrast /u/ with the other vowel phonemes that you have mastered: /u/–/i/, /u/–/a/, /u/–/i/–/a/. Note how your lips and tongue change position, and how your mouth opens and closes. Then produce /u/ with some consonant phonemes: /mu, fu, chu, mucha, fucha, chucha, chufa/.

The positions of your lips and tongue during the production of /a/, /i/, and /u/ are convenient points of reference to describe the production of these and the other Spanish vowel phonemes. To produce /i/, your tongue is as high and as far forward as possible, whereas in /u/ it is as high and as far back as possible. Hence, /i/ and /u/ can be described, respectively, as **high front** and **high back** vowels. The descriptions can be completed by adding terms referring to the lip positions. The term **spread** describes the lips during the production of /i/, and **rounded** serves to describe the lips during the production of /u/. Thus, /i/ can be described concisely as a **high front spread** vowel, and /u/, on the other hand, as a **high back rounded** vowel. In contrast to these extreme high and front or back positions, /a/ is a low central vowel. As the lips are spread, /a/ is described as a **low central spread** vowel.

/e/: The Spanish phoneme /e/ has two allophones: [e] and [ɛ]. The former is a mid front spread vowel. To produce [e], the mouth is opened slightly, the lips are spread, the front of the tongue is raised not quite as high as possible, and at the same time, it is pushed as far forward as possible. In other words, [e] is like /i/, except that the tongue is not as high as in the production of /i/. When you can mimic your teacher's production of [e], contrast it with /i/, with /a/, and finally with /u/. Then practice the following: [me, fe, che, eme, efe, eche, echa, ache].

The allophone [ɛ] is produced like [e], but with the tongue somewhat lower in the mouth, and with the lips not spread quite as much. Listen to the difference between the allophones of /e/ when your teacher produces them in isolation: [e, ɛ, e, ɛ]. Later you will learn when [ɛ] occurs; for the present you will hear and imitate [e] only.

/o/: The Spanish phoneme /o/ has two allophones: [o] and [ɔ]. The former is a mid back rounded vowel. To produce [o], the mouth is opened slightly, the lips are rounded, the back of the tongue is raised not quite as high as for /u/, and it is pushed toward the back of the mouth. In other words, [o] is like /u/, except that the tongue is not as high as in the production of /u/. When you can imitate your teacher's production of [o], contrast it with /u/, and then with /a/, /i/, and [e] in turn. Then practice the following combinations of [o] with the consonant phonemes: [mo, fo, cho, ocho, fofo, focha, echo, acho, chucho, mucho, macho].

The allophone [ɔ] is produced like [o], but the tongue is somewhat lower in the mouth. Listen to the difference between the allophones of /o/ when your teacher produces them in isolation: [o, ɔ, o, ɔ]. Later you will learn when [ɔ] occurs; for the present you will hear and imitate [o] only.

Now review your knowledge of the vowel and consonant phonemes by repeating the following sets of "words" after your teacher (from here on, for simplification, all models will be in square brackets):

1. fama	2. echa	3. mofo	4. facha	5. macho	6. muchacho
fuma	eche	mofa	fecha	mecha	muchacha
fumo	echo	mofe	ficha	mucha	

1.5 VOICE

If you place your fingers on your throat and then produce /a/, /i/, /u/ and the allophones of /e/ and /o/, you can feel the vibration of your vocal cords. The technical term for this vibration is **voice**. All the Spanish vowel phonemes are voiced. Some Spanish consonant phonemes are voiced, as is /m/, whreas others, such as /f/ and /ch/, are voiceless. The presence of voice is all that differentiates between the allophones of /s/:

/s/: The Spanish phoneme /s/ has two allophones: [s] and [z]. The former is voiceless, and for all practical purposes, the Spanish sound represented by [s] may be considered almost identical to the initial English sound in the English word *seal*. On the other hand, Spanish [z] is voiced, and for all practical purposes, [z] may be considered almost identical to the initial English sound in the English word *zeal*.

The voiceless allophone is more common, for [z] occurs only before voiced consonants, such as /m/: [mizmo, mizma, chizme, chuzma, azma].

Before, after, and between vowels, the Spanish phoneme /s/ is always represented by [s]: [si, se, su, as, asa, ase, use, uso, mesa, masa, misa, musa, fosa].

The /s/ just described is produced differently in some parts of Spain: the tongue tip is raised toward the gum ridge behind the upper front teeth, producing a sound suggestive of a hiss. If you can do this without becoming tongue-tied, fine. If not, forget it, because the /s/ of most North Americans is the /s/ of South America.

1.6 SOME DIFFICULT SPANISH PHONEMES

/x/: To produce the voiceless sound that represents the Spanish phoneme /x/, raise the back of your tongue toward (but do not touch) the rear of the roof of the mouth, keeping the tongue tip down below the level of the front teeth, and exhale strongly. When the air stream passes through the narrow space between the tongue and the velum, the result is a sound somewhat like the initial English /h/ of the English words *hoot* and *heel*, but the Spanish /x/ is a rougher sound. Practice /x/ followed by the vowel phonemes and allophones: [xa, xi, xu, xe, xo]. Then practice /x/ between vowels: [axa, axo, maxa, maxo, ixa, ixo, fixa, fixo, faxa].

Before /x/, the phonemes /e/ and /o/ are represented, respectively, by [ɛ] and [ɔ]: [ɛxa, ɛxo, ɛxe, ɔxa, ɔxe, ɔxo, mɔxa, mɔxo].

/r/: To produce the voiced sound that represents the Spanish phoneme /r/, the tongue is tensed along the bottom of the mouth, and then sprung upwards so that the tip of the tongue briefly taps the gum ridge behind the upper front teeth. Since this is just what your tongue does when you pronounce the English /d/ in words like *caddy*, *ladder*, and *madder*, you cannot claim that you are unable to produce Spanish /r/. Practice /r/ now between vowels, as in [ara, era, ira, ora, ura, mira, mire, miro, muro, moro]. When you have mastered /r/ in this position, then try a more difficult /r/, stressing the vowel phoneme following it: [ara, ira, ire, mire, miro]. Then practice /r/ in longer sequences of sounds: [fumara, fumare, mirara, mirare]. The real test of your ability to produce /r/ occurs when /r/ precedes a consonant or is final, as in [arma, irma, firma, mar, mesar, marchar].

/rr/: To produce the voiced sound that represents the Spanish phoneme /rr/, draw the body of your tongue a little way back in your mouth, tense the tip of your tongue upward against the gum ridge behind your upper front teeth, and exhale forcefully, producing voice at the same time. The pressure of your breath over and around the tongue tip strikes the gum ridge, forcing the tongue away and causing it to "flutter." (This sound is sometimes used by children to imitate a motorcycle, or a pre-jet age airplane.) Place your tongue in the correct position, exhale forcefully, and practice /rr/ in the following: [rrasa, rrama, rracha, rrisa, rrima, rrusa]. Although /rr/ may at first sound to you like an English /d/ followed by a Spanish /r/, such is not the case. Spanish /rr/ cannot be produced by consciously moving the tip of the tongue; strong exhalation is vital. Keep practicing until you can produce /rr/ at will. Then you are ready to try /rr/ between vowel phonemes: [arra, irra, urra, chirra, farra, mirra, amarra].

Before and after /rr/, the phonemes /e/ and /o/ are represented by [ɛ] and [ɔ], respectively. Practice the following: [arrɛ, irrɛ, urrɛ, ɛrrɛ, arrɔ, irrɔ, urrɔ, ɔrrɔ, ɔrrɛ, ɛrrɔ, rrɔma, rrɔsa].

Before /rr/, the phoneme /s/ usually disappears. Thus, for example, you will not hear [miz rrimas], but rather [mi rrimas].

The phoneme /r/ never occurs at the beginning of a word; instead, /rr/ is found in this position. The phoneme /rr/ does not occur before a consonant or at the end of a word; instead, /r/ is found in these positions. However, both /r/ and /rr/ can occur between vowels, and in this position the use of the wrong phoneme can lead to misunderstanding. The actual Spanish words that comprise the following pairs are distinguished from each other only by /r/ and /rr/:

[1. fara–farra   2. mira–mirra   3. amara–amarra]

Can you make this very necessary distinction? And, can you produce both phonemes in the same "word," as: [rrara, rrimara, arrasara, rraxara]?

/l/: To the untrained ear, the voiced sound that represents the Spanish phoneme /l/ appears to be identical to the initial English sound in the English word *law*. But there is a difference. In the production of both English /l/ and Spanish /l/, the tip of the tongue is placed against the gum ridge behind the upper front teeth (the **alveolar ridge**). However, in the English /l/ the middle of the tongue is low, whereas in the Spanish /l/ the middle of the tongue is arched slightly. To produce Spanish /l/ correctly, place the tip of your tongue in the proper position, and then consciously arch the middle of your tongue, being careful not to touch the roof of your mouth. Try this now: [la, le, lo, loma, lima, lucha, leche, luche]. When you have mastered /l/ in an initial position, try producing it in the same way between vowel phonemes: [fila, filo, chile, chula, chulo].

Although the difference between English /l/ and Spanish /l/ may seem insignificant and unimportant to you, a native speaker of Spanish will notice your "foreign accent" if you do not master the Spanish /l/.

Now to the language laboratory, where you will have a chance to compare your efforts with the pronunciation of an educated Spaniard from Madrid. (Note: For typographical reasons, the stressed phonemes are underlined on your Lab Drill pages.)

Lesson 2

2.1 ASPIRATION

Hold your fingers about one inch in front of your lips and say the English words *can, kill, cool.* The puff of air that you felt after the initial consonant sound is called **aspiration.** In English, aspiration accompanies not only initial /k/, but also initial /p/ and /t/. On the other hand, after /s/ the English /k/, /p/, and /t/ are not aspirated. You can prove this to yourself by holding your fingers an inch before your mouth and repeating the following pairs of English words: *can–scan, pill–spill, tall–stall.*

The Spanish phonemes /k/, /p/, and /t/ are never aspirated. No matter how well you produce the other Spanish sounds, unless you learn to produce unaspirated /k/, /p/, and /t/, you will be speaking Spanish with an English accent.

/k/: Except for being unaspirated, the sound that represents the voiceless Spanish phoneme /k/ may be considered, for all practical purposes, almost identical to the initial English sound in the English word *kill.* To produce an unaspirated /k/, position the back of your tongue against the rear of the upper palate (as in English), and let the pressure build up. As soon as you release the pressure by moving your tongue away from the velum, immediately produce the following vowel sound: [ka, ki, ku, ke, ko]. To determine whether you are successful, hold your fingers in front of your lips when you practice. If you still feel the aspiration, another method of eliminating it is to start with a hissing sound (sssss), and while producing it, concentrate on positioning your tongue and on releasing it. Prolong the hiss, gradually lowering its volume, and when the hiss has died out, produce the /k/ and then immediately produce the following vowel sound. After you are successful with the examples given above, try longer sequences: [kasa, kosa, kiso, keso, kema].

Once you succeed in eliminating the aspiration of your initial /k/, you will be ready to practice unaspirated /k/ between vowels. This is somewhat trickier. One way to avoid the aspiration is to produce [loko] as if the /k/ were a double sound, prolonging it *slightly* before producing the following vowel. Do *not* say [lok-ko], but rather [lo-kko]. And be careful not to move the stress from the first [o] to the second. After you can produce an acceptable [loko], go on to: [choka, seka, chika]. Then practice with the stress after the /k/: [choko, seko, seke].

/p/: Except for being unaspirated, the sound that represents the voiceless Spanish phoneme /p/ may be considered, for all practical purposes, almost identical to the initial English sound in the English word *pill*. You can learn to produce the unaspirated Spanish /p/ by applying the methods described under /k/. Concentrate on tensing your lips and letting the pressure build up; then release the pressure by opening your lips, and immediately produce the following vowel sound: [pa, pi, pu, pe, po]. When you can produce an unaspirated initial /p/, then practice the Spanish /p/ between vowels, producing it as described above: [sepa, sapo, sopa, supo]. The next step will be to practice unaspirated /p/ as well as /k/ in the following: [peka, pike, poko, piko, kepa, kapa, kupo].

/t/: The sound that represents the voiceless Spanish phoneme /t/ presents two problems to speakers of English: articulation and aspiration. A convenient point of reference for describing Spanish /t/ is the initial English sound in the English word *tall*. The English /t/ is produced by touching the tip of the tongue against the gum ridge behind the upper front teeth. In contrast, Spanish /t/ is produced by touching the tongue tip against the back of the upper front teeth. The correct position for your tongue is easily found by preparing to say the English word *too*, and then moving the tip of the tongue forward until you feel it touch your upper front teeth. Position your tongue correctly, and repeat: [ta, ti, tu, te, to]. Once you are accustomed to producing /t/ in this manner, you must learn to produce /t/ without aspiration. The methods described under /k/ may be helpful. When you have mastered this unaspirated dental /t/ in an initial position, then practice producing it between vowels: [ata, ato, mato, mate, mito, moto, meto, meta, sota].

Then practice the unaspirated consonant phonemes of: [toko, topo, tipo, pito, kito, kota]. Finally, practice the consonant cluster /tr/; concentrate on producing the unaspirated /t/ by touching the front teeth, not the gum ridge above them: [tres, otra, metro].

2.2 SPANISH NASAL PHONEMES

The term **nasal** is used to describe consonant phonemes that are produced by air passing through the nose, rather than through the mouth. Acceptable production of the Spanish nasal phonemes should not offer you any difficulty. All Spanish nasal phonemes are consonants. As indicated in 1.3, the Spanish nasal consonant /m/ may be considered, for all practical purposes, almost identical to the initial English sound in the English word mat.

/n/: The Spanish phoneme /n/ has three allophones. Two of them are represented by the same symbol: [n]. They differ merely in the part of the mouth contacted by the tongue, and they may be considered, for all practical purposes, almost identical to two English /n/ allophones. Before and between vowel phonemes, Spanish [n] is almost identical to the initial English sound in the English word no. In the production of Spanish intervocalic [n], the tongue contacts the alveolar ridge, as it does in English: [no, ni, ana, uno, fino]. Before dental consonants, such as Spanish /t/, the tongue contacts the back of the upper front teeth: [ante, xuntar, un tema]. Since you are already accustomed to producing a dental [n] in English words, such as anthem, there will be no particular difficulty for you—as long as you remember that Spanish /t/ is dental, and that /t/ is not the only dental phoneme in Spanish (you will learn others later).

The third allophone, represented by [ŋ], occurs before /k/, /g/, and /x/. Again, there is a similarity to an English sound, the [ŋ] before the /k/ and /g/, respectively, of the English words anchor and angry. Since you are accustomed to producing [ŋ] before /k/ and /g/ in many English words, all you will have to do is to learn to produce [ŋ] before /x/: [maŋxar, fiŋxe, uŋ xaro, naraŋxa]

You will sometimes hear a sound resembling the English [ŋ] at the end of the English word sing when /n/ is final in Spanish. You need not strive to imitate this, for it is not universal among speakers of Spanish.

/ñ/: The sound represented by the Spanish phoneme /ñ/ is roughly comparable to the sound given to ni in the English word onion. The tip of the tongue touches the lower teeth, the middle of the tongue presses against the front part of the roof of the mouth while the air escapes through the nose, and practically at once the tongue moves away from the hard palate, producing a short sound like the initial sound of the English word yard. Since /ñ/ is not easy to produce in isolation, practice it between vowel phenemes: [aña, oño, eño, iñi, uña, uñe].

2.3 SPANISH FRICATIVE SOUNDS

A consonant sound produced by narrowing the air passage at some point so that the air stream is forced out with an audible hissing or friction is called a **fricative.** The initial sounds of the English words *fun, sun, thin, shin, veal, zeal,* and *thine* are English fricatives. A sound produced by completely stopping the air flow is called a **stop.** Examples of English stop consonants are the initial sounds of the English words *pat, bat, top, do, cat,* and *go.* Three of the phonemes of Spanish have stop and fricative allophones, and it is with these that you may experience great difficulty.

/d/: The Spanish phoneme /d/ has two allophones: stop [d] and fricative [đ]. The voiced Spanish sound represented by [d] differs from the initial sound of the English word *do* in one very important respect: Spanish [d] is dental. That is, in the production of Spanish [d] the tip of the tongue touches the back of the upper front teeth. In the English /d/, on the other hand, the tongue touches the alveolar ridge. To learn to produce a dental [d], start to pronounce the English word *do,* and stop before you pronounce the vowel sound. Then move your tongue forward and downward until it touches the back of the upper teeth. With your tongue in this position, practice [da, di, du, de, do]. This allophone occurs in Spanish **only** at the beginning of an utterance, and after /n/ or /l/: [manda, mundo, falda, umilde, dando]. Note that before [d], the allophone [n] is dental.

In all other positions, /d/ is represented by the voiced fricative allophone [đ]. This is produced by touching the bottom of the upper incisors lightly and briefly with the tip of the tongue. The resultant sound is somewhat like the initial English sound in the English word *thine.* Since [đ] does not occur initially in Spanish, practice it between vowels, before and after consonants other than /n/ and /l/, and at the end of words: [ađa, iđa, ođa, seđa, muđo, mađre, pađre, mađriđ, arđe, urđe, mirađ, eđađ].

It is important that you become accustomed to producing [đ] between vowels, otherwise you run the risk of being misunderstood. The reason is the similarity in sound of [d] and /r/, and a Spaniard may misinterpret your incorrect [oda] as [ora], your incorrect [todo] as [toro], etc. Note that it is possible to have both allophones of /d/ in a few words. Can you hear the difference when your teacher says [deđo, dađo] and [ađonde]? More important, can you reproduce the difference?

/g/: The Spanish phoneme /g/ has two allophones: stop [g] and fricative [g]. The voiced Spanish sound represented by [g] may be considered, for all practical purposes, almost identical to the initial English sound in the English word *go*. Stop [g] occurs **only** at the beginning of an utterance and after /n/: [gasa, goma, maŋgo, taŋgo, saŋgre].

In all other positions, /g/ is represented by the voiced fricative allophone [g̶], which has no commonly heard counterpart in English. To produce the sound represented by [g̶], place your tongue in position to pronounce the initial sound of the English word *go*, and then lower the rear of your tongue slightly so that it does not quite contact the soft palate. The air will thus pass through a small space and produce the desired sound. As [g̶] does not occur initially, practice it between vowels: [ag̶a, eg̶a, og̶a, ig̶o, ug̶o]. Then practice [g̶] before and after consonants: [sig̶lo, dig̶no, og̶re, tig̶re, alg̶o, salg̶o, karg̶o, purg̶a].

Learning to produce [g̶] at will requires considerable practice. But do not neglect everything else in order to master this allophone. Although failure to produce [g̶] in the proper position will mark you as a foreigner, it will not lead to misunderstanding.

/b/: The Spanish phoneme /b/ has two allophones: stop [b] and fricative [b̶]. The voiced Spanish sound represented by [b] may be considered, for all practical purposes, almost identical to the initial English sound in the English word *bat*. Stop [b] occurs **only** at the beginning of an utterance and after /m/: [ba, ban, rrumba].

In all other positions, /b/ is represented by the voiced fricative allophone [b̶], which has no counterpart in English. When you hear [b̶], you may "interpret" the sound as the equivalent of English /b/ or /v/. The English sound /v/ does not exist in Spanish! The fricative [b̶] differs from stop [b] in that the lips are not pressed together; rather they are merely brought close to each other, allowing the air stream to pass between them. It may help you to draw the corners of your mouth back at the same time. Since [b̶] does not occur in an initial position, practice it between vowel phonemes, and before and after consonant phonemes: [ab̶a, ub̶a, ib̶a, ub̶e, ub̶o, sub̶o, kub̶re, lib̶ro, dob̶le, alb̶a, ob̶eso].

Although this is the most difficult sound for non-Spaniards to produce, it is not impossible. Watch your teacher, and above all, practice in front of a mirror, taking care not to let your lips touch each other. Do not attempt to replace [b̶] with English /w/ or /v/. After you acquire the ability to produce intervocalic fricative [b̶] at will, try the following "words" containing both allophones of /b/: [beb̶e, bib̶e, bib̶o, beb̶o, beb̶a, bib̶a].

2.4 "AMERICAN" SPANISH AND "SPANISH" SPANISH

Just as you can usually tell a North American from a Briton by the way each produces certain English sounds, so you can distinguish a South American from many (but not all) peninsular Spaniards by listening for the following phoneme.

/θ/: The Spanish phoneme /θ/ has two allophones: voiceless [θ] and voiced [z̧]. The sound represented by the allophone [θ] may be considered, for all practical purposes, almost identical to the initial English sound in the English word *think*. Your main problem with [θ] will be getting used to producing it in unfamiliar contexts: [iθe, iθo, θeta, rraθa, aθ, tiθa]. Before [θ], [n] is dental: [danθa, panθa].

Before voiced consonant phonemes, the phoneme /θ/ is represented by its voiced allophone [z̧]. For all practical purposes, this sound may be considered almost identical to the initial English sound in the English word *there*. Practice [z̧] in the following: [tiz̧ne, xuz̧gar, biz̧ma, kab̧iz̧b̧axo].

In the phonemic system of South America, Central America, and some parts of Spain, /s/ is used instead of /θ/. In central and northern Spain, /θ/ and /s/ are distinct phonemes, whereas in some other parts of Spain, /θ/ is used instead of /s/. First-year students would be well advised to make the distinction between /θ/ and /s/—not because such a distinction is "correct," or a sign of social superiority, but for two practical reasons. First, the distinction is made in orthography, and, therefore, it will be easier to spell Spanish correctly when you get around to writing it. Second, if you want to sound like a South American, you must do more than merely drop /θ/: you must adopt several other South Americanisms, depending on the region of South America that you choose to imitate. Doing so will probably confuse you completely. Do not worry about being ridiculed on account of your /θ/ when you go to South or Central America; it is perfectly acceptable in a foreigner.

2.5 /LL/ AND /Y/

More complicated than the distinction between "Spain" and "Spanish America" is the distribution of the phonemes /ll/ and /y/.

/ll/: The voiced sound represented by /ll/ is produced in two stages. First, the tip of the tongue touches the lower front teeth and the middle of the tongue is raised to contact the roof of the mouth as well as the back of the alveolar ridge. Then the middle of the tongue moves slightly forward and downward. The resultant sound is roughly similar to the sound given to the letters *ly* in the English word *halyard*. However, the English sound is produced with the tip of the tongue raised, whereas in Spanish the tip of the tongue is in contact with the lower front teeth. To accustom yourself to producing /ll/ in a different manner, practice the following: [llama, llanto, kalla, kallo, alla, elle, ella].

/y/: The Spanish phoneme /y/ has two allophones: [y] and [ŷ]. The voiced fricative sound represented by [y] can be compared to the initial English sound in the English word *young*. However, Spanish [y] is a more "forceful" sound—almost, but not quite, like the English [j] of the English name *Jesse*. First practice [y] before a stressed vowel in order to become accustomed to articulating it more strongly than you do in English: [yate, yema, sayal, kayaɖa, ayuɖa]. Then practice it in other positions: [mayo, rrayo, bayo, baya, suya].

The voiced sound represented by the allophone [ŷ] may be considered, for all practical purposes, almost identical to the initial English sound in the English word *gentleman*. You will not hear or use [ŷ] very often, for it represents /y/ only after /n/ and /l/: [un ŷuŋke, al ŷaŋki].

Although Spanish phoneticians consider /ll/ and /y/ distinct phonemes, there are parts of Spain in which /ll/ is not found. In Madrid, for example, /ll/ has been replaced generally by /y/. In most of Spanish America, too, /ll/ has been replaced by [y], which, in turn, is replaced by [ŷ] in some regions. Since your tapes were recorded by a *madrileño*, you will not hear /ll/. You are to imitate the tapes unless your teacher tells you otherwise. (Note: Remember that the stressed phonemes are underlined on your Lab Drill pages.)

Lesson 3

3.1 SPANISH DIPHTHONGS

A diphthong is formed by the subordination of one vowel phoneme to an adjacent vowel phoneme. In Spanish, such subordination is possible only if one of the adjacent vowel phonemes is unstressed /i/ or unstressed /u/. Thus, fourteen diphthongs are possible:

/ai/ /ei/ /oi/ /au/ /eu/ /ou/ /iu/
/ia/ /ie/ /io/ /ua/ /ue/ /uo/ /ui/

Although the only way to learn the correct pronunciation of these diphthongs is by listening closely to your teacher and mimicking him, some English sounds offer convenient points of departure. It should be clearly understood that the English sounds given in the following pages are merely approximations, not equivalents.

/ai/: The Spanish diphthong /ai/ is somewhat similar to the *ai* of the English word *aisle*. However, in Spanish /ai/ the tongue glides further toward the front and top of the mouth. Can you hear the difference between [das] and [dais], and between [bas] and [bais] when your teacher pronounces them? Now imitate your teacher's pronunciation of: [ai, aire, baila, daifa, naipe, xaiƀa, laiko, gaita].

/ei/: The Spanish diphthong /ei/ is somewhat similar to the *ey* of the English word *they*. However, in Spanish /ei/ the tongue glides further toward the front and top of the mouth. Listen to the difference between [le] and [lei], between [bes] and [beis], and between [des] and [deis] when your teacher pronounces them. Then try the following: [seis, rrei, rreina, peina, peine, beinte, θeiƀa].

/oi/: The Spanish diphthong /oi/ is somewhat similar to the *oi* of the English word *loiter*. However, as in the preceding diphthongs, the difference between the English sound and the Spanish /oi/ is that in Spanish the tongue glides further toward the front and top of the mouth. Can you contrast [do] and [doi], [bo] and [boi]? Imitate your teacher's pronunciation of: [oi, oigo, koi, boina, koima].

/au/: The Spanish diphthong /au/ is somewhat similar to the *ou* of the English word *loud*. But in order to produce the correct Spanish sound, the lips should be more rounded at the end of /au/, and the tongue should move further back in the mouth. Can you hear and reproduce the difference between [ala] and [aula], between [xala] and [xaula], and between [kasa] and [kausa]? Practice the pronunciation of: [kaucho, kauđa, fauna, fausto, gaucho, lauro, nauta, pausa, pauta, rrauđo, sauθe].

/eu/: There is no English sound similar to the Spanish diphthong /eu/, and an accurate, comprehensible description of /eu/ is almost impossible. Imitate your teacher, and remember that the lips should be rounded at the end of /eu/, with the tongue well back in the mouth: [deuđo, deuđa, feuđo, feuđal, neutro, neutral, rreunir, seuđo, teuton].

/ou/: Since the diphthong /ou/ occurs in only one word, and that one a borrowing from Catalonian, you may safely ignore it.

/ia/: The Spanish diphthong /ia/ is somewhat similar to the *ya* of the English word *yacht*. However, in Spanish /ia/ the initial sound is produced more "forcefully" than in *yacht*. Imitate your teacher's pronunciation of: [fiar, piafa, miaxa, piano, fiađo, miazma, biaxa].

/ie/: The Spanish diphthong /ie/ is somewhat similar to the English word *yea* in the expression *yea team!* But in Spanish the initial sound is enunciated more "forcefully" than in English. Practice with: [ierra, bien, θien, dieθ, fiel, pie, siesta, biento, biexo, tierra, dieta, fiesta, θienθia].

/io/: The Spanish diphthong /io/ is somewhat similar to the *yo* of the English word *yolk*. However, in Spanish /io/ the initial sound is more "forceful" than in *yolk*, and the final sound is more open. Imitate your teacher's pronunciation of: [io, diosa, miope, pioxo, rrioxa, biola].

/ua/: The Spanish diphthong /ua/ is somewhat similar to the *wa* of the English word *watch*. However, to produce Spanish /ua/ correctly, the lips must be more rounded than in *watch*. Practice with: [kual, dual, xuan, guano, guapo, kuando, kuatro, rruana, agua, guagua].

/ue/: The Spanish diphthong /ue/ is between the *we* of the English word *wet* and the *wai* of the English word *wait*. Spanish /ue/ is not as short as the former and not as long as the latter. In addition, in the production of /ue/ the lips are rounded. Practice with: [ueso, bueno, kueŋka, kuento, kuero, duelo, fuente, muela, sueño].

/uo/: The Spanish diphthong /uo/ is somewhat similar to the *wo* of the English word *woke*. But the lips should be more rounded and the final sound should be more open than in English. This diphthong is not encountered as frequently as some of the others: [kuota, bakuo].

/ui/: The Spanish diphthong /ui/ is somewhat similar to the *wee* in the English word *weep*. However, in Spanish /ui/ the lips are more rounded, and the tongue glides further toward the front and top of the mouth. Imitate your teacher's pronunciation of: [uir, kuito, buitre, rruina, kuiđađo].

/iu/: The Spanish diphthong /iu/ is somewhat similar to the *ew* of the English word *few*. However, in Spanish /iu/ the lips are more rounded and the tongue moves further back in the mouth. Imitate your teacher's pronunciation of: [biuđa, diurno, θiuđađ]. Be careful not to confuse the last of these words with the last word of the preceding drill: [kuiđađo–θiuđađ].

The Spanish phonemic system also contains four triphthongs: /iai/, /iei/, /uai/, and /uei/. Although you will not come across them very often, you must at least master the correct pronunciation of [paraguai] and [uruguai].

3.2 SPANISH ORTHOGRAPHY

The conventions of written Spanish will be child's play to anyone who has mastered the vagaries of English spelling. The Spanish vowel phonemes /a/, /e/, /o/, and /u/ are always represented by the letters a, e, o, and u, respectively. Although /i/ is usually represented by i, the one word that consists of /i/ alone is written y.

Orthography of the Spanish consonant phonemes (in the order studied) is shown in the following table:

PHONEME	LETTER	EXAMPLES AND COMMENT
/m/	m	*me, amo, alma*
	n	*un par, un beso, ninfa;* before /p/, /b/, and /f/, the letter n represents /m/
/f/	f	*fino, efe, marfil*
/ch/	ch	*chufa, ocho, marcha*
/s/ — [s]	s	*sota, fosa, este, mapas*
/s/ — [z]	s	*mismo, desde, rasgo*

PHONEME	LETTER	EXAMPLES AND COMMENT
/x/	j	jefe, caja, jinete, manjar
	g	general, gime; **g** only before /e/ and /i/
/r/	r	ara, arma, mar; /r/ does not occur initially
/rr/	rr	perro, carro; the letter **rr** occurs only inter-vocalically
	r	ropa, alrededor, Enrique; when /rr/ is initial or follows /l/ or /n/, it is written **r**
/l/	l	lo, ala, molde, moral
/k/	c	cama, coma, cuba, saca
	qu	queso, quise, saque; **qu** only before /e/ and /i/
	k	kilo; only in foreign words
/p/	p	pifo, mapa
/t/	t	te, ata, antes
/n/ — [n]	n	nato, uno, dental, tan
/n/ — [ŋ]	n	finca, tengo, monja
/ñ/	ñ	ñame, año
/d/ — [d]	d	da, andar, falda
/d/ — [ð]	d	ida, arde, pasad
/g/ — [g]	g	gala, golpe, gula, tengo
	gu	guerra, guisar; **gu** only before /e/ and /i/
/g/ — [ǥ]	g	siga, algo, alguno
	gu	pague, seguir; **gu** only before /e/ and /i/
/b/ — [b]	b	bien, ambos
	v	vino, enviar
/b/ — [ƀ]	b	lobo, sorbo, cubre
	v	uva, polvo
/θ/ — [θ]	z	zapato, zona, zumo, caza, rozo, coz
	c	cero, cima, dice, fácil; **c** only before /e/ and /i/
/θ/ — [ẓ]	z	juzgar, gozne
/ll/	ll	llano, olla

PHONEME	LETTER	EXAMPLES AND COMMENT
/y/ < [y]	y	yate, mayor
[ŷ]	y	*inyectar*
	x	before a vowel phoneme, x represents /ks/: *éxito*; before a consonant phoneme, x represents /s/: *extra*; in a few words the letter x represents /x/: *México, Quixote*
	h	has no phonemic value in Spanish: *hace* [aθe]
	w	occurs only in foreign words, and is pronounced as English /w/ by some speakers and as English /v/ by others: *Wáshington, wagón*

As you can see from the preceding table, the only significant difference between the English and Spanish alphabets is that in the latter *ch*, *ll*, and *rr* are inseparable double letters. In alphabetical lists, *ch* follows all other *c* entries, *ll* follows all other *l* entries, and *rr* follows *rq* and precedes *rs*. The *ñ* follows all other *n* entries.

As shown by the examples in the table, most Spanish consonant phonemes can occur initially, intervocalically, and before as well as after other consonant phonemes. However, the only consonant phonemes that occur at the end of a word (excluding foreign "loan" words such as *golf* and *coñac*) are /s/, /r/, /l/, /n/, /d/, and /θ/. Although a few Spanish words end with the letter *j*, most speakers do not pronounce /x/ in final position: for example, *reloj* [rrɛlo].

Unlike English, Spanish orthography has only two doubled consonants. The sequence *-cc-* is pronounced as /kθ/ in words such as *accidente* and *lección*. Much rarer is the sequence *-nn-*, which is pronounced as a lengthened /n/ in words such as *innoble* and *perenne*.

As you have undoubtedly deduced from the preceding table, the only problems you will have in transcribing speech are the inclusion of the silent *h*, the graphic representation of /x/ before /e/ and /i/, and the choice of *b* or *v* to represent /b/. There are no "rules of thumb" to help you; you will have to depend on your memory—as Spaniards do. Reading Spanish aloud offers only one difficulty: your eyes may cause you to make a distinction between *b* and *v*. Remember that both letters represent *the same phoneme* and that the English phoneme /v/ does not exist in Spanish.

Certain conventions govern the orthography of the diphthongs. When /ai/, /ei/, /oi/, or /ui/ are final in a word, they are written as ay, ey, oy, and uy: hay, ley, doy, muy. When /ua/, /ue/, and /ui/ begin a word, they are preceded by h: huaco, hueso, huir. In some words initial /ie/ is preceded by h (hielo), whereas in others the initial /ie/ is written as ye (yerro). When /ia/ and /io/ are initial, they are written as ya and yo: yambo, yodo. When the triphthongs /uai/ and /uei/ are final, they are written as uay and uey: Paraguay, buey.

3.2.1 *Capitalization and Punctuation.* Capital letters appear less frequently in Spanish than in English. They are used in Spanish only for the first word of a sentence, the Deity, and the names of people (*Juan*) and places (*España*). The days of the week, the months, "I," and adjectives of nationality (*Canadian*) are not capitalized in Spanish when they do not begin a sentence. When initial ch and ll must be capitalized, they are written Ch and Ll.

Punctuation is similar to English, except for the ¿ preceding a question, the ¡ preceding an exclamation, and the use of a dash or « » to indicate a direct quotation.

3.3 SPANISH SYLLABIFICATION

In order (a) to stress Spanish words correctly, and (b) to divide words at the end of a line, you must first learn how to divide Spanish words into syllables. The principles of Spanish syllabification are quite simple:

(1) A word has as many syllables as vowels and/or diphthongs:

    me   ama   muchacho   seis   reinar   cigarro

(2) A syllable consists of a consonant and the following vowel or diphthong:

    mu-cha-cho   ba-ta-lla   ci-ga-rro   pia-no   hie-na

(3) An initial vowel stands alone as a syllable, whereas a final consonant belongs to the same syllable as the preceding vowel or diphthong:

    a-ma   o-cho   a-ni-mal   co-piar

(4) Adjacent vowels that do not form a diphthong are divided:

    le-er   re-al   ca-er   dí-a   re-ú-ne

(5) Two adjacent consonants are divided, unless the second is l or r:

    mis-mo   lec-ción   cin-co   **but: **o-tro   a-ma-ble

(6) Exceptions to the l or r "rule" given above are sl, sr, nr, rl, and tl, which are divided:

    mus-lo   Is-ra-el   hon-ra   bur-la   At-lán-ti-co

(7) Three successive consonants are divided as $2 + 1$, unless the third consonant is *l* or *r*, in which case the division is $1 + 2$.

ins-tan-te   *but:* com-ple-to   en-tre   mos-trar

(8) Four successive consonants are divided as $2 + 2$:

mons-truo   abs-trac-to   ins-truir

(9) Prepositional prefixes always form separate syllables, unless the prefix precedes *s* + consonant, in which case the *s* is joined to the prefix, because in Spanish a syllable cannot begin with *s* + consonant:

des-a-tar   *sub*-ra-yar   *in*-ap-to   *but: ins*-pi-rar

3.4 STRESS AND WRITTEN ACCENT MARKS

As you recall from 1.2, **stress** is the relative prominence given in speech to some particular syllable of a word that has more than one syllable. The principles of Spanish stress are few and simple:

(1) Words ending in a vowel phoneme or /n/ or /s/ are stressed on the next-to-last syllable, and no accent mark is used in writing:

ro-jo   ma-*ña*-na   *a*-man   *mar*-tes   bus-*ca*-mos

(2) Words ending in a consonant phoneme other than /n/ or /s/ are stressed on the last syllable, and no accent mark is used in writing:

mo-*ral*   ciu-*dad*   ve-*jez*   en-tre-*gar*

(3) Exceptions to these two principles are indicated by an acute accent (´) above the vowel phoneme of the stressed syllable:

bus-*có*   sar-*tén*   mar-*qués*   *fá*-cil   com-*prá*-ba-mos

(4) When /i/ or /u/ and an adjacent vowel phoneme do not form a diphthong, an accent is written above the /i/ or /u/ to indicate that it is stressed:

dí-a   o-*í*-mos   re-*ú*-ne   *pú*-a

(5) In writing, an accent mark is used to distinguish between the different meanings and/or functions of certain pairs of words that are pronounced identically. Such accents are always placed above the stressed vowel:

como	as	el	the	este	this
¿cómo?	how?	él	he	éste	this one

3.5 "CLOSED" SYLLABLES

A syllable ending in a consonant is said to be **closed**. In all closed syllables, the phoneme /o/ is represented by the allophone [ɔ]:

dos	[dɔs]	conde	[kɔnde]	comprar	[kɔmprar]
golpe	[gɔlpe]	lorca	[lɔrka]	costar	[kɔstar]

In syllables closed by /k/, /l/, /p/, /t/, and /r/, the phoneme /e/ is represented by the allophone [ɛ]:

secta	[sɛkta]	inepto	[inɛpto]	verde	[bɛrđe]
papel	[papɛl]	étnico	[ɛtniko]	comer	[komɛr]

(Note that orthographic x represents /ks/ before a vowel. A syllable preceding /ks/ is closed by the /k/ of this consonant cluster. Thus, the phoneme /e/ is represented by [ɛ] before /ks/: **éxito** [ɛk-si-to], **eximo** [ɛk-si-mo], **exultar** [ɛk-sul-tar].)

In syllables closed by /θ/, /d/, /m/, /n/, and /s/, however, the phoneme /e/ is represented by the allophone [e]:

pez	[peθ]	hembra	[embra]	mes	[mes]
sed	[seđ]	tengo	[teŋgo]	extra	[estra]

However, not all native speakers of Spanish make this allophonic distinction, and, therefore, you may hear [sɛđ] rather than [seđ], [ɛste] rather than [este], and [dɛn] rather than [den], etc.

3.6 INTONATION

The rise and fall in pitch of the voice during speech is called **intonation**. In Spanish, as in English, there are various patterns of intonation, depending on whether you are making a statement, asking a question, being emphatic, enumerating, etc. These different intonation patterns can be described in terms of **pitch levels, terminals,** and **stress.**

Conversational Spanish has three **pitch** (or tone) **levels.** The lowest is indicated by /1/, the middle level is indicated by /2/, and the highest by /3/. For all practical purposes, these levels may be considered almost identical to three of the levels that you use in English. When you make the statement *John went home,* your voice begins at /2/ and remains there until *home,* where it rises to (3) and rapidly descends to /1/ (and then continues falling as the sound fades out). Unlike Spanish, English also has a level /4/, which is above /3/. If you say *John went home* and emphasize his destination, at *home* your voice rises to /4/ before descending to /1/. Your problems in speaking Spanish will be omitting /4/ and using /1/, /2/, and /3/ in sequences different from those of English.

Terminals refers to the manner of ending an utterance. A drop in pitch level accompanied by a gradual fade-out of sound is called **falling terminal** and is symbolized by / ↓ /. Falling terminal can be illustrated in English by the end of the statement *John went home.* A sharp rise in pitch level accompanied by an abrupt cessation of sound is called **rising terminal** and is symbolized by / ↑ /. The end of the English question *John went home?*

illustrates rising terminal. The third type, **level terminal,** consists of no change in pitch level accompanied by an abrupt cessation of sound. It is symbolized by /→/. Level terminal can be illustrated in English by *Well,* /→/ *no, I don't think so.*

Stress is very important in Spanish intonation because when changes in pitch occur, they take place on the first and the last stressed syllables of an utterance.

Spanish intonation patterns are described by four numbers and an arrow, all placed between slant lines, for example: /1211↓/. The first number indicates the pitch level of the syllable (or syllables) preceding the first stressed syllable. When an utterance begins with a stressed syllable, the level indicated by the first number is not heard. The second number indicates the pitch of the first stressed syllable. An utterance beginning with a stressed syllable begins at this level. The third number indicates the pitch of the last stressed syllable, and the fourth number indicates the pitch of the syllable (or syllables) following the last stressed syllable. When an utterance ends with a stressed syllable, the level indicated by the fourth number is not heard unless it is different from the level indicated by the third number, as in /1231↓/. The arrow indicates what happens to the sound at the end of the utterance. Two basic Spanish intonation patterns are described below; make sure that you understand them before you go to the laboratory to drill them. Other important intonation patterns will be described later.

3.6.1 Statement Patterns. The English intonation pattern for a brief declarative statement, such as *John went home,* is /231↓/. In Spanish, however, a brief declarative statement has a very different pattern: /1211↓/. **Compramos queso,** a statement whose meaning is deliberately withheld for the present, is uttered as:

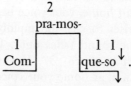

A statement beginning with a stressed syllable, **Compro queso,** starts at /2/:

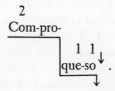

Although this intonation may sound odd to you because in English you may be accustomed to using a /211↓/ pattern to signify boredom or disinterest, be careful not to transfer your English /231↓/ intonation to Spanish; a similar Spanish pattern, /1231↓/, is emphatic. Patterns for longer declarative statements need not concern you now: merely remember that regardless of the length of an unemphatic Spanish statement, the pitch of its last stressed syllable does not rise, but instead falls.

PATTERN DRILL (A). Say each sentence below, using the /1211↓/ intonation pattern. The meanings of these sentences need not concern you. The important thing is to become familiar with them so that you will recognize them later when you hear them in the laboratory.

1. Compramos queso.   5. Comemos poco.
2. Compramos mucho.   6. Comemos queso.
3. Compramos poco.   7. Buscamos flores.
4. Comemos mucho.   8. Buscamos libros.

PATTERN DRILL (B). Say each of the following sentences, which begin with a stressed syllable at level /2/. These, too, will be heard in the laboratory.

1. Compro queso.   5. Como poco.
2. Compro mucho.   6. Como queso.
3. Compro poco.   7. Busco flores.
4. Como mucho.   8. Busco libros.

3.6.2 "Yes" and "No." Many of the lab drills will require you to answer questions affirmatively or negatively. The intonation pattern of **Sí** and **No** before a statement is /21↓/. Thus, the reply **Sí, compramos mucho** has the following intonation:

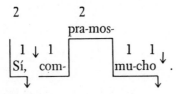

When **Sí** and **No** stand alone, their pattern is /21↓/ also. Sometimes you may hear **Sí** and **No** with a /21→/ intonation before a statement.

PATTERN DRILL.   Say each of the sentences below, using the /21↓1211↓/ pattern. Practice them often, so that the words will not sound strange to you in the lab.

1. Sí, compramos mucho.   5. Sí, compro mucho.
2. Sí, compramos queso.   6. Sí, compro queso.
3. Sí, comemos poco.   7. Sí, como poco.
4. Sí, buscamos flores.   8. Sí, busco flores.

Lesson 4

4.1 NOUNS

Spanish words that are preceded by **el** or **la** are called *nouns*. Those given below will be used in this lesson. Next to each is the corresponding English term. Practice pronouncing them.

1.	**el muchacho**	*the boy*	7.	**la pluma**	*the pen*
2.	**la muchacha**	*the girl*	8.	**el lápiz**	*the pencil*
3.	**el padre**	*the father*	9.	**el libro**	*the book*
4.	**la madre**	*the mother*	10.	**la ciudad**	*the city*
5.	**el clavel**	*the carnation*	11.	**la casa**	*the house*
6.	**la rosa**	*the rose*	12.	**la lección**	*the lesson*

4.2 GENDER

All Spanish nouns are either masculine or feminine in gender. Those preceded by **el** are masculine (except for some to be explained in a later lesson); those preceded by **la** are feminine. Although it is quite logical for nouns referring to males to be masculine (1, 3 above), and for nouns referring to females to be feminine (2, 4 above), the original (that is, mainly the Latin) choices of genders for inanimate things are largely inexplicable (5–12 above). In such cases the correct gender must be learned along with the noun itself. Should you forget whether a noun is preceded by **el** or **la**, the following "rules of thumb" are useful:

4.2.1 Nouns ending in **-o** are regularly masculine (1, 9 above). One important exception is **la mano,** *the hand.*

4.2.2 Nouns ending in **-a** are usually feminine (2, 6, 11 above). One important exception is **el día,** *the day.*

4.2.3 Nouns ending in **-dad** and **-ción** are regularly feminine (10, 12 above).

4.3 DEFINITE ARTICLES

The forms **el** and **la** are called, respectively, the singular masculine and the singular feminine *definite articles*. Their respective plural forms are **los** and **las**. All four forms correspond to *the* in English, although their use does not always correspond to the English use of the definite article.

4.4 PLURALIZATION OF NOUNS

What can you deduce about the plurals of nouns from the following groups of articles and nouns?

Group 1	Group 2	Group 3	Group 4
el muchacho	el padre	el clavel	el lápiz
los muchachos	los padres	los claveles	los lápices
la muchacha	la madre	la ciudad	la lección
las muchachas	las madres	las ciudades	las lecciones

4.4.1 The forms in Groups 1 and 2 show that regardless of gender, nouns ending in an unaccented vowel add /-s/, written -s, to indicate the plural.

4.4.2 The forms in Groups 3 and 4 show that regardless of gender, nouns ending in a consonant add /-es/, written -es, to indicate the plural.

4.4.3 The forms in Group 4 show two changes that are of importance only in writing. What are these changes, and why do they not matter in speech?

PATTERN DRILL. On the basis of the examples given in the preceding section, you can accurately form the plural of any given noun. Do so with the following new nouns. First say each as it appears, then say its plural.

1. el caballo	*the horse*	7. la cuchara	*the spoon*
2. la yegua	*the mare*	8. la cucharita	*the teaspoon*
3. la flor	*the flower*	9. el tenedor	*the fork*
4. el árbol	*the tree*	10. el cuchillo	*the knife*
5. la mesa	*the table*	11. la taza	*the cup*
6. la silla	*the chair*	12. el platillo	*the saucer*

4.5 VERBS

Spanish verbs are inflected to indicate mood, tense, person, and number. For example, in **compro** (*I buy*), the **-o** attached to the stem **compr-** designates indicative mood, present tense, first person, singular number.

Inflections form certain patterns, thereby providing a convenient means of classifying and learning most Spanish verbs. A so-called *regular verb* has an inflectional pattern that can be foretold from its *infinitive*, the form ending in -r. Infinitives ending in -ar (**comprar, buscar**) indicate an inflectional pattern conventionally referred to as the *first conjugation.* Infinitives ending in -er (**vender, comer**) indicate an inflectional pattern conventionally referred to as the *second conjugation.* Infinitives ending in -ir (**abrir, escribir**) indicate an inflectional pattern conventionally referred to as the *third conjugation.* Verbs whose inflections lie outside these three patterns are called *irregular* verbs.

The *stem* of a verb is that part of the verb preceding the -ar, -er, or -ir of the infinitive. For example, **comprar** consists of the stem **compr-** plus -ar. Similarly, **vender** can be divided into **vend-** plus -er, and **escribir** consists of **escrib-** plus -ir. It is to these stems that most mood-tense-person-number markers are added.

Since such markers clearly indicate person and number in most moods and tenses, the so-called *subject pronouns,* vital in English, are usually unnecessary in Spanish. Consequently, their use is limited to occasions when contrast or emphasis is desired. Using them when they are not required is incorrect. (Experience has shown that students whose native language is English have a strong tendency to make this mistake. To counteract this "carryover" from English, the usually unnecessary Spanish subject pronouns are deliberately omitted from this lesson.)

4.6 PRESENT INDICATIVE: FIRST CONJUGATION

4.6.1 *First Person Singular.* To indicate the first person singular, the -ar of the infinitive is replaced by -o. The infinitive **buscar** means *to look for.* The Spanish equivalent of *I'm looking for* is **busco.** *I'm looking for the book* is **Busco el libro.** *I'm not looking for the book* is **No busco el libro.**

PATTERN DRILL (A). Practice *aloud* using **busco** to form sentences with the nouns given in the first column below. Next to each noun is the Spanish sentence that you are to form, followed by its English equivalent. Remember that the inflectional pattern is /1211↓/, and that the first /1/ is not heard because **busco** begins with a stressed syllable.

1. la pluma	Busco la pluma.	*I'm looking for the pen.*
2. las rosas	Busco las rosas.	*I'm looking for the roses.*
3. el lápiz	Busco el lápiz.	*I'm looking for the pencil.*
4. el clavel	Busco el clavel.	*I'm looking for the carnation.*
5. la ciudad	Busco la ciudad.	*I'm looking for the city.*
6. los caballos	Busco los caballos.	*I'm looking for the horses.*
7. la lección	Busco la lección.	*I'm looking for the lesson.*
8. los árboles	Busco los árboles.	*I'm looking for the trees.*

PATTERN DRILL (B). Now use **no busco** with the same nouns to form sentences meaning *I'm not looking for the* . . . . Remember that all the Pattern Drills are to be done aloud.

4.6.2 *First Person Plural.* The first person plural is indicated by replacing the **-ar** of the infinitive with **-amos: buscamos.** *We're looking for the flower* is **Buscamos la flor.** The negative, *We're not looking for the flower,* is **No buscamos la flor.**

PATTERN DRILL (A). Practice aloud using **buscamos** to form sentences with the nouns in the first column below. One such sentence is given as a guide, followed by its English equivalent. Do you know the equivalents of the others? The inflectional pattern of these sentences is /1211↓/.

1. el caballo   Buscamos el caballo.   *We're looking for the horse.*
2. la silla
3. los lápices
4. la taza
5. el platillo
6. las plumas
7. los libros
8. la casa

PATTERN DRILL (B). Now use **compramos,** *we're buying* (from **comprar,** *to buy*) to form sentences with the same nouns.

4.6.3 *Second Person.* The second person is the so-called "intimate you." The formation and use of the second person will be studied in a subsequent lesson. The "non-intimate" (or "polite") Spanish *you* will be explained in 4.6.6.

4.6.4 *Third Person Singular.* The third person singular is indicated by replacing the **-ar** of the infinitive by **-a: busca.** This form is used with all singular subjects that are not in the first or second persons: *the boy, John, Mary,* etc.

> *The boy is looking for the house.*   **El muchacho busca la casa.**
> *John isn't buying the books.*   **Juan no compra los libros.**

This form is also used with *he* and *she.* The distinction between them is made, when necessary for clarity or emphasis, by employing the subject pronouns **él** and **ella,** respectively. *He is buying the cups and she is looking for the saucers* is **Él compra las tazas y ella busca los platillos.**

PATTERN DRILL (A). Use **busca** to connect the nouns in the first column below with the nouns in the second column. One model sentence is given to aid you. What is the English equivalent of each sentence?

1. La muchacha . . . las flores.   La muchacha busca las flores.
2. Ella . . . la mesa.
3. La madre . . . el tenedor.
4. El padre . . . los cuchillos.
5. Juan . . . la yegua.
6. Él .. . . las flores.
7. El muchacho . . . las rosas.
8. Ella . . . las cucharitas.

PATTERN DRILL (B). Now use **compra** in the same way. The first sentence is **La muchacha compra las flores.**

4.6.5 *Third Person Plural.*

The third person plural is indicated by replacing the **-ar** of the infinitive by **-an: buscan.** This form is used with all plural subjects that are not in the first or second persons: *the boys, John and Mary,* etc.

The boys are looking for the table.   **Los muchachos buscan la mesa.**
John and Mary look for the chairs.   **Juan y María buscan las sillas.**
They aren't looking for the spoons.   **No buscan las cucharas.**

Unlike English, Spanish can distinguish between masculine *they* and feminine *they.* This distinction is made, when necessary for clarity or emphasis, by employing the subject pronouns **ellos** and **ellas,** respectively. *They* [the boys] *are buying the forks and they* [the girls] *are buying the spoons* is **Ellos compran los tenedores y ellas compran las cucharas.**

PATTERN DRILL (A). Use **buscan** to connect the nouns in the first column below with the nouns in the second column. The meaning of each new word will be found at the end of the sentence in which it is introduced.

1. Juan y María . . . las tazas.   Juan y María buscan las tazas.
2. Los muchachos . . . el caballo.
3. María y Elena . . . las cucharas.
4. Ellas . . . el mantel. (*tablecloth*)
5. Ellos . . . los cuchillos.
6. Las muchachas . . . las flores.
7. Juan y Pedro . . . el animal. (*animal*)
8. Las madres . . . los manteles.

PATTERN DRILL (B). Now use **no compran** to connect the same two columns. The first sentence will be **Juan y María no compran las tazas.**

4.6.6 *Spanish "You."* The Spanish equivalent of the English you is **usted** in the singular and **ustedes** in the plural. In writing, these forms are often abbreviated as **Vd., Ud.,** or **V.** in the singular, and as **Vds., Uds.,** or **VV.** in the plural. **Usted** is used with a third person singular verb (**usted busca**), and **ustedes** is used with a third person plural verb (**ustedes buscan**). This is so because **usted** and **ustedes** are modern Spanish developments of earlier forms of address (**Vuestra Merced** and **Vuestras Mercedes**) that required third person verb forms, as in the case of the English Your Grace.

For reasons of courtesy as well as clarity, **usted** and **ustedes** generally accompany their respective third person verb forms. However, they are not as vital as you is in English, and in direct address **usted** is usually used only once, in the first sentence. For example: "*Good morning, Mr. González. How are you? When did you return from Lima? Did you have a good trip? Do you plan to go back soon?*" etc. In the preceding dialogue, **usted** normally would have been used only in "*How are you?*" Unnecessary repetition of **usted** can be insulting.

Eventually you will become accustomed to this. For the time being, make it a "rule of thumb" always to employ **usted** and **ustedes**, especially in answers to questions and in unrelated sentences (as in the Pattern Drills).

You're looking for the tablecloth is either **Usted busca el mantel** or **Ustedes buscan el mantel,** depending on the number of people being addressed. Similarly, *You are not looking for the cups* is either **Usted no busca las tazas** or **Ustedes no buscan las tazas.**

PATTERN DRILL (A). Practice aloud using **usted busca** to form sentences with the nouns below:

1. las cucharas   Usted busca las cucharas.
2. la mesa
3. los lápices
4. el vaso (*glass*)
5. el mantel
6. la casa
7. los vasos
8. el plato (*plate*)

PATTERN DRILL (B). Practice aloud using **ustedes compran** to form sentences with the nouns in the preceding drill.

4.7 NEGATION

As you have undoubtedly deduced from the examples in the preceding sections, negation is expressed in Spanish by using **no** immediately before a verb:

No busco el vaso.   *I'm not looking for the glass.*
Vds. no compran la casa.   *You're not buying the house.*

PATTERN DRILL. Say each sentence below. Then repeat it as a negative sentence, using **no** immediately before the verb:

1. Las muchachas buscan las tazas.   Las muchachas no buscan las tazas.
2. Buscamos el mantel.
3. Compro la servilleta. (*napkin*)
4. Vd. compra los tenedores.
5. Juan busca los platos.
6. Ellas buscan la sartén. (*frying pan*)
7. María y él buscan los vasos.
8. Vds. compran las servilletas.

4.8 INTERROGATION

In Spanish, as in English, there are two basic types of questions. A question that begins with an interrogative word—such as *What are you buying?*—is called an *information* question. In a Spanish information question, the initial interrogative word is followed by a verb, which, in turn, is followed by the subject of that verb (if the subject is expressed by a separate word). The Spanish equivalent of the English *what?* is **¿qué?** In writing, all Spanish questions are preceded by an inverted question mark:

¿Qué compra Vd.?   *What are you buying?*
¿Qué busca Juan?   *What is John looking for?*
¿Qué buscamos?   *What are we looking for?*

Some speakers of Spanish use a /1211↓/ intonation pattern to ask information questions; others use a /1321↓/ intonation. The first /1/ of either pattern is rarely heard because most Spanish interrogative words are stressed monosyllables, or have a stressed initial syllable. The changes in pitch levels of **¿Qué buscamos?** can be seen in the following diagrams:

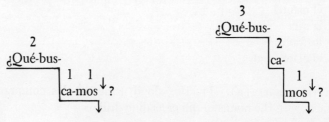

PATTERN DRILL. Use the /1211↓/ intonation pattern to ask each information question below:

1. ¿Qué buscamos?
2. ¿Qué compramos?
3. ¿Qué buscan ustedes?
4. ¿Qué busca María?
5. ¿Qué compra usted?
6. ¿Qué deseamos? (**desear**, *to want*)
7. ¿Qué desean ustedes?
8. ¿Qué desea el hombre? (*man*)

4.8.1 *The Second Type of Question.* A question that does not begin with an interrogative word—such as *Are you looking for the chair?*—is called a yes-no question. Spanish yes-no questions do not have a fixed word order. They can have either the inverted order "verb + subject (if a separate word) + remainder of sentence" or the statement order "subject (if a separate word) + verb + remainder of sentence":

¿Busca Vd. la silla?   ¿Vd. busca la silla?

The position of the subject and the verb with respect to each other is not important because in Spanish the interrogative character of such utterances is clearly indicated by intonation. Some speakers use a /2322↑/ pattern for yes-no questions:

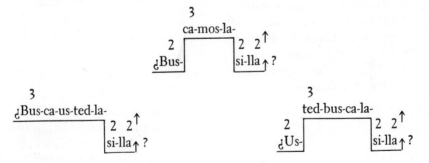

Other speakers use /1222↑/ for such questions. In both patterns, the rising terminal is abrupt:

PATTERN DRILL. Say each sentence below. Then repeat it as a yes-no question, placing the subject after the verb and using the /2322↑/ intonation pattern:

1. Juan busca el plato.   ¿Busca Juan el plato?
2. María desea el vaso.
3. Vd. compra las flores.
4. Los muchachos buscan la casa.
5. El hombre busca las servilletas.
6. La madre desea la rosa.
7. Ellas buscan las tazas.
8. Vds. buscan los árboles.

4.9 ADDITIONAL REGULAR «–AR» VERBS

estudiar	to study	**Estudio la lección.**	*I'm studying the lesson.*
hallar	to find	**Hallo las rosas.**	*I find the roses.*
tomar	to take	**Tomo el plato.**	*I take the plate.*
mirar	to look at	**Miro el libro.**	*I'm looking at the book.*

PATTERN DRILL. Answer each of the following questions affirmatively, using **Sí** and a complete sentence:

1. ¿Estudia Vd. las lecciones?   —Sí, estudio las lecciones.
2. ¿Miran Vds. las flores?
3. ¿Toman Vds. las servilletas?
4. ¿Hallan los muchachos el caballo?
5. ¿Estudia María la lección?
6. ¿Toma Vd. la sartén?
7. ¿Hallan Vds. los manteles?
8. ¿Mira Vd. las rosas?

Lesson 5

5.1 INDEFINITE ARTICLES

Compro un libro means *I'm buying a book*. **Compro una manzana** means *I'm buying an apple*. The Spanish words **un** and **una** are called, respectively, the masculine and the feminine *indefinite articles*. They correspond to the English a (and an). They always precede the noun with which they are used, and agree with that noun in gender. Sometimes, as in the preceding sentences, the Spanish usage of **un** and **una** parallels the English use of a. However, there are occasions when English requires the indefinite article and Spanish does not. These differences will be studied later.

PATTERN DRILL. Say each of the following sentences as it appears. Then repeat it, replacing **el** and **la** with the corresponding forms of **un** and **una**, as in the model sentence. At the right are the English meanings of your sentences:

1. Compro el queso.   Compro un queso.   *I'm buying a cheese.*
2. Compro la naranja.   *I'm buying an orange.*
3. Compro el huevo.   *I'm buying an egg.*
4. Compro la manzana.   *I'm buying an apple.*
5. Compro el melocotón.   *I'm buying a peach.*
6. Compro la toronja.   *I'm buying a grapefruit.*
7. Compro el pescado.   *I'm buying a fish.*
8. Compro el pan.   *I'm buying a loaf of bread.*

5.2 QUANTITY

To express the specific quantity represented by the English one, Spanish uses **un** and **una**. *I'm buying one egg* is **Compro un huevo.** *I'm buying one orange* is **Compro una naranja.** Although written Spanish does not distinguish between **un** signifying "1" and the indefinite article **un**, in speech **un**

40

and **una** are stressed slightly in order to indicate the quantity "1." In contrast, unstressed **un** and **una** are equivalent to the English indefinite *a*. Other specific quantities, such as *two eggs, seven oranges,* etc., will be studied in a later lesson.

5.2.1 To *Express an Indeterminate Large Quantity.* English employs *a great deal of, a lot of, many,* and *lots of.* Spanish employs **mucho** for the same purpose. What can be deduced about **mucho** from the following sentences?

1. **Compramos mucho pan.**	*We buy a great deal of bread.*
¿Compran Vds. mucho pan?	*Do you buy a lot of bread?*
2. **Compramos mucha carne.**	*We're buying a lot of meat.*
¿Compran Vds. mucha carne?	*Are you buying a great deal of meat?*
3. **Compramos muchos huevos.**	*We buy many eggs.*
¿Compran Vds. muchos huevos?	*Do you buy lots of eggs?*
4. **Compramos muchas fresas.**	*We buy lots of strawberries.*
¿Compran Vds. muchas fresas?	*Are you buying many strawberries?*

5.2.1.1 The preceding examples show that **mucho** precedes the noun with which it is used, and agrees with that noun in number and gender.

PATTERN DRILL. Say each sentence below, and then repeat it, replacing the article with the correct form of **mucho,** as in the model:

1. Compro el pescado.   Compro mucho pescado.
2. Compran la carne.
3. Compramos los huevos.
4. Juan compra las naranjas.
5. Compro las manzanas.
6. Vds. compran el queso.
7. ¿Compra Vd. las fresas?
8. No compro los melocotones.

5.2.2 To *Express an Intermediate Small Quantity.* English employs *little* or *few.* Spanish employs **poco** for the same purpose. What you learned about **mucho** also applies to **poco:**

1. **Compramos poco pan.**	*We buy little bread.*
2. **Compramos poca carne.**	*We buy little meat.*
3. **Compramos pocos huevos.**	*We buy few eggs.*
4. **Compramos pocas fresas.**	*We buy few strawberries.*

PATTERN DRILL (A). Say each sentence below, and then repeat it, replacing the article with the correct form of **poco,** as in the model:

1. Compro el queso.   Compro poco queso.
2. Compro la leche. (*milk*)
3. Compramos las fresas.
4. Juan compra el pescado.
5. Vds. compran las toronjas.
6. ¿Compra Vd. la leche?
7. María compra las naranjas.
8. ¿Compran Vds. los huevos?

PATTERN DRILL (B). Answer each of the following questions with **No** and, as in the model answer, the opposite of the quantity expressed in the question:

1. ¿Compran Vds. mucho pescado?   —No, compramos poco pescado.
2. ¿Compran Vds. poco queso?
3. ¿Compran Vds. poca carne?
4. ¿Compran Vds. mucha leche?
5. ¿Compra Vd. muchos huevos?
6. ¿Compra Vd. muchas fresas?
7. ¿Compra Vd. poca leche?
8. ¿Compra Vd. pocas naranjas?

5.2.3 *To Express an Indeterminate Intermediate Quantity.* English employs *some* or *any*. In Spanish this concept is usually expressed by the complete absence of any quantitative word at all:

1. **Compramos leche.**   We're buying some milk.
   ¿Compra Vd. leche?   Are you buying any milk?
   No compro leche.   I'm not buying any milk.
2. **Compramos fresas.**   We're buying some strawberries.
   ¿Compra Vd. fresas?   Are you buying any strawberries?
   No compro fresas.   I'm not buying any strawberries.

Note that English has a parallel construction: We're buying bread; Are you buying bread? and I'm not buying bread.

PATTERN DRILL. Repeat each sentence below, changing it to express the concept of *some* or *any*:

1. José compra los tenedores.   5. ¿Compra Vd. las cucharas?
2. Elena compra las rosas.   6. No compran los platillos.
3. No compro los vasos.   7. ¿Compro mucha carne?
4. Compramos las naranjas.   8. Vds. no compran mucha leche.

5.3 DEMONSTRATIVE ADJECTIVES

An adjective is conventionally defined as a word used in conjunction with a noun for the purpose of providing information about the noun. A *demonstrative* adjective points out a particular noun (English *this book* and *that book*). Although Spanish has four demonstrative adjectives, only three of them have a direct demonstrative character. The other, **el**, is used as the definite article. All the Spanish demonstrative adjectives are inflected to agree in gender and number with the nouns with which they are used, and they normally precede these nouns.

5.3.1 *Association with the Speaker.* **Compro este queso** means *I'm buying this cheese. I'm buying these cheeses* is **Compro estos quesos.** The forms of **este** and **estos** used before feminine nouns are, respectively, **esta** and **estas.** The forms of **este** are employed, as the English *this* and *these* are, to denote what is near to, or associated with, the speaker.

PATTERN DRILL. Say each of the following sentences as it appears. Then repeat it, replacing **el, la, los,** and **las** with the corresponding forms of **este:**

1. Compro el pescado.
2. No compro el huevo.
3. Compramos la toronja.
4. No compramos la manzana.
5. No compro los melocotones.
6. ¿Compramos los quesos?
7. ¿Compro las naranjas?
8. Compro las fresas.

5.3.2 *Association with the Hearer.* **Vd. compra ese melocotón** means *You're buying that peach. You're buying those peaches* is **Vd. compra esos melocotones.** The forms of **ese** and **esos** used before feminine nouns are, respectively, **esa** and **esas.** The forms of **ese** are employed, as the English *that* and *those* are, to denote what is near to, or associated with, the person spoken to. Unlike English *that* and *those*, **ese** does not also refer to what is remote from both speaker and hearer.

PATTERN DRILL. Say each of the following sentences as it appears. Then repeat it, replacing **el, la, los,** and **las** with the corresponding forms of **ese:**

1. Vd. compra el pan.
2. Vds. compran el queso.
3. ¿Compra Vd. la manzana?
4. Vd. no compra la naranja.
5. ¿Compran Vds. los melocotones?
6. ¿Compra Vd. los huevos?
7. Vds. no compran las uvas. (*grapes*)
8. ¿Compran Vds. las toronjas?

5.3.3 *Remoteness from Speaker and Hearer.* **Juan compra aquel queso** means *John is buying that cheese over there. John is buying those cheeses over there* is **Juan compra aquellos quesos.** The forms of **aquel** and **aquellos**

used before feminine nouns are, respectively, **aquella** and **aquellas.** The forms of **aquel** are employed, as the archaic English *yonder* (and the current English *that . . . over there*), to denote what is remote from both the speaker and the person spoken to.

PATTERN DRILL.   Say each of the following sentences as it appears. Then repeat it, replacing el, la, los, and las with the corresponding forms of **aquel:**

1. Juan compra el caballo.	5. El padre compra los melones.
2. Ella compra el melón. (*melon*)	6. ¿Compra José la naranja?
3. María y él compran la toronja.	7. ¿Compran las fresas?
4. No compran la manzana.	8. Ellas compran las uvas.

5.4   PRESENT INDICATIVE: SECOND CONJUGATION (INFINITIVES IN «–ER»)

5.4.1   *First Person Singular.* To indicate the first person singular, the -er of the infinitive is replaced by -o. The infinitive **comer** means *to eat.* The Spanish equivalent of *I'm eating the egg* is **Como el huevo.** *I'm not eating the egg* (or *I don't eat the egg*) is **No como el huevo.**

PATTERN DRILL (A).   Practice aloud using **como** to form statements with the expressions given below:

1. la manzana   Como la manzana.
2. las uvas
3. esta toronja
4. una naranja
5. mucha carne
6. el melocotón
7. muchos huevos
8. muchas fresas

PATTERN DRILL (B).   Now use **no como** with the same expressions to form sentences meaning *I'm not eating. . . .*

5.4.2   *First Person Plural.* To indicate the first person plural, the -er of the infinitive is replaced by -emos: comemos. *We're eating the bread* is **Comemos el pan.** *We're not eating the bread* is **No comemos el pan.**

PATTERN DRILL (A). Practice aloud using **comemos** to form statements with the expressions given below:

1. esta toronja   Comemos esta toronja.
2. muchas uvas
3. este melón
4. pan y queso
5. mucho pescado
6. los melocotones
7. las cerezas (*cherries*)
8. estas fresas

PATTERN DRILL (B). Now use **no comemos** with the same expressions to form sentences meaning We're not eating. . . .

5.4.3 *Third Person Singular.* To indicate the third person singular, the -er of the infinitive is replaced by -e: **come.** Remember that **come** is used not only with all singular subjects not in the first or second persons, but also with **usted.**

Helen is eating the cherries.	**Elena come las cerezas.**
The man is eating fish.	**El hombre come pescado.**
Do you eat a lot of cheese?	**¿Come Vd. mucho queso?**

PATTERN DRILL. Use **come** to connect the nouns in the first column below with the nouns in the second column. Do you understand all the sentences?

1. Este hombre . . . mucho pan.   Este hombre come mucho pan.
2. Elena   . . . muchas cerezas.
3. Usted   . . . poca carne.
4. Ese muchacho . . . una toronja.
5. Ese hombre   . . . fresas.
6. La madre   . . . muchas uvas.
7. José   . . . aquellas manzanas.
8. Vd.   . . . pan y queso.

PATTERN DRILL. Now use **¿Come Vd.?** followed by each of the expressions in the second column above in order to form questions. The first is **¿Come Vd. mucho pan?**

5.4.4 *Third Person Plural.* To indicate the third person plural, the -er of the infinitive is replaced by -en: **comen.** Remember that **comen** is used with **ustedes** as well as with all plural subjects not in the first or second persons.

The men are eating cheese.	**Los hombres comen queso.**
John and Helen eat a lot of bread.	**Juan y Elena comen mucho pan.**
You're eating fish.	**Ustedes comen pescado.**

PATTERN DRILL (A). Use **comen** to connect the nouns in the first column below with the nouns in the second column. The first sentence will be **Estos hombres comen mucha carne.**

1. Estos hombres . . . mucha carne.
2. Juan y Elena . . . el melón.
3. Los muchachos . . . muchas fresas.
4. Ustedes . . .· estas cerezas.
5. Vds. . . . mucho pan.
6. Ellos . . . aquel queso.
7. Esos hombres . . . muchas uvas.
8. Vds. . . . huevos.

PATTERN DRILL (B). Now use **¿Comen Vds.?** followed by each of the expressions in the second column above to form questions. The first is **¿Comen Vds. mucha carne?**

5.5 PRESENT INDICATIVE: THIRD CONJUGATION (INFINITIVES IN «–IR»)

With two exceptions, infinitives ending in **-ir** are inflected with the same markers used for infinitives ending in **-er**. **Vivir** means *to live,* and the first person singular is indicated by replacing the **-ir** with **-o**: **Vivo en el Canadá** means *I live in Canada.*

The third person singular is indicated by replacing the **-ir** of the infinitive with **-e**: **José vive en el Canadá. Vd. vive en los Estados Unidos.**

The third person plural is indicated by replacing the **-ir** of the infinitive with **-en**: **José y Elena viven en el Canadá. ¿Viven Vds. en el Brasil?**

One of the exceptions mentioned above is the first person plural, which is indicated by replacing the **-ir** of the infinitive with **-imos**: **Vivimos en el Brasil. No vivimos en la Argentina.**

The other exception, the second person plural, will be studied later.

PATTERN DRILL (A). Say each sentence below, and then repeat it as a negative sentence, with **no** immediately preceding the verb. Make sure that you pronounce the names of the countries correctly.

1. Vivo en el Canadá.
2. Juan vive en el Japón.
3. Vd. vive en el Perú.
4. Vivimos en la Argentina.

5. Aquellos hombres viven en la China.
6. Vivimos en el Uruguay.
7. Vds. viven en el Paraguay.
8. Vivimos en los Estados Unidos.

PATTERN DRILL (B). Say each sentence below, and then repeat it as a question, placing the subject, if expressed, immediately after the verb:

1. Vivo en el Canadá.   ¿Vivo en el Canadá?
2. Vivimos en el Perú.
3. José vive en la Argentina.
4. Vd. vive en el Uruguay.
5. Vds. viven en los Estados Unidos.
6. Esos hombres viven en el Ecuador.
7. Vivimos en la India.
8. Vivo en el Brasil.

PATTERN DRILL (C). Answer each of the following questions affirmatively, using Sí, the proper form of vivir, and then the remainder of the question:

1. ¿Vive Vd. en los Estados Unidos?   —Sí, vivo en los Estados Unidos.
2. ¿Vive José en el Ecuador?
3. ¿Viven Vds. en el Canadá?
4. ¿Viven Vds. en el Perú?
5. ¿Viven Juan y María en la China?
6. ¿Vive Vd. en la India?
7. ¿Viven ellas en el Brasil?
8. ¿Viven Vds. en el Japón?

PATTERN DRILL (D). Now answer each of the preceding questions negatively, using No, and then a negative sentence: No, no vivo en los Estados Unidos.

5.6 SPECIAL USE OF THE DEFINITE ARTICLE

In Spanish the definite article always precedes the names of some countries, most of which are given in 5.5. Such usage is comparable to the American English usage of the definite article in *the United States*. Far more numerous are the names of countries before which the definite article is not ordinarily used, such as those below. Do you recognize them?

España	Italia	Inglaterra	Noruega	Dinamarca	Grecia
Francia	Rusia	Alemania	Bélgica	Polonia	Suiza
Escocia	Suecia	Hungría	Turquía	Panamá	Haití

5.7 OTHER REGULAR «–ER» AND «–IR» VERBS

beber	*to drink*	**Bebo mucha cerveza.**	*I drink a lot of beer.*
vender	*to sell*	**Vendo mucho vino.**	*I sell a lot of wine.*
leer	*to read*	**Leo el periódico.**	*I'm reading the newspaper.*
abrir	*to open*	**Abro la puerta.**	*I open the door.*
recibir	*to receive*	**Recibo el regalo.**	*I receive the present.*
escribir	*to write*	**Escribo la carta.**	*I'm writing the letter.*

PATTERN DRILL. Answer each of the following questions affirmatively, using **Sí** and a complete sentence:

1. ¿Bebe Vd. mucha leche?
2. ¿Lee Vd. ese periódico?
3. ¿Abre Vd. la puerta?
4. ¿Escribe Vd. muchas cartas?

5. ¿Beben Vds. poca cerveza?
6. ¿Venden Vds. mucho pescado?
7. ¿Reciben Vds. muchas cartas?
8. ¿Abren Vds. los regalos?

5.8 EMPHATIC INTONATION

The main difference between the English /241 ↓ / emphatic intonation and the Spanish /1231 ↓ / emphatic pattern is the pitch level of the last stressed syllable. In an emphatic English utterance, such as *John went home!*, the voice rises to level /4/ at the heavily stressed syllable (*home*) before falling to /1/. In Spanish, however, the last stressed syllable is no higher than level /3/. The other difference between English emphasis and Spanish emphasis is the lower level of an unstressed initial syllable in Spanish. The emphatic ¡**Compramos mucho!** changes pitch as follows:

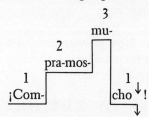

Emphatic utterances that begin with a stressed syllable, such as ¡**Compro mucho!** start at level /2/ (as in English):

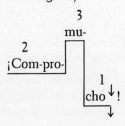

PATTERN DRILL. Say each sentence below using the /1211↓/ statement intonation. Then repeat each sentence, this time using the /1231↓/ emphatic intonation pattern:

1. Compramos mucho.
2. Comemos mucho.
3. Comemos muchas uvas.
4. Comemos mucho pescado.

5. Compro mucho.
6. Como mucho.
7. Como muchas uvas.
8. Como mucho pescado.

Lesson 6

6.1 INTIMATE "YOU"

In addition to **usted** and **ustedes,** Spanish has two other subject pronouns that are equivalent to the English you: **tú** and its plural, **vosotros** (feminine, **vosotras**). They, together with their corresponding verb endings, object pronouns, and possessives, comprise the so-called *second person* in Spanish. As a result of the circumstances governing the use of the second person, it is often referred to as the "intimate you" or the "informal you."

In very general terms, the intimate you is employed when addressing members of your family, close friends, inferiors (children, animals, some servants), and equals (such as classmates). However, usage varies from region to region as well as among social classes. Inopportune use of the intimate forms can be insulting.

A good "rule of thumb" is *never to initiate* the use of the intimate you, but rather to let the native Spanish speaker be the first to employ it. And when this happens, you are expected to reply in kind; not to do so consti- tutes a rebuff. Therefore, you had better drill and learn the proper forms.

In South America and some parts of Spain, **vosotros** has dropped out of use as the plural of **tú,** and has been replaced by **ustedes** (with its corre- sponding third person plural forms).

6.1.1 Regular Verbs: Second Person Singular. In verbs inflected according to the **buscar** pattern, singular intimate you is indicated by replacing the **-ar** of the infinitive with **-as: Buscas el libro. ¿Compras mucha cerveza?**

In verbs inflected according to the **comer** and **vivir** patterns, singular intimate you is indicated by replacing the **-er** and **-ir** of the infinitive with **-es: Comes mucha carne. ¿Vives en el Canadá?**

A useful "rule of thumb" is that the second person singular is the same as the third person singular plus /-s/:

Vd. busca	**buscas**
Vd. come	**comes**
Vd. vive	**vives**

This pattern holds true for most moods and tenses of regular as well as irregular verbs. Note that the subject pronoun **tú** is unnecessary.

PATTERN DRILL (A). Say each sentence below as it appears, and then repeat it as a negative sentence with **no** immediately preceding the verb:

1. Buscas la lección.
2. Compras muchas fresas.
3. Vendes esa casa.
4. Vives en el Perú.

5. Lees el periódico.
6. Abres la ventana. (*window*)
7. Recibes muchos regalos.
8. Necesitas ese mantel.

PATTERN DRILL (B). Say each sentence below as it appears, and then repeat it using the intimate you:

1. Vd. busca las servilletas.
2. Vd. estudia la lección.
3. ¿Desea Vd. esa pluma?
4. ¿Come Vd. mucho pan?

5. Vd. bebe mucha cerveza.
6. ¿Vive Vd. en la Argentina?
7. Vd. no escribe muchas cartas.
8. ¿Qué busca Vd.?

PATTERN DRILL (C). Answer the following questions according to the pattern given beside the first:

1. ¿Buscas el libro?   —Sí, busco el libro.
2. ¿Deseas la pluma?
3. ¿Bebes mucha leche?
4. ¿Vives en el Ecuador?
5. ¿Comes mucho queso?
6. ¿Vendes la casa?
7. ¿Escribes muchas cartas?
8. ¿Hallas las fresas?

PATTERN DRILL (D). Change the sentences below into questions beginning with ¿**Qué?** according to the pattern given beside the first sentence:

1. Buscas el libro.   ¿Qué buscas?
2. Hallas la pluma.
3. Abres la ventana.
4. Recibes el regalo.
5. Lees el periódico.
6. Estudias la lección.
7. Necesitas los tenedores.
8. Deseas la naranja.

6.1.2 *Regular Verbs: Second Person Plural.* In verbs inflected according to the **buscar** pattern, plural intimate you is indicated by replacing the **-ar** of the infinitive with **-áis**:

Buscáis las cartas.   ¿Qué compráis?

In verbs inflected according to the **comer** pattern, plural intimate you is indicated by replacing the **-er** of the infinitive with **-éis**:

Coméis muchas uvas.   ¿Vendéis la casa?

In verbs inflected according to the **vivir** pattern, plural intimate you is indicated by replacing the **-ir** of the infinitive with **-ís**:

Vivís en el Canadá.   ¿Recibís las cartas?

PATTERN DRILL (A). Say each of the sentences below as it appears, and then repeat it as a negative sentence with **no** immediately before the verb:

1. Buscáis los caballos.
2. Necesitáis la sartén.
3. Deseáis ese mantel.
4. Coméis las manzanas.
5. Bebéis mucha cerveza.
6. Vivís en los Estados Unidos.
7. Leéis los periódicos.
8. Abrís esa puerta.

PATTERN DRILL (B). Say each sentence below as it appears, and then repeat it with the verb in the plural intimate you:

1. Vds. desean los vasos.
2. Vds. no compran mucha carne.
3. Vds. comen mucho pan.
4. ¿Hallan Vds. el caballo?
5. ¿Leen Vds. muchos libros?
6. Vds. viven en el Uruguay.
7. ¿Qué buscan Vds.?
8. Vds. escriben muchas cartas.

PATTERN DRILL (C). Answer the following questions aloud according to the pattern given beside the first:

1. ¿Buscáis las plumas?   —Sí, buscamos las plumas.
2. ¿Estudiáis la lección?
3. ¿Coméis muchas fresas?
4. ¿Leéis los periódicos?
5. ¿Bebéis vino?
6. ¿Vivís en el Brasil?
7. ¿Abrís la ventana?
8. ¿Escribís las cartas?

6.2 TENER

This verb is *irregular* because of the changes that occur as it is inflected. **Tener** is the equivalent of English *to have*, and it assumes the following forms in the present indicative.

6.2.1 *First Person Singular.*

Tengo el libro.	*I have the book.*
No tengo el libro.	*I don't have the book.*
¿Tengo el libro?	*Do I have the book?*

In addition to the primary meaning *I have*, **tengo** is the equivalent of English *I am* in the following expressions:

Tengo calor.	*I'm warm.*	**Tengo mucho calor.**	*I'm very warm.*
Tengo frío.	*I'm cold.*	**Tengo mucho frío.**	*I'm very cold.*

PATTERN DRILL (A). Practice aloud using **tengo** to form sentences with each of the expressions below. Do you understand all of them?

1. los tenedores
2. muchas fresas
3. la manzana
4. frío

5. estas cucharas
6. calor
7. mucho frío
8. mucho calor

PATTERN DRILL (B). Now use **no tengo** with the preceding expressions.

6.2.2 *First Person Plural.*

Tenemos el libro.	*We have the book.*
Tenemos calor.	*We are warm.*
Tenemos frío.	*We are cold.*
Tenemos hambre.	*We're hungry.*
Tenemos sed.	*We're thirsty.*
Tenemos mucha hambre.	*We're very hungry.*
Tenemos mucha sed.	*We're very thirsty.*

Note that before **calor** and **frío** the equivalent of *very* is **mucho**, and that before **hambre** and **sed** its equivalent is **mucha**.

PATTERN DRILL. Practice aloud using **tenemos** to form sentences with each of the expressions below. Then use **no tenemos** in the same way.

1. mucho pan
2. estas tazas
3. sed
4. mucha sed

5. toronjas
6. frío
7. mucho calor
8. mucha hambre

6.2.3 *Second Person Singular and Plural.*

Tienes el libro.	*You have the book.*	**Tenéis el libro.**
Tienes frío.	*You are cold.*	**Tenéis frío.**
No tienes sed.	*You're not thirsty.*	**No tenéis sed.**
¿Tienes hambre?	*Are you hungry?*	**¿Tenéis hambre?**

PATTERN DRILL. Practice aloud using **tienes** to form statements with each of the following expressions. Then use **tenéis** in the same way.

1. mucha sed	5. ese caballo
2. mucho calor	6. mucho frío
3. esos melocotones	7. esas naranjas
4. mucha cerveza	8. mucha hambre

6.2.4 Third Person Singular and Plural.

Vd. tiene el libro.	You have the book.	Vds. tienen el libro.
¿Tiene Vd. la pluma?	Do you have the pen?	¿Tienen Vds. la pluma?
¿Tiene Vd. hambre?	Are you hungry?	¿Tienen Vds. hambre?
¿Tiene Vd. mucha sed?	Are you very thirsty?	¿Tienen Vds. mucha sed?

PATTERN DRILL (A). Practice aloud using **tiene** to connect the nouns in the first column below to the expressions in second column:

1. Juan	. . .	la pluma.
2. Elena	. . .	las sillas.
3. El hombre	. . .	muchos caballos.
4. Vd.	. . .	mucho frío.
5. La madre	. . .	aquella casa.
6. El muchacho	. . .	muchas fresas.
7. José	. . .	mucha sed.
8. Vd.	. . .	mucha hambre.

PATTERN DRILL (B). Practice aloud using **tiene** or **tienen**, as required, to connect the nouns in the first column below to the expressions in the second column:

1. Aquel hombre	. . .	mucho frío.
2. Juan	. . .	el mantel.
3. Vds.	. . .	sed.
4. Elena y María	. . .	las cucharas.
5. Las muchachas	. . .	hambre.
6. Vd.	. . .	mucha cerveza.
7. Aquella madre	. . .	frío.
8. Vds.	. . .	mucha hambre.

PATTERN DRILL (C). Practice aloud answering the following questions with **Sí,** the proper form of **tener,** and the remainder of the question:

1. ¿Tiene Vd. calor?	—Sí, tengo calor.
2. ¿Tienes frío?	Sí, tengo frío.
3. ¿Tienen Vds. mucha sed?	Sí, tenemos mucha sed.

4. ¿Tenéis mucho pan?   Sí, tenemos mucho pan.
5. ¿Tiene Juan aquellas sillas?   Sí, Juan tiene aquellas sillas.
6. ¿Tienen los hombres mucha hambre?   Sí, los hombres tienen mucha hambre.
7. ¿Tengo mucha cerveza?   Sí, Vd. tiene mucha cerveza.
8. ¿Tenemos aquella casa?   Sí, Vds. tienen aquella casa.

6.3 CONTRACTION

Whenever the Spanish word **de** immediately precedes the masculine singular definite article, the two contract to form **del**.

6.4 POSSESSION

What can you deduce about possession in Spanish from the following set of English statements and their Spanish equivalents?

1. *I have John's car.*   **Tengo el coche de Juan.**
2. *I have Mary's car.*   **Tengo el coche de María.**
3. *I have the boy's car.*   **Tengo el coche del muchacho.**
4. *I have the girl's car.*   **Tengo el coche de la muchacha.**
5. *I have the boys' car.*   **Tengo el coche de los muchachos.**
6. *I have the girls' car.*   **Tengo el coche de las muchachas.**
7. *I have this man's car.*   **Tengo el coche de este hombre.**
8. *I have this woman's car.*   **Tengo el coche de esta mujer.**
9. *I have John's father's car.*   **Tengo el coche del padre de Juan.**

6.4.1 The preceding examples show that English use of 's (*John's, the boy's*) to indicate possession is parallel to the Spanish use of **de** for the same purpose.

PATTERN DRILL. Complete the sentences below so as to indicate the possession of the items preceding the dots by the persons following the dots:

1. Busco el lápiz   . . . Juan.   Busco el lápiz de Juan.
2. ¿Tienes el mantel   . . . la muchacha?
3. ¿Buscas los caballos   . . . los hombres?
4. No tengo la sartén   . . . la mujer.
5. Deseo el caballo   . . . el muchacho.
6. ¿Abres la puerta   . . . María?
7. Buscamos el coche   . . . el profesor. (*teacher*)
8. Vivo en la casa   . . . José

6.5 POSSESSIVE ADJECTIVES

The function of the so-called *possessive* adjectives is to indicate the possessor of the noun with which the adjective is used: *my book, our houses,* etc. Spanish possessive adjectives, like English ones, precede the nouns with which they are used: *my book,* **mi libro.** Unlike the English, however, Spanish possessive adjectives are inflected. All add /-s/ before a plural noun, and some have a feminine form before a feminine noun.

6.5.1 *First Person Singular.* The Spanish equivalent of *my* is **mi** before a singular noun of either gender, and **mis** before a plural noun of either gender:

Tengo mi libro.	**Tengo mi revista.** (*magazine*)
Tengo mis libros.	**Tengo mis revistas.**

PATTERN DRILL. Say each sentence below, and then repeat it, replacing the definite article with the proper form of **mi** or **mis:**

1. Tengo el caballo.
2. Tengo los libros.
3. Tengo las cucharitas.
4. Tengo la pluma.
5. Tengo los melocotones.
6. ¿Tiene Vd. las revistas?
7. Juan tiene los tenedores.
8. Tenemos los caballos.

6.5.2 *Second Person Singular.* When addressing one person, the Spanish intimate *your* is **tu** before a singular noun of either gender, and **tus** before a plural noun of either gender:

Tienes tu periódico.	**Tienes tu revista.**
Tienes tus periódicos.	**Tienes tus revistas.**

PATTERN DRILL. Say each sentence below, and then repeat it, replacing the definite article or demonstrative with the proper form of **tu** or **tus:**

1. Tienes las yeguas.
2. Tienes la cuchara.
3. Tienes el platillo.
4. Tienes los periódicos.
5. Tienes la pluma.
6. ¿Tengo esos cuchillos?
7. ¿Tenemos la revista?
8. No tengo esas tazas.

6.5.3 *First Person Plural.* The Spanish equivalent of *our* is **nuestro** before a masculine singular noun, and **nuestra** before a feminine singular noun. Before plural nouns their respective forms are **nuestros** and **nuestras:**

Tenemos nuestro libro.	**Tenemos nuestra libreta.** (*notebook*)
Tenemos nuestros libros.	**Tenemos nuestras libretas.**

PATTERN DRILL. Say each sentence below, and then repeat it, replacing the definite article or demonstrative with the proper form of **nuestro**:

1. Tenemos este mantel.
2. Tenemos las cucharas.
3. Tenemos los claveles.
4. Tenemos estas naranjas.

5. Tenemos los caballos.
6. ¿Tiene Vd. la revista?
7. Tengo estas libretas.
8. Vds. no tienen los lápices.

6.5.4 Second Person Plural. When addressing more than one person, the Spanish intimate your is **vuestro** before a masculine singular noun, and **vuestra** before a feminine singular noun. Before plural nouns their respective forms are **vuestros** and **vuestras**:

> **Tenéis vuestro perro. (dog)   Tenéis vuestra vaca. (cow)**
> **Tenéis vuestros perros.   Tenéis vuestras vacas.**

PATTERN DRILL. Say each sentence below, and then repeat it, replacing the definite article or demonstrative with the proper form of **vuestro**:

1. Tenéis esa sartén.
2. Tenéis los periódicos.
3. Tenéis las libretas.
4. ¿Tenéis el perro?

5. Tenéis las fresas.
6. Tengo esos platillos.
7. No tenemos las servilletas.
8. Juan tiene esas vacas.

6.5.5 Third Person Singular and Plural. Spanish has only two third-person possessive adjectives: **su,** which precedes singular nouns of either gender, and **sus,** which precedes plural nouns of either gender. Depending on context, **su** can indicate *his, her,* or *their.* In addition, since **Vd.** and **Vds.** are in the third person, **su** can indicate *your.*

Although in isolation the value of **su** can be confusing, in context, on the other hand, the meaning of **su** offers little difficulty. For example, in **Juan tiene su libro** (or **sus libros**), **su** is obviously *his.* Similarly:

María tiene su libro   (or **sus libros**)
                                        Mary has her book (or *her books*)
Ellos tienen su libro   (or **sus libros**)
                                        They have their book (or *their books*)
Vd. tiene su libro   (or **sus libros**)
                                        You have your book (or *your books*)

Su normally refers either to the subject of the preceding third-person verb, as in the preceding examples, or, if there is no third-person verb, then **su** refers to the most recently mentioned *he, she, they,* or *you,* as in the following related sentences: **María desea los libros, y no tenemos sus libros.** Here **sus** is obviously *her.* In cases where ambiguity is possible, such as *He has her book*, exactness can be obtained by replacing **su** (or **sus**) in the following ways:

Juan tiene su libro	*his book*
" " el libro de ella	*her book*
" " el libro de ellos	*their book*
" " el libro de Vd.	*your book*
" " los libros de Vd.	*your books*
" " la pluma de Vd.	*your pen*
" " las plumas de ella	*her pens*
" " las plumas de ellos	*their pens*

In the same manner, *He has his pen, her pencil, and their notebook* is clearly indicated by **Él tiene su pluma, el lápiz de ella y la libreta de ellos.**

PATTERN DRILL (A). Say each sentence below, and then repeat it, replacing the definite article with the proper form of **su** to indicate possession by the subject of the sentence:

1. Juan tiene el periódico.
2. José tiene las plumas.
3. Ellas tienen el coche.
4. Ellas tienen la casa.
5. María tiene el platillo.
6. Elena tiene las tazas.
7. Vd. tiene el tenedor.
8. Vd. tiene las cucharas.

PATTERN DRILL (B). Say each sentence below, and then repeat it, using the proper form of **su** to indicate possession:

1. Tengo el lápiz de Juan.   Tengo su lápiz.
2. ¿Tenemos los libros de María?
3. No tenemos la revista de María.
4. ¿Tienes el perro de ellos?
5. ¿Tienes la libreta de ella?
6. ¿Tienes las libretas de ella?
7. No tengo el libro de Vd.
8. No tengo las revistas de Vd.

PATTERN DRILL (C). Practice answering the following questions affirmatively, using **Sí**, the proper form of **tener**, and the correct possessive adjective:

1. ¿Tiene Vd. mi periódico?   —Sí, tengo su periódico.
2. ¿Tiene Vd. mis libretas?   Sí, tengo sus libretas.
3. ¿Tiene Vd. nuestra vaca?   Sí, tengo su vaca.
4. ¿Tiene Vd. nuestros platillos?   Sí, tengo sus platillos.
5. ¿Tienes mi coche?   Sí, tengo tu coche.
6. ¿Tienes mis plumas?   Sí, tengo tus plumas.

7. ¿Tienes tu coche?	Sí, tengo mi coche.
8. ¿Tienes tus manzanas?	Sí, tengo mis manzanas.
9. ¿Tiene Vd. su carta?	Sí, tengo mi carta.
10. ¿Tienen Vds. su mesa?	Sí, tenemos nuestra mesa.

6.5.6 Possession of Several Things. In Spanish, unlike English, the possessive adjective is usually repeated before each noun:

I have my pen and pencil.	**Tengo mi pluma y mi lápiz.**
I have your books and magazines.	**Tengo tus libros y tus revistas.**
We have our cups and saucers.	**Tenemos nuestras tazas y nuestros platillos.**

PATTERN DRILL. Practice answering the following questions affirmatively, using **Sí**, the proper form of **tener**, and the correct possessive adjectives:

1. ¿Tienen Vds. su libro y su pluma?
   —Sí, tenemos nuestro libro y nuestra pluma.
2. ¿Tienen Vds. mi perro y mi vaca?
   —Sí, tenemos su perro y su vaca.
3. ¿Tienes mi vino y mi cerveza?
   —Sí, tengo tu vino y tu cerveza.
4. ¿Tengo tu taza y tu platillo?
   —Sí, tienes mi taza y mi platillo.
5. ¿Tiene Vd. su tenedor y sus cucharas?
   —Sí, tengo mi tenedor y mis cucharas.
6. ¿Tenemos su revista y sus periódicos?
   —Sí, Vds. tienen mi revista y mis periódicos.
7. ¿Tiene Vd. su cuchillo y su tenedor?
   —Sí, tengo mi cuchillo y mi tenedor.
8. ¿Tienes tu mesa y tus sillas?
   —Sí, tengo mi mesa y mis sillas.

Lesson 7

7.1 CONTRACTION

In Spanish whenever **a** immediately precedes the masculine singular definite article, the two contract to form **al**:

Escribimos al hombre.   *We're writing to the man.*

PATTERN DRILL.   Say each sentence below, and then repeat it as a negative sentence with **no** immediately preceding the verb:

1. Escribo al hombre.
2. Vd. escribe a la mujer.
3. Leo esta carta al padre de José.
4. Escribimos a las mujeres.

5. Juan lee el libro a aquel hombre.
6. Escribo una carta al profesor.
7. Vendo esta revista al muchacho.
8. Vds. leen a las muchachas.

7.2 IR

The irregular verb **ir** is the Spanish equivalent of *to go*. **Ir** and a destination are connected by **a**: **Ir a la Argentina**, *to go to Argentina*. In the present tense, indicative mood, **ir** assumes the following forms.

7.2.1 *First Person Singular.*

Voy a España.   *I'm going to Spain.*
No voy al Brasil.   *I'm not going to Brazil.*

PATTERN DRILL (A).   Practice aloud using **voy** to form sentences with each of the following destinations:

1. a los Estados Unidos
2. al Perú
3. a la tienda (*to the store*)
4. al Canadá

5. al cine (*to the movies*)
6. a la tienda de Juan
7. a la ciudad
8. al campo (*to the country*)

PATTERN DRILL (B). Now use **no voy** with the same destinations.

7.2.2 *The Other Persons.* In all the remaining persons, **ir** is inflected as a regular -ar verb whose stem is **v-**:

Singular:	vas	¿Vas al centro?	*Are you going downtown?*
	va	Juan va al centro.	*John is going downtown.*
		¿Va Vd. al centro?	*Are you going downtown?*
Plural:	vamos	Vamos al centro.	*We're going downtown.*
	vais	¿Vais al centro?	*Are you going downtown?*
	van	No van al centro.	*They're not going downtown.*
		¿Van Vds. al centro?	*Are you going downtown?*

Why is no accent mark necessary in writing **vais** (unlike **compráis**)?

PATTERN DRILL (A). Practice aloud using **Vd. va** to form sentences with each of the following destinations:

1. al cine
2. al centro
3. al hospital (*to the hospital*)
4. a la tienda
5. al mercado (*to the market*)
6. al campo
7. a la ciudad
8. al teatro (*to the theater*)

PATTERN DRILL (B). Now use **¿Van Vds.?** with the same destinations.

PATTERN DRILL (C). Practice aloud using **a la escuela** (*to school*) to complete each of the sentences begun below:

1. Enrique va . . .
2. No vamos . . .
3. El padre del muchacho va . . .
4. ¿Va Vd. . . . ?
5. ¿Van José y Elena . . . ?
6. Esa muchacha no va . . .
7. Voy . . .
8. Vds. van . . .

PATTERN DRILL (D). Now use **a la universidad** (*to college*) to complete the sentences begun above.

7.2.3 *Where?* The Spanish equivalent of *Where are you going?* is **¿Adónde va Vd.?**

PATTERN DRILL (A). Practice aloud using **¿Adónde?** and **ir** to form questions with each of the subjects below:

1. Juan   ¿Adónde va Juan?
2. Vds.
3. Elena y María
4. el padre de José
5. tú
6. tu padre
7. aquellos hombres
8. Vd.

PATTERN DRILL (B). Practice aloud using **ir a casa** (*to go home*) to answer each of the questions below:

1. ¿Adónde va Vd.? —Voy a casa.
2. ¿Adónde va Enrique?
3. ¿Adónde van aquellas mujeres?
4. ¿Adónde vas?

5. ¿Adónde van Vds.?
6. ¿Adónde va tu hermano? (*brother*)
7. ¿Adónde va tu hermana? (*sister*)
8. ¿Adónde van tus hermanos?

7.3 FUTURE ACTION

In place of the future tense (*I'll buy the house*), English often substitutes the verb go: *I'm going to buy the house.* In Spanish, **ir a** followed by an infinitive is used in the same way:

Voy a comer esta manzana.	*I'm going to eat this apple.*
¿Vas a comprar ese libro?	*Are you going to buy that book?*
Juan no va a vender el coche.	*John isn't going to sell the car.*
Vamos a beber mucha cerveza.	*We're going to drink a lot of beer.*
¿Vais a estudiar esta lección?	*Are you going to study this lesson?*
Van a escribir al hombre.	*They're going to write to the man.*
¿Van Vds. a comer ese pescado?	*Are you going to eat that fish?*

PATTERN DRILL (A). Practice aloud using **voy a** to form sentences with each of the following expressions:

1. comer mucha carne
2. leer las revistas de Juan
3. beber este vino
4. recibir muchos regalos

5. comprar esta corbata (*tie*)
6. escribir al muchacho
7. abrir las ventanas
8. tener mucha sed

PATTERN DRILL (B). Now use **Vd. va a** with the same expressions.

PATTERN DRILL (C). Say each sentence below. Then express it in the future, replacing each verb with **vamos a** and the infinitive of the original verb:

1. Buscamos aquella casa.   Vamos a buscar aquella casa.
2. Comemos mucho pescado.
3. Escribimos al hombre.
4. Leemos muchos libros.
5. Vendemos este coche.
6. Vivimos en la casa de Elena.
7. Estudiamos estas lecciones.
8. Compramos los pantalones. (*trousers*)

PATTERN DRILL (D). Say each sentence below. Then express the same thought in the future, replacing the verb in each sentence with the form of **ir a** that the sentence's subject indicates, plus the infinitive of the original verb:

1. ¿Beben Vds. mucha cerveza?   ¿Van Vds. a beber mucha cerveza?
2. Vd. compra la casa.
3. Juan desea aquellas manzanas.
4. María compra esa falda. (*skirt*)
5. No compramos aquellos pantalones.
6. ¿Comes mucha carne?
7. ¿Tienen Vds. mucha hambre?
8. Vd. no necesita mi corbata.

7.4 DESCRIPTIVE ADJECTIVES

The function of the so-called *descriptive* adjectives is to indicate the color, size, shape, quality, condition, nationality, or other attribute of the noun with which the adjective is used. For example, in *I have a red book, red* is a descriptive adjective.

Although in Spanish the position of descriptive adjectives is not as rigidly fixed as it is in English, this need not confuse or worry first-year students. Most Spanish descriptive adjectives usually follow the nouns to which they refer. The reasons why this statement is qualified by "most" and "usually" will be explained in a later lesson.

A good "rule of thumb" is always to place descriptive adjectives that you learn in this lesson after the nouns to which they refer.

Unlike their English counterparts, Spanish descriptive adjectives are inflected. All assume plural forms when used with plural nouns, and, in addition, some of them show feminine gender when referring to feminine nouns. This is called *agreement*, a concept that you are already familiar with from your previous studies of the demonstrative and possessive adjectives.

7.4.1 Agreement: Number. Used with singular nouns, Spanish descriptive adjectives are singular. When referring to plural nouns, they indicate plural number in exactly the same ways that Spanish nouns do. Descriptive adjectives ending in a vowel in the singular add /-s/, written -s, when used with plural nouns:

Tengo el libro rojo. (red)   **Tengo el libro verde.** (green)
Tengo los libros rojos.   **Tengo los libros verdes.**

Descriptive adjectives terminating in a consonant in the singular add /-es/, written -es, when they are used with plural nouns:

Tengo el libro azul. (*blue*)   Tengo el mantel gris. (*grey*)
Tengo los libros azules.   Tengo los manteles grises.

PATTERN DRILL. Say each of the following sentences as it appears. Then repeat it, changing all articles, nouns, and adjectives to the plural:

1. Voy a buscar el vaso rojo.   5. No deseamos aquel coche gris.
2. Deseo el libro azul.   6. ¿Tiene Vd. mi lápiz azul?
3. ¿Vas a comprar el mantel rojo?   7. No compro este melón verde.
4. No tengo tu mantel azul.   8. ¿Buscas este clavel blanco? (*white*)

7.4.2 Agreement: Gender. When a descriptive adjective whose masculine singular form ends in -o (**rojo, blanco**) is used in reference to a feminine noun, the final -o is replaced by -a:

Tengo el mantel blanco.   Tengo la servilleta blanca.
Leo el libro mexicano.   Leo la revista mexicana. (*Mexican*)
Bebo vino italiano.   Bebo cerveza italiana. (*Italian*)

Such adjectives end in -as when referring to plural feminine nouns:

Tengo las servilletas blancas.   Leo las revistas mexicanas.

PATTERN DRILL (A). Say each of the sentences below, supplying the correct form of **rojo** after the nouns:

1. Necesito el clavel . . .   5. Vamos a necesitar esas rosas . . .
2. No necesitas la taza . . .   6. María va a comprar muchas flores . . .
3. ¿Vas a buscar ese coche . . .?   7. Mi hermano vive en aquella casa . . .
4. Deseo este sombrero . . . (*hat*) 8. No deseo esa camisa . . . (*shirt*)

PATTERN DRILL (B). Say each of the sentences above, supplying the correct form of **amarillo** (*yellow*) after the nouns.

7.4.3 Agreement: Gender. Descriptive adjectives ending in a vowel other than -o do not show feminine gender when referring to feminine nouns:

Leo el periódico canadiense. (*Canadian*)
Leo la revista canadiense.

Feminine gender is not shown by most descriptive adjectives ending in a consonant:

Busco el lápiz azul.   Leo este libro difícil. (*difficult*)
Busco la pluma azul.   Leo esta lección difícil.

PATTERN DRILL (A). Say each of the sentences below, supplying the correct form of **verde** after the nouns:

1. Elena compra un sombrero . . .
2. ¿Tiene Vd. mi camisa . . .?
3. Voy a vender el coche . . . al hombre.
4. ¿Buscas las servilletas . . .?
5. ¿Necesita Vd. ese zapato . . .? (*shoe*)
6. Voy a comprar una corbata . . .
7. Mi hermana tiene muchos zapatos . . .
8. No voy a comer ese queso . . .

PATTERN DRILL (B). Say each of the sentences above, supplying the correct form of **azul** after the nouns.

PATTERN DRILL (C). Say each of the sentences above, supplying the correct form of **blanco** after the nouns.

7.4.4 Agreement: Gender. Descriptive adjectives that end in a consonant and indicate nationality, such as **francés** (*French*) and **español** (*Spanish*), are the most important exceptions to 7.4.3. Referring to feminine nouns, such adjectives add -a to the masculine singular form:

> **Leo el periódico francés.**   **Bebo mucho vino español.**
> **Leo la revista francesa.**   **Bebo mucha cerveza española.**

Such adjectives end in -as when referring to plural feminine nouns:

> **Leo las revistas francesas.**   **Compro naranjas españolas.**

Why do adjectives like **francés** and **alemán** (*German*) not need an accent mark over their feminine form or their plural forms in writing?

PATTERN DRILL (A). Say each of the sentences below, supplying the correct form of **francés** after the noun:

1. ¿Venden Vds. ese coche . . .?
2. José busca una camisa . . .
3. Tengo zapatos . . .
4. Compramos muchos vinos . . .
5. ¿Lees muchas revistas . . .?
6. No deseo aquella corbata . . .
7. Juan recibe muchos periódicos . . .
8. María vive en aquella ciudad . . .

PATTERN DRILL (B). Say each of the sentences above, supplying the correct form of **español** after the nouns.

PATTERN DRILL (C). Say each of the sentences above, supplying the correct form of **inglés** (*English*) after the nouns.

PATTERN DRILL (D). Say each of the sentences above, supplying the correct form of **italiano** after the nouns.

7.4.5. *Agreement with Different Nouns.* What do the following sentences show about a descriptive adjective that refers to different nouns?

1. Busco un vaso y un plato rojos.
2. Busco una camisa y una corbata rojas.
3. Busco una taza y un platillo rojos.

A. Sentences 1, 2, and 3 show that a descriptive adjective referring to two different nouns is plural.

B. Sentences 1 and 2 show that when a descriptive adjective refers to different nouns of the same gender, the plural of that gender is used.

C. Sentence 3 shows that when a descriptive adjective refers to different nouns of different genders, the masculine plural is used.

PATTERN DRILL (A). Say each of the sentences below, supplying the correct form of **caro** (*expensive*) after the nouns:

1. Compro una corbata y una camisa . . .
2. Juan tiene un sombrero y un abrigo . . . (*overcoat*)
3. María busca un sombrero y una falda . . .
4. No deseamos cuchillos y cucharitas . . .
5. ¿Van Vds. a buscar una casa y un auto . . .?
6. ¿Tienes mi falda y mi blusa . . .? (*blouse*)
7. No vamos a comprar estas servilletas y este mantel . . .
8. Aquel hombre vende melocotones y fresas . . .

PATTERN DRILL (B). Say each of the sentences above, supplying the correct form of **barato** (*inexpensive, cheap*) after the nouns.

7.4.6 *Position: Two Descriptive Adjectives Referring to the Same Noun.* When two descriptive adjectives follow the same noun, they are usually joined by **y**. There are no "rules" for the sequence of two adjectives connected by **y**:

Vivimos en esta casa roja y amarilla.	*We live in this red and yellow house.*
María compra una falda azul y blanca.	*Mary is buying a blue and white skirt.*
¿Deseas mi corbata verde y cara?	*Do you want my expensive green tie?*
Busco zapatos blancos y baratos.	*I'm looking for cheap white shoes.*

PATTERN DRILL (A). Say each sentence below, placing the correct form of **rojo y blanco** in the proper position:

1. Voy a comprar este coche.
2. Enrique vive en nuestra casa.
3. ¿Tienes mi corbata?
4. Busco estos lápices.

5. María no desea aquella falda.
6. Necesitamos muchas servilletas.
7. Como muchas uvas.
8. ¿Desea Vd. estos zapatos?

PATTERN DRILL (B). Say each sentence below, placing the correct form of the adjectives in parentheses in the proper position:

1. (blanco y azul)   No voy a vivir en aquella casa.
2. (azul y caro)   Juan tiene mi corbata.
3. (amarillo y caro)   No deseamos aquella mesa.
4. (gris y barato)   ¿Busca Vd. una camisa?
5. (verde y barato)   No voy a necesitar este abrigo.
6. (amarillo y verde)   José no tiene pantalones.
7. (rojo y amarillo)   ¿Desean Vds. estas servilletas?
8. (francés y alemán)   Bebemos muchos vinos.

Lesson 8

8.1 ESTAR

Spanish has two verbs that correspond in use to the English *to be*. They are not freely interchangeable. One of these verbs is **estar,** which is often connected by **en** to a noun indicating a location: **Estar en el centro,** *to be downtown.* In the present tense, indicative mood, **estar** assumes the following forms.

8.1.1 *First Person Singular.*

Estoy en el Canadá.	*I'm in Canada.*
No estoy en el cine.	*I'm not at the movies.*

Note that after **estar, en** is equivalent to the English *at* as well as *in.*

PATTERN DRILL (A). Practice aloud using **estoy** to form sentences with each of the following locations:

1. en el hospital
2. en el campo
3. en mi cuarto (*room*)
4. en el Uruguay

5. en la sala (*living room*)
6. en el cuarto de Carlos
7. en el centro
8. en la cocina (*kitchen*)

PATTERN DRILL (B). Now use **no estoy** with each of the same locations.

8.1.2 *The Other Persons.* In the remaining persons, **estar** is inflected as a regular **-ar** verb, except that the /-a/ of the person and number markers is stressed:

Singular:	estás	**¿Estás en el campo?**	*Are you in the country?*
	está	**Juan no está aquí.**	*John isn't here.*
		¿Cómo está Vd.?	*How are you?*

Plural: estamos   **No estamos aquí.**   *We're not here.*
           estáis   **¿Cómo estáis?**   *How are you?*
           están   **No están aquí.**   *They're not here.*
                      ¿Cómo están Vds.?   *How are you?*

PATTERN DRILL (A). Practice aloud using **María está** to form sentences with each of the following locations:

1. en la sala
2. en nuestro cuarto
3. en el comedor (*dining room*)
4. en aquella ciudad española
5. en la biblioteca (*library*)
6. en la cocina
7. en el centro
8. en el restorán (*restaurant*)

PATTERN DRILL (B). Now use **¿Están Vds.?** with the same locations.

PATTERN DRILL (C). Practice aloud using **en casa** (home, at home) to complete each of the sentences below:

1. Mis hermanas están . . .
2. ¿Está Vd. . . .?
3. No voy a estar . . .
4. Vds. no están . . .
5. No estamos . . .
6. Carlos y Elena están . . .
7. ¿Estás . . .?
8. La criada va a estar . . . (*maid*)

PATTERN DRILL (D). Now use **aquí** to complete the sentences above.

PATTERN DRILL (E). Practice aloud using **¿Cómo?** and the appropriate form of **estar** to inquire about the health of the following persons:

1. María y Elena
2. Juan
3. tú
4. tu padre
5. el hermano de Carlos
6. Vds.
7. sus muchachos
8. Vd.

8.2 WHERE?

With **estar**, where? is **¿dónde?**: **¿Dónde están las muchachas?**

PATTERN DRILL. Practice aloud using **¿Dónde?** and the appropriate form of **estar** to ask the location of each item or person below:

1. mi revista francesa
2. Carlos
3. Elena y la criada
4. Vd.
5. tus zapatos negros
6. la cerveza
7. tú
8. el cuarto de baño (*bathroom*)

8.3 AGREEMENT

Descriptive adjectives used with **estar** are inflected to agree with the subject of **estar**:

Este hombre está enfermo. (*sick*)	Juan está triste. (*sad*)
Esta mujer está enferma.	Elena está triste.
Ellos no están enfermos.	Ellos están tristes.
Ellas no están enfermas.	Ellas están tristes.

Similarly, a man says "**Estoy enfermo**"; a woman says "**Estoy enferma**"; men say "**Estamos enfermos**"; and women say "**Estamos enfermas**." Men and women together say "**Estamos enfermos**."

PATTERN DRILL (A). Practice aloud using **bueno** (*well*) to complete each of the sentences below:

1. Carlos está . . .
2. Tu madre está . . .
3. Mis hermanos no están . . .
4. Mi abuela está . . . (*grandmother*)
5. El padre de María está . . .
6. Nuestros padres están . . . (*parents*)
7. Elena va a estar . . .
8. Aquellos hombres no están . . .

PATTERN DRILL (B). Now use **cansado** (*tired*) to complete the sentences above.

8.4 QUESTIONS

When **estar** and a descriptive adjective are used in a question, the adjective is often found between **estar** and a noun subject:

¿Está cansado Juan?   ¿Están cansadas las muchachas?

The same pattern holds true for **estar** and **aquí**: ¿Está aquí la criada?

PATTERN DRILL. Practice aloud making questions out of the following statements:

1. María está cansada.   ¿Está cansada María?
2. Nuestro profesor está ocupado. (*busy*)
3. Esta mujer está enferma.
4. La puerta está cerrada. (*closed*)
5. Juan y su hermana están enfermos.

6. Elena y María están sentadas. (*sitting down*)
7. Esas ventanas están cerradas.
8. Las criadas están ocupadas.

8.5 SER

The irregular verb **ser** is the other Spanish equivalent of *to be*. **Ser** is used with **de** and a location to indicate the origin of someone or something: **Ser de la Argentina,** *to be from Argentina*. **Ser** is also used with a noun to indicate what someone or something is: **Ser estudiante,** *to be a student*. Note that no indefinite article followed **ser** in the preceding Spanish sentence. In the present tense, indicative mood, **ser** assumes the following forms.

8.5.1 First Person Singular.

Soy del Canadá.	*I'm from Canada.*
No soy soldado.	*I'm not a soldier.*
¿Soy tu criada?	*Am I your maid?*

PATTERN DRILL (A). Practice aloud using **soy** to form sentences with each of the following expressions:

1. de los Estados Unidos
2. abogado (*lawyer*)
3. estudiante
4. hombre de negocios (*businessman*)
5. el hermano de Carlos
6. médico (*doctor*)
7. de esa ciudad francesa
8. abuelo (*grandfather*)

PATTERN DRILL (B). Now use **no soy** with each of the same expressions.

8.5.2 First Person Plural.

Somos de Escocia.	*We're from Scotland.*
No somos dentistas.	*We're not dentists.*

PATTERN DRILL. Practice aloud using **somos** to form sentences with each of the following expressions:

1. del Uruguay
2. abogados
3. ingenieros (*engineers*)
4. médicos
5. profesores
6. del campo
7. hombres de negocios
8. soldados

8.5.3 Second Person Singular and Plural.

Eres estudiante.	You're a student.	
Sois estudiantes.	You're students.	
¿Eres del Perú?	Are you from Peru?	¿Sois del Perú?

PATTERN DRILL. Practice aloud using **¿eres?** to form questions with each of the following expressions. Then use **¿sois?** making whatever changes are required by this plural form:

1. de la República Dominicana
2. arquitecto (*architect*)
3. soldado
4. abogado
5. médico
6. ingeniero
7. de esa ciudad inglesa
8. dentista

8.5.4 Third Person Singular.

Juan es de la Habana.	John's from Havana.
¿De dónde es Vd.?	Where are you from?
María es actriz.	Mary's an actress.

Another use of **ser** is with **de** to indicate possession:

Ese libro es de Juan.	That book is John's.
Es de María.	It's Mary's.
No es de Vd.	It isn't yours.

PATTERN DRILL (A). Practice aloud using **es** to complete the sentences below:

1. Mi abuelo . . . del Ecuador.
2. Carlos . . . hombre de negocios.
3. Esta pluma . . . de tu hermano.
4. Mi abuela . . . de esta ciudad.
5. Aquel hombre . . . profesor.
6. Vd. . . . estudiante.
7. El coche rojo . . . de Juan.
8. Este cuarto . . . la cocina.

PATTERN DRILL (B). Now use **no es** to complete the sentences above.

8.5.5 Third Person Plural.

Son del Japón.	They're from Japan.
Vds. no son estudiantes.	You're not students.
Las plumas son de Juana.	The pens are Jane's.

PATTERN DRILL (A). Practice aloud using **son** to complete the sentences below:

1. Estas casas . . . de mi padre.
2. Mis hermanos . . . soldados.
3. Estas camisas blancas . . . de Vd.
4. Esas toronjas . . . de la Florida.

5. Aquellas muchachas . . . criadas.   7. Los perros . . . de esta mujer.
6 Vds. . . . médicos.   8. Estos cuartos . . . comedores.

PATTERN DRILL (B). Now use **no son** to complete the sentences above.

PATTERN DRILL (C). Practice aloud using **es** or **son,** as indicated by context, to complete the sentences below:

1. Enrique . . . abogado.   5. Carlos y María . . . estudiantes.
2. ¿De dónde . . . Vds.?   6. Estos zapatos . . . de mi hermano.
3. Las corbatas rojas . . . de ellos. 7. Nuestra criada . . . de la Argentina.
4. Vd. no . . . profesor.   8. Esta mujer . . . mi abuela.

8.6 AGREEMENT

Descriptive adjectives used with **ser** are inflected to agree with the subject of **ser:**

> **Este hombre es alto.** (*tall*)   **Juan es joven.** (*young*)
> **Esta mujer es alta.**   **Juana es joven.**
> **Ellos no son altos.**   **Ellos son jóvenes.**
> **Ellas no son altas.**   **Ellas son jóvenes.**

Similarly, a man says "**Soy francés**"; a woman says "**Soy francesa**"; men say "**Somos franceses**"; and women say "**Somos francesas.**" Men and women together say "**Somos franceses.**" (Why in writing is an accent necessary above the /-o-/ of **jóvenes?**)

PATTERN DRILL. Practice aloud using **inglés** to complete the sentences below:

1. Ese actor es . . .   5. María y Elena son . . .
2. Mi madre es . . .   6. Estos zapatos negros son . . .
3. La abuela de Carlos es . . .   7. Aquella actriz es . . .
4. Esas mujeres no son . . .   8. Nuestro tío es . . . (*uncle*)

8.7 QUESTIONS

When **ser** and a descriptive adjective are used in a question, the adjective is often found between **ser** and a noun subject:

> **¿Es roja tu casa?   ¿Son jóvenes esas mujeres?**

The same pattern holds for **ser** and a noun indicating an occupation:

> **¿Es médico tu abuelo?   ¿Son criadas sus hermanas?**

PATTERN DRILL. Practice aloud making questions out of the following statements:

1. Tus hermanas son altas.   ¿Son altas tus hermanas?
2. Los padres de Juan son españoles.
3. Aquel hombre es rico. (*rich*)
4. Este libro es interesante.
5. Mi tío es joven.
6. Nuestra tía es bonita. (*pretty*)
7. Muchas mujeres son ricas.
8. Aquellas muchachas son bonitas.

8.8 «SER» AND «ESTAR» COMPARED

Non-Spaniards often have difficulty deciding whether to choose **ser** or **estar** as the equivalent of the English *to be*. In some cases, the answer is provided by another word in the same sentence. The pattern drills that you have practiced indicate three useful "rules of thumb":

8.8.1   **En, ¿dónde?** and **aquí** are used with **estar**:

   Estoy en la cocina.   *¿Dónde está* Juan?   *¿Está* Vd. *aquí?*

8.8.2   **De** is usually used with **ser**:

   ¿De dónde *es* Vd.?   Juan *es de* México.   El libro *es de* Elena.

8.8.3   The subject of a sentence is usually connected to a noun by **ser**:

   [Tú] *Eres profesor.*   *Soy abogado.*   *La muchacha es criada.*

(Exceptions to the above, such as idioms containing **estar** and **de**, need not concern you now.)

   Descriptive adjectives generally offer no such syntactic clues, and in order to decide on **ser** or **estar**, meaning must be taken into account. When you want to indicate "what" you think someone or something normally or usually is, choose **ser**. In this category of "what" are physical, mental, and moral qualities, age, nationality, religion, and economic status. For example:

Juan no es *alto.*	physical quality	María es *bonita.*	
El coche es *rojo.*	physical quality	La casa es *grande.* (big)	
Eres *inteligente.*	mental quality	Eres *estúpido.*	
Vd. es *hipócrita.*	moral quality	Son *malos.* (evil)	
Carlos es *joven.*	age	Soy *viejo.* (old)	
No soy *francés.*	nationality	Somos *canadienses.*	
Son *protestantes.*	religion	Son *católicos.*	
Juana es *rica.*	economic status	Carlos es *pobre.* (poor)	

On the other hand, when you want to indicate the "condition" or the "way" or "how" something or someone is, or happens to be at a particular time, choose **estar**. In this category of "how" are health, physical condition or position, and life or death. For example:

Juan está *enfermo.*	health	Estoy *bueno.*
Estoy *cansado.*	physical condition	Está *roto.* (broken)
Está *sucio.* (dirty)	physical condition	Está *lleno.* (full)
Está *cerrado.*	physical position	Estoy *sentado.*
Juan está *vivo.*	life or death	María está *muerta.*

A change from a norm is indicated by **estar**. For example, you know that coffee in a cup is usually hot, but when the cup of coffee that has been served to you is cold, you complain to the waiter, saying **"Este café está frío."** When *to be* means *has become*, or *looks*, or *feels*, or *tastes*, use **estar**. On the other hand, when neither immediate experience nor the possibility of change enters into your concept of something or someone, use **ser**.

Some descriptive adjectives have different connotations with **estar** and **ser**:

Mi profesor *está aburrido.* (bored)	**Mi profesor** *es aburrido.* (boring)
María *está cansada.* (tired)	**María** *es cansada.* (tiresome)
Juan *está listo.* (ready)	**Juan** *es listo.* (clever)
Las uvas *están verdes.* (unripe)	**Las uvas** *son verdes.* (color)
Juan *está malo.* (sick)	**Juan** *es malo.* (evil)
Juan *está bueno.* (well)	**Juan** *es bueno.* (good)

Finally, note the difference between:

¿Cómo está Juan?	How is John? and
¿Cómo es Juan?	What's John like?

PATTERN DRILL. Complete aloud the Spanish sentences below:

1. *My sister is young.*   Mi hermana . . . joven.
2. *My mother looks young.*   Mi madre . . . joven.
3. *Mary is pretty.*   María . . . bonita.
4. *Mary looks pretty with that hat.*   María . . . bonita con ese sombrero.
5. *That expensive glass is Italian.*   Ese vaso caro . . . italiano.
6. *This glass is broken.*   Este vaso . . . roto.
7. *Our house is white.*   Nuestra casa . . . blanca.
8. *My white tablecloth is dirty.*   Mi mantel blanco . . . sucio.
9. *This soup doesn't taste good.*   Esta sopa no . . . buena.
10. *My young brother has become old.*   Mi hermano joven . . . viejo.

8.9 COGNATES

The discussion of **ser** and **estar** in 8.8 introduced some Spanish words whose English meanings were deliberately withheld. You probably had no difficulty understanding **inteligente, protestante, estúpido,** and **hipócrita** because of their similarity to the English words *intelligent, Protestant, stupid,* and *hypocrite*. These resemblances are obvious signs of the common root of each of these pairs of Spanish and English terms. Words of related origin in different languages are called *cognates*. Many Spanish and English cognates have not only similar written forms, but also the same meanings in both languages and, therefore, require no explanation:

original	*original*	**inmediato**	*immediate*
rápido	*rapid*	**moción**	*motion*
silencio	*silence*	**acción**	*action*
invitar	*invite*	**misión**	*mission*

Other Spanish and English cognates do not, at first glance, resemble each other as closely as the words just mentioned. These not-so-obvious cognates will be explained when they are introduced. Eventually, you will learn to recognize relationships like those of **solitario** and *solitary,* **sagaz** and *sagacious,* and **caridad** and *charity*. The ability to spot cognates will save you considerable time when you start to read Spanish.

There are some Spanish and English cognates that currently do not have the same meanings in both languages. **Parientes** and *parents* are an example of these so-called *deceptive* cognates: **mis parientes** are *my relatives,* whereas *my parents* are **mis padres**. There are so few deceptive cognates that you should have no trouble remembering them.

PATTERN DRILL. Pronounce carefully each Spanish word below, and then give its English cognate:

1. nación	5. sección	9. pasión
2. estación	6. ficción	10. ocasión
3. iniciación	7. instrucción	11. concesión
4. nacionalización	8. elección	12. discusión

Lesson 9

9.1 DESCRIPTION

In Spanish, some attributes of nouns are not indicated by means of descriptive adjectives. Instead, **de** and a noun are used:

> **Voy a comprar un abrigo de lana.** *a woolen overcoat*
> **Vivimos en una casa de ladrillo.** *a brick house*
> **¿Tienes mi lápiz de oro?** *my gold pencil*
> **Deseo helado de chocolate.** *some chocolate ice cream*

Although Spanish uses **de** and a noun mainly to indicate what something is made of, sometimes this construction indicates what something is about, or for:

> **No voy a la clase de matemáticas.** *the mathematics class*
> **No tengo tu libro de español.** *your Spanish book*

The difference between **un libro de español** and **un libro español** is that the latter is from Spain or in Spanish, whereas the former is about Spanish. Similarly, **un profesor de francés** teaches French, whereas **un profesor francés** is French.

With **de** and a noun, *to be* is **ser**:

> **La camisa es de seda.** (*silk*)   **Estos pantalones son de lana.**

PATTERN DRILL (A). Answer the following questions affirmatively, using **Sí** and a complete sentence:

1. ¿Compras esa casa de ladrillo?
2. ¿Tiene Vd. su libro de español?
3. ¿Desea María una falda de seda?
4. ¿Comes mucho helado de fresa?
5. ¿Es de oro ese reloj? (*watch*)
6. ¿Son de seda estas corbatas caras?
7. ¿Es de madera tu casa? (*wood*)
8. ¿Son de lana esos abrigos?

PATTERN DRILL (B). Now answer the same questions negatively, using **No** and a complete negative sentence.

84

9.2 "YES, I AM"

The Spanish equivalent of the reply Yes, I am in answer to a question with ser or estar and a descriptive adjective, or to a question with ser or ser de and a noun, is **Sí, lo soy,** or **Sí, lo estoy.** The **lo** is invariable:

¿Está Vd. enfermo?	—Sí, lo estoy.	Yes, I am.
¿Es Vd. abogado?	—Sí, lo soy.	
¿Están Vds. cansados?	—Sí, lo estamos.	Yes, we are.
¿Son Vds. inteligentes?	—Sí, lo somos.	
¿Es de España tu abuelo?	—Sí, lo es.	Yes, he is.
¿Está buena María?	—Sí, lo está.	Yes, she is.
¿Son inglesas esas mujeres?	—Sí, lo son.	Yes, they are.
¿Están cerradas las puertas?	—Sí, lo están.	
¿Es de oro ese reloj?	—Sí, lo es.	Yes, it is.

The equivalent of No, I'm not, etc., is **No, no lo soy** or **No, no lo estoy,** etc.

PATTERN DRILL (A). Answer the following questions affirmatively, using **lo** and the corresponding form of **ser** or **estar:**

1. ¿Están listas las muchachas?
2. ¿Son altos tus padres?
3. ¿Son estudiantes Vds.?
4. ¿Es de algodón esa camisa? (cotton)
5. ¿Es de lana ese traje? (suit)
6. ¿Son del Canadá Vds.?
7. ¿Es de chocolate ese helado?
8. ¿Están cerradas las ventanas?

PATTERN DRILL (B). Now answer the preceding questions negatively, using **lo.**

9.3 STEM-CHANGING VERBS

The stems of some Spanish verbs undergo certain changes as the verbs are inflected to indicate various persons, tenses, and moods. There are no "rules of thumb" for recognizing the infinitives of such verbs. There are three types of changes in the present tense, indicative mood.

9.3.1 *Empezar.* The verb **empezar** is the Spanish equivalent of to begin. When **empezar** is followed by an infinitive, the two are connected by a: **Empezar a estudiar,** to begin to study. In all three singular persons, and in the third person plural, the /-e-/ immediately preceding the final consonant of the stem diphthongizes to /-ie-/:

Empiezo a estudiar.	I'm beginning to study.
¿Empiezas esa novela?	Are you starting that novel?

| Juan no empieza a comer. | *John isn't beginning to eat.* |
| ¿Empiezan Vds. a trabajar? | *Are you beginning to work?* |

In the first and second persons plural, the /-e-/ does not become /-ie/:

| Empezamos a tener hambre. | *We're starting to be hungry.* |
| ¿Empezáis a estar cansados? | *Are you beginning to be tired?* |

These two forms are "regular" because they are not stressed on the /-e-/ preceding the inflectional ending, but rather on the ending itself.

PATTERN DRILL (A). Say each sentence below as it appears. Then repeat it as a negative sentence, with **no** immediately preceding the verb:

1. Empezamos esta lección.
2. Empiezo a comer muchas manzanas.
3. Elena empieza a estar cansada.
4. El muchacho empieza a leer.
5. Los caballos empiezan a tener sed.
6. Empiezas a trabajar mucho. (*hard*)
7. Vds. empiezan a estudiar.
8. Este libro empieza a ser aburrido.

PATTERN DRILL (B). Answer the following questions affirmatively, using **Sí** and a complete sentence:

1. ¿Empiezas a leer el periódico?
2. ¿Empiezas a tener frío?
3. ¿Empieza Vd. a abrir las ventanas?
4. ¿Empiezas a buscar una casa barata?
5. ¿Empiezan Vds. esa novela?
6. ¿Empiezan tus padres a comer?
7. ¿Empieza Carlos a trabajar mucho?
8. ¿Empieza a estar frío el café?

9.3.2 *Other /-ie-/ Verbs.* The diphthongization of /-e-/ to /-ie-/ occurs in verbs of all conjugations. Reference works usually indicate such verbs in the following way: **querer (ie)**, *to want;* **preferir (ie)**, *to prefer.*

Quiero ser ingeniero.	Juan prefiere ir al centro.
¿Quieres este traje de lana?	¿Prefieren Vds. helado de fresa?
Queremos una casa de madera.	Preferimos esa cerveza canadiense.

Note that **querer** and **preferir** are not connected to a following infinitive by any preposition.

PATTERN DRILL (A). Answer the following questions affirmatively, using **Sí** and a complete sentence:

1. ¿Quiere Vd. ir al Japón?
2. ¿Quiere ser médico Enrique?
3. ¿Quieres trabajar en mi tienda?
4. ¿Quieren Vds. mis libros de español?
5. ¿Prefiere Vd. helado de chocolate?
6. ¿Prefiere María estar en su cuarto?
7. ¿Prefieres ese restorán francés?
8. ¿Prefieren Vds. este vino barato?

PATTERN DRILL (B). Now answer the same questions negatively, using **No** and a complete negative sentence.

9.3.3 *Volver.* The verb **volver** is the Spanish equivalent of *to return.* **Volver** and a destination are connected by **a**: **Volver a la ciudad**, *to return to the city.* To indicate *return from,* **volver** and a place are connected by **de**: **Volver del campo**, *to return from the country.* In all three singular persons, and in the third person plural, the /-o-/ immediately preceding the final consonants of the stem diphthongizes to /-ue-/:

Vuelvo al centro.	*I'm going back downtown.*
¿Vuelves de París?	*Are you returning from Paris?*
María no vuelve.	*Mary isn't coming back.*
¿Vuelven Vds. al campo?	*Are you returning to the country?*

In the first and second persons plural, /-o-/ does not become /-ue-/ because in these two forms the stress does not fall on the /-o-/ preceding the inflectional ending, but rather on the ending itself:

Volvemos a casa.	*We're returning home.*
¿Volvéis a casa?	*Are you going back home?*

PATTERN DRILL (A). Say each sentence below as it appears. Then repeat it as a negative sentence, with **no** immediately preceding the verb:

1. Carlos vuelve a su cuarto.
2. Mis parientes vuelven de Londres.
3. Vuelvo a aquella tienda.
4. Volvemos a casa.
5. Vds. vuelven al centro.
6. Mi tía vuelve al Perú.
7. Vd. vuelve a la sala.
8. Mis hermanos vuelven de la escuela.

PATTERN DRILL (B). Answer the following questions affirmatively, using **Sí** and a complete sentence:

1. ¿Vuelves a ese restorán caro?
2. ¿Vuelve Vd. a casa?
3. ¿Vuelven tus padres de Inglaterra?
4. ¿Vuelven Vds. a Europa?
5. ¿Vuelve Juan a la biblioteca?
6. ¿Vuelve la criada al comedor?
7. ¿Vuelve Vd. a los Estados Unidos?
8. ¿Vuelves a tu cuarto?

9.3.4 *Other /-ue-/ Verbs.* The diphthongization of /-o-/ to /-ue-/ occurs in verbs of all conjugations: **contar** (**ue**), *to count;* **dormir** (**ue**), *to sleep.*

Cuento mis libros.	**Juan no duerme en casa.**
¿Cuentas esos ladrillos?	**¿Duermen Vds.?**
Contamos las fresas.	**Dormimos en ese hotel.**

PATTERN DRILL (A). Answer the following questions affirmatively, using **Sí** and a complete sentence:

1. ¿Duerme Juan en esta clase?
2. ¿Cuenta Vd. sus lápices?
3. ¿Duermen Vds. en la biblioteca?
4. ¿Duermes mucho? (*a lot*)

5. ¿Cuenta la criada las cucharitas?   7. ¿Cuentas esas corbatas de seda?
6. ¿Duerme Vd. en el cine?   8. ¿Cuentan Vds. los relojes?

PATTERN DRILL (B). Now answer the preceding questions negatively, using **No** and a complete negative sentence.

9.3.5 *Pedir*. The verb **pedir** is the Spanish equivalent of *to ask for* and *to order*: **Pedir helado de vainilla,** *to order some vanilla ice cream.* In all three persons of the singular, and in the third person plural, the /-e-/ immediately preceding the final consonant of the stem becomes /-i-/:

Pido un reloj de plata.	*I'm asking for a silver watch.*
¿Pides café?	*Are you ordering coffee?*
Juan no pide vino.	*John doesn't ask for wine.*
¿Piden Vds. queso?	*Are you ordering cheese?*

In the first and second persons plural, the /-e-/ does not become /-i-/ because in these two forms the stress does not fall on the /-e-/ preceding the inflectional ending, but rather on the ending itself:

No pedimos ir al campo.	*We're not asking to go to the country.*
¿Pedís ese vino francés?	*Are you ordering that French wine?*

Note that no preposition is required to connect **pedir** and either a following infinitive or a following noun.

PATTERN DRILL (A). Answer the following questions affirmatively, using **Sí** and a complete sentence:

1. ¿Pide Vd. helado de vainilla?   5. ¿Pides cerveza mexicana?
2. ¿Piden Carlos y Juan tu coche?   6. ¿Pide Vd. pan y queso?
3. ¿Pides pescado en ese restorán?   7. ¿Pide tu hermano ir a Europa?
4. ¿Piden Vds. café?   8. ¿Pide el muchacho un vaso de leche?

PATTERN DRILL (B). Now answer the preceding questions negatively, using **No** and a complete negative sentence.

9.3.6 *Other /-i-/ Verbs*. The replacement of /-e-/ by /-i-/ is limited to certain **-ir** verbs, such as **servir (i)**, *to serve.*

Sirvo leche a las muchachas.	*I serve milk to the girls.*
¿Sirves vino en casa?	*Do you serve wine at home?*
La criada sirve el café.	*The maid is serving the coffee.*
¿Qué sirven Vds.?	*What are you serving?*
No servimos cerveza.	*We don't serve beer.*

PATTERN DRILL (A). Answer the following questions affirmatively, using
Sí and a complete sentence:

1. ¿Sirve Vd. helado en casa?   5. ¿Sirve tu madre muchas fresas?
2. ¿Sirve cerveza ese restorán?   6. ¿Sirve Vd. mucho pescado?
3. ¿Sirves vino a tus hijos? (*children*) 7. ¿Sirves cerveza en casa?
4. ¿Sirven Vds. café en la sala?   8. ¿Sirven tus padres mucha carne?

PATTERN DRILL (B). Now answer the preceding questions negatively, using
No and a complete negative sentence.

9.4 NUMBERS

The Spanish cardinal numbers from 0 through 15 are:

0	cero	4	cuatro	8	ocho	12	doce
1	uno	5	cinco	9	nueve	13	trece
2	dos	6	seis	10	diez	14	catorce
3	tres	7	siete	11	once	15	quince

The cardinal numbers normally precede the nouns to which they refer:
dos libros, quince toronjas, etc. Although the numbers are adjectives, all
but **uno** are invariable in form. Before a masculine singular noun, **uno**
becomes **un: un mantel.** Before a feminine singular noun, **uno** becomes
una: una servilleta.

9.4.1 *Arithmetical Signs.*

$1 + 1$ is read as **uno más uno.**
$2 - 1$ is read as **dos menos uno.**

With numbers, *to be* is **ser:**

Uno más uno son dos.
Dos menos uno es uno.

PATTERN DRILL. Complete aloud the following sentences:

1. Uno más dos son . . .   5. Ocho menos dos son . . .
2. Dos más dos son . . .   6. Diez menos cinco son . . .
3. Cuatro más tres son . . .   7. Siete menos cuatro son . . .
4. Seis más cinco son . . .   8. Nueve menos cuatro son . . .

9.4.2 *How much?* In arithmetic, *How much are* . . .? is **¿Cuántos son** . . .?:

¿Cuántos son uno más seis?   ¿Cuántos son once menos tres?

PATTERN DRILL. Answer the following questions with complete sentences:

1. ¿Cuántos son siete más dos?
2. ¿Cuántos son cinco más cuatro?
3. ¿Cuántos son once más cuatro?
4. ¿Cuántos son diez más cinco?

5. ¿Cuántos son trece menos ocho?
6. ¿Cuántos son quince menos tres?
7. ¿Cuántos son catorce menos cinco?
8. ¿Cuántos son catorce menos nueve?

9.4.3 Numbers. The Spanish cardinal numbers from 16 through 30 are:

16	dieciséis	21	veintiuno	26	veintiséis
17	diecisiete	22	veintidós	27	veintisiete
18	dieciocho	23	veintitrés	28	veintiocho
19	diecinueve	24	veinticuatro	29	veintinueve
20	veinte	25	veinticinco	30	treinta

Before a masculine noun, **veintiuno** becomes **veintiún: veintiún mucha-chos**. Before a feminine noun, **veintiuno** becomes **veintiuna: veintiuna muchachas**.

9.4.4 Arithmetical Signs.

2×2 is read as **dos por dos.**
$4 \div 2$ is read as **cuatro dividido por dos.**

PATTERN DRILL (A). Complete aloud the following sentences:

1. Tres por tres son . . .
2. Diez por tres son . . .
3. Cuatro por seis son . . .
4. Siete por tres son . . .

5. Dieciséis dividido por dos son . . .
6. Veintiocho dividido por siete son . . .
7. Treinta dividido por seis son . . .
8. Dieciocho dividido por seis son . . .

PATTERN DRILL (B). Answer the following questions with complete sentences:

1. ¿Cuántos son catorce más catorce?
2. ¿Cuántos son trece más ocho?
3. ¿Cuántos son dieciséis más nueve?
4. ¿Cuántos son doce más once?
5. ¿Cuántos son treinta menos ocho?
6. ¿Cuántos son veinte menos dos?
7. ¿Cuántos son veinticuatro menos nueve?
8. ¿Cuántos son veintidós menos ocho?

PATTERN DRILL (C). Complete aloud the following sentences:

1. $10 + 4$ son . . .
2. $30 - 16$ son . . .

3. 7×4 son . . .
4. $14 \div 7$ son . . .

5. 8 ÷ 2 son . . .   7. 15 + 14 − 6 son . . .
6. 7 + 3 − 8 son . . .   8. 8 × 2 − 13 son . . .

9.5 COGNATES

Spanish nouns ending in **-dad** and **-tad** and English nouns ending in *-ty* are usually cognates:

serenidad	*serenity*	**vanidad**	*vanity*
libertad	*liberty*	**caridad**	*charity*

The explanation of this relationship is that such nouns have come into both English and Spanish from Latin. Spanish nouns ending in **-dad** and **-tad** are always feminine in gender.

PATTERN DRILL. Pronounce carefully each Spanish word below, and then give its English cognate:

1. curiosidad   5. deidad   9. castidad
2. eternidad   6. equidad   10. debilidad
3. mortalidad   7. capacidad   11. iniquidad
4. sociedad   8. maternidad   12. dificultad

Lesson 10

10.1 TIME

In Spanish, the hours of the clock are indicated with a feminine definite article and the cardinal numbers from **una** through **doce. La** precedes **una,** and **las** precedes **dos** through **doce:**

la una	*one o'clock*	**las ocho**	*eight o'clock*
las dos	*two o'clock*	**las doce**	*twelve o'clock*

With the time, **ser** is the equivalent of the English *to be.* **Es** is used with **la una,** and **son** is used with the remaining hours:

Es la una.	*It's one o'clock.*
¿Son las cuatro?	*Is it four o'clock?*
No son las cinco.	*It's not five o'clock.*

Minutes after an hour are indicated by **y** and the cardinal numbers from **uno** through **treinta:**

Es la una y diez.	*It's ten after one.*
Son las tres y cinco.	*It's five past three.*
Son las seis y treinta.	*It's six-thirty.*

The inclusion of **minutos** is optional:

Son las siete y veintiún minutos.
Son las siete y veintiuno.

The half-hour is often indicated by **media: ¿Es la una y media?** The quarter-hour is often indicated by **cuarto: Son las nueve y cuarto.**

Minutes beyond **treinta** are usually indicated by subtracting them from the following hour:

Es la una menos veintinueve.	*It's twelve-thirty-one.*
¿Es la una menos diez?	*Is it ten to one?*
Son las once menos veinte.	*It's twenty of eleven.*
Son las cuatro menos cuarto.	*It's a quarter to four.*

The Spanish equivalent of *What time is it?* is **¿Qué hora es?**

PATTERN DRILL. Answer each of the following questions aloud, using **Sí** and a sentence containing the form of **ser** necessary to express the time suggested:

1. ¿Qué hora es?   ¿Las 7?   —Sí, son las siete.
2. ¿Qué hora es?   ¿Las 3 y 30?
3. ¿Qué hora es?   ¿La 1 y 15?
4. ¿Qué hora es?   ¿Las 12 menos 20?
5. ¿Qué hora es?   ¿Las 8 y 10?
6. ¿Qué hora es?   ¿La 1 y 30?
7. ¿Qué hora es?   ¿Las 4 menos 15?
8. ¿Qué hora es?   ¿Las 11 y 25?

10.2 "A.M." AND "P.M."

A.M. or *in the morning* is indicated by **de la madrugada** for times between midnight and sunrise: **Es la una de la madrugada.** Times between sunrise and noon are indicated by **de la mañana: Son las diez de la mañana.** P.M. is also indicated in two ways. With times between noon and sunset, **de la tarde** is used: **Es la una de la tarde,** *It's one in the afternoon.* Times between sunset and midnight are indicated by **de la noche: Son las ocho de la noche,** *It's eight in the evening* or *It's eight at night.* The equivalent of *It's noon* is **Son las doce del día.** *It's midnight* is **Son las doce de la noche.**

PATTERN DRILL (A). Say each sentence below. Then repeat it, adding fifteen minutes to the original time:

1. Son las dos de la tarde.
2. ¿Es la una y cuarto de la tarde?
3. Son las diez y media de la mañana.
4. Es la una y veinte de la madrugada.
5. Son las doce y media de la tarde.
6. ¿Son las siete y diez?
7. Son las once menos cinco.
8. Es la una menos siete.

PATTERN DRILL (B). Now subtract half an hour from the original times above.

10.3 "WHEN?" AND "AT"

When? can be asked in two ways:

¿Cuándo vas al centro?   ¿A qué hora vas al centro?

In replies to such questions, **a** precedes a specific time:

Voy al centro a las ocho y media de la mañana.
Comemos a las seis de la tarde.
Juan vuelve a casa a las once menos cuarto de la noche.

PATTERN DRILL (A).   Answer each of the following questions aloud with **Sí** and a complete sentence containing the time suggested:

1. ¿Cuándo vuelves? ¿A las tres?   —Sí, vuelvo a las tres.
2. ¿Cuándo vas a comer? ¿A las doce y cuarto?
3. ¿A qué hora quieres ir? ¿A las once y media de la mañana?
4. ¿Cuándo vas al cine? ¿A las siete de la noche?
5. ¿A qué hora vuelven Vds. a casa? ¿A las cinco de la tarde?
6. ¿Cuándo empiezen Vds. a comer? ¿A las ocho?
7. ¿A qué hora vas a estar aquí? ¿A la una de la madrugada?
8. ¿Cuándo va Vd. al teatro? ¿A las ocho menos cuarto?

PATTERN DRILL (B).   Answer the preceding questions with **No** and a sentence changing the suggested time to fifteen minutes later. Your first answer will be: **No. Vuelvo a las tres y cuarto.**

10.4 DIRECT OBJECTS: NOUNS

The term *direct object* is applied to a person or a thing that is directly affected by the action of a verb: *John is buying a car. Are you looking for the teacher?* In Spanish, when the direct object of a verb is a noun that refers to a definite person, that noun is preceded by **a**:

Buscamos aquel restorán.	but	**Buscamos a tu hermano.**
¿Hallas mi lápiz azul?	but	**¿Hallas a Juan y a María?**
No hallo las cucharitas.	but	**No hallo a nuestra criada.**

This so-called *personal* **a**, which has no English equivalent, is omitted when the speaker does not have a definite person in mind: **Busco una criada francesa.** The **a** is usually omitted after **tener**: **Tengo una hermana en el Perú.**

PATTERN DRILL (A).   Say each sentence below. Then repeat it as a negative sentence, with **no** immediately preceding the verb:

1. Busco a mi hermano.
2. Espero a Juan. (*to wait for*)
3. Queremos hallar a María.
4. Mi padre espera a mi madre.
5. Vamos a buscar al profesor.
6. Quiero a mis padres. (*to love*)
7. Estos hombres buscan a tu abuelo.
8. Esperamos a Juana y a Elena.

PATTERN DRILL (B).   Answer the following questions affirmatively, using **Sí** and a complete sentence:

1. ¿Quieres a tus hermanos?
2. ¿Busca Juan al profesor?
3. ¿Halla Vd. a su criada?
4. ¿Esperan Vds. a María y a Elena?
5. ¿Quieren Vds. a su tío rico?
6. ¿Quieres esperar a aquella mujer?
7. ¿Necesitan Vds. a Pedro?
8. ¿Buscas a tu esposa? (*wife*)

10.5   PARTIALLY IRREGULAR VERBS

In the present indicative, a number of Spanish verbs have irregular forms to indicate the first person singular. Three such verbs are explained below; others will be presented from time to time.

10.5.1   *Ver: to see.*   *I see* is **veo**:

> **Veo a María en la sala.**   **No veo el coche azul de Juan.**

To indicate the other persons, **ver** is inflected as a regular -er verb:

> **¿Ves aquellos árboles altos?**   **Juan y María no ven a sus padres.**

PATTERN DRILL (A). Practice aloud using **veo** to form sentences with each of the persons or things below:

1. a nuestro profesor de francés
2. muchas películas buenas (*films*)
3. ese mantel sucio
4. a mi hijo aquí (*son*)
5. a la esposa de Carlos
6. al padre de Juan en el centro
7. la sartén en la cocina
8. a mi hija en esa tienda

PATTERN DRILL (B). Now use **¿Ve Vd.?** with the same persons and things.

10.5.2   *Conocer: to be acquainted with.*   *I am acquainted with* is **conozco**:

> **Conozco a tu abuela.**   **No conozco esa ciudad inglesa.**

To indicate the other persons, **conocer** is inflected like a regular -er verb:

> **¿Conoce Vd. a mi hermano?**   **No conocemos a la esposa de Juan.**

PATTERN DRILL (A). Practice aloud using **conozco** to form sentences with each of the persons or things below:

1. al esposo de Elena (*husband*)
2. esa ciudad interesante
3. a esos hombres de negocios
4. al hijo de esa mujer
5. ese museo famoso (*museum*)
6. al abuelo de Roberto
7. a las hijas de Carlos
8. aquel restorán francés

PATTERN DRILL (B). Now use **¿Conocen Vds.?** with the same persons and things.

10.5.3   *Salir: to leave, to go out.*   *I'm going out* is **salgo**. **Salir** and a location are connected by **de** to indicate *direction from*, and by **a** to indicate *direction toward*:

> **Salgo de la cocina.**   *I'm leaving the kitchen.*
> **Salgo al jardín.**   *I'm going out into the garden.*

To indicate the other persons, **salir** is inflected like a regular **-ir** verb:

Juan sale de Madrid. **No salimos a las once de la noche.**

PATTERN DRILL (A). Practice aloud using **salgo** to form sentences with each of the expressions below:

1. a la una menos veinte
2. de la universidad a las seis
3. de casa a las ocho y cuarto
4. al jardín a las cuatro

5. de la biblioteca a las nueve
6. al patio ahora (*now*)
7. del centro a las cinco y media
8. del Canadá a las doce de la noche

PATTERN DRILL (B). Now use **salimos** with the same expressions.

10.6 PARTIALLY IRREGULAR, STEM–CHANGING VERBS

Some Spanish stem-changing verbs are irregular in the first person singular of the present indicative. You have mastered one such verb already: **tener**. The next is similar.

10.6.1 *Venir* (ie): *to come.* I'm coming is **vengo**. **Venir** and a noun indicating a location are connected by **a** to express *direction toward*, and by **de** to express *direction from*:

Vengo a tu casa ahora. **No vengo de la biblioteca.**

In the second and third persons singular, and in the third person plural, the /-e-/ of the stem diphthongizes to /-ie-/:

¿A qué hora vienes? When are you coming?
Juan viene del Brasil. John's on his way from Brazil.
¿Vienen Vds. ahora? Are you coming now?

The first and second persons plural are "regular":

Venimos a la una y diez. **¿Cuándo venís a mi casa?**

PATTERN DRILL (A). Practice aloud using **vengo** to form sentences with each of the expressions below:

1. a la escuela a las diez
2. a la universidad con Elena (*with*)
3. a las cuatro menos cuarto
4. al baile (*dance*)

5. del centro al mediodía (*noon*)
6. al baile con Teresa
7. con mucha cerveza
8. a la fiesta (*party*)

PATTERN DRILL (B). Now use **¿Viene Vd.?** with each of the expressions above.

PATTERN DRILL (C). Answer the following questions affirmatively, using **Sí** and a complete sentence:

1. ¿Viene Juan a la fiesta?
2. ¿Vienen tus hermanos ahora?
3. ¿Vienes con Elena?
4. ¿Viene Vd. a las tres y cuarto?
5. ¿Vienen esos hombres al mediodía?
6. ¿Vienen Vds. a nuestra casa?
7. ¿Vienes a nuestro baile?
8. ¿Venís a la fiesta de Teresa?

10.7 THE PRETERITE TENSE

In Spanish, as in English, there are several ways of indicating the past. Spanish uses the *preterite* to express something that was done (*I bought the car*) or that happened (*He left*) at some past time. For the time being, you may consider the Spanish preterite the equivalent of the English past tense: *I bought, I didn't buy, Did you buy?* etc. Infinitives that end in **-ar** assume the following forms in the preterite indicative.

10.7.1 *First Person Singular.* To indicate the first person singular, the **-ar** of the infinitive is replaced by **-é**. The infinitive **comprar** means *to buy*. The Spanish equivalent of *I bought* is **compré: Compré zapatos negros,** *I bought black shoes. I didn't buy black shoes* is **No compré zapatos negros.** In the preterite, **-ar** verbs do not undergo any stem changes: **Conté los libros,** *I counted the books.*

PATTERN DRILL (A). Practice aloud using **compré** to form sentences with each of the expressions below:

1. un abrigo de lana
2. mucha cerveza
3. un reloj de plata
4. una gabardina barata (*raincoat*)
5. tres corbatas de seda
6. dos pañuelos (*handkerchiefs*)
7. helado de vainilla
8. un paraguas negro (*umbrella*)

PATTERN DRILL (B). Now use **no compré** with each of the expressions above.

PATTERN DRILL (C). Say each sentence below. Then repeat it, beginning the sentence with **ayer** (*yesterday*) and changing the verb to the preterite:

1. No hallo tu pluma de oro.
2. Estudio la lección de español.
3. Cuento mis corbatas rojas.
4. Pinto el comedor. (*to paint*)
5. No trabajo mucho.
6. Empiezo a trabajar a la una.
7. Busco a Juan en la biblioteca.
8. Llego a las dos. (*to arrive*)

10.7.1.1 Orthography. How would you represent orthographically the forms [buské] and [llegé]? Why? What convention governs the orthography of [empeθé]?

10.7.2 First Person Plural. To indicate the first person plural, the -ar of the infinitive is replaced by -amos: **compramos.** Although this form is identical to the present tense form, context usually clarifies the meaning. Or, you can avoid possible confusion by using time words, such as **anoche,** *last night:* **Anoche compramos aquella casa,** *We bought that house last night.*

PATTERN DRILL. Practice aloud using **anoche compramos** to form sentences with each of the expressions below:

1. muchos pañuelos de lino (*linen*)
2. nuestros libros de español
3. el tocadiscos (*phonograph*)
4. este coche inglés
5. naranjas y toronjas
6. estas gabardinas blancas
7. aquella casa de ladrillo
8. muchos discos (*records*)

10.7.3 Second Person Singular. To indicate the singular intimate you, the -ar of the infinitive is replaced by -aste: **compraste.** *What did you buy?* is **¿Qué compraste?** *You didn't buy many records* is **No compraste muchos discos.**

PATTERN DRILL (A). Practice aloud using **¿Compraste?** to form questions with each of the expressions below:

1. esa gabardina ayer
2. muchos regalos caros ayer
3. un traje de lana anoche
4. ese paraguas de seda ayer
5. mucha cerveza ayer
6. aquella casa de madera ayer
7. aquel tocadiscos anoche
8. esos pañuelos ayer

PATTERN DRILL (B). Say each sentence below. Then repeat it, beginning the sentence with **anoche,** and changing the verb to the preterite:

1. ¿Pintas el cuarto de baño?
2. No estudias esta lección.
3. ¿Esperas a María a las ocho?
4. ¿Hallas la sartén en la cocina?
5. Llegas a las nueve y cuarto.
6. ¿Cuentas los lápices de Juan?
7. ¿Buscas a tu hermano?
8. ¿Empiezas a comer a las seis?

10.7.4 Second Person Plural. To indicate the plural intimate you, the -ar of the infinitive is replaced by -asteis: **comprasteis.** *When did you buy that car?* is **¿Cuándo comprasteis ese coche?**

PATTERN DRILL. Say each sentence below. Then repeat it, beginning the sentence with **ayer,** and changing the verb to the preterite:

1. Empezáis a trabajar mucho.
2. No pintáis la sala.
3. ¿Halláis a Juan?
4. ¿Buscáis vuestros libros?
5. Llegáis a la una y media.
6. ¿Compráis aquella casa grande?
7. No esperáis a María.
8. No estudiáis vuestras lecciones.

10.7.5 Third Person Singular. To indicate the third person singular, the -ar of the infinitive is replaced by -ó: compró. *John bought a suit* is **Juan compró un traje.** *What did you buy?* is **¿Qué compró Vd.?** *My father didn't buy any beer last night* is **Mi padre no compró cerveza anoche.**

PATTERN DRILL (A). Practice aloud using **compró** to connect the nouns in the first column below with the nouns in the second column:

1. Mi madre . . . mucha carne.
2. María . . . un vestido ayer. (*dress*)
3. Vd. no . . . esta corbata en mi tienda.
4. Carlos . . . esos guantes. (*gloves*)
5. Vd. . . . muchos discos.
6. Mi hijo . . . ese coche rojo.
7. La muchacha . . . una blusa de seda.
8. Tu esposa . . . un vestido caro.

PATTERN DRILL (B). Practice aloud using **¿Compró Vd.?** to form sentences with each of the expressions below:

1. esa gabardina en esta tienda
2. un vestido de algodón
3. muchos regalos en Europa
4. muchas rosas blancas ayer
5. guantes de lana
6. aquel tocadiscos ayer
7. esa novela interesante
8. ese coche en Francia

10.7.6 Third Person Plural. To indicate the third person plural, the -ar of the infinitive is replaced by -aron: compraron. **¿Cuándo compraron Vds. esta casa?** means *When did you buy this house? Those men didn't buy the restaurant* is **Aquellos hombres no compraron el restorán.**

PATTERN DRILL (A). Practice aloud using **compraron** to complete each of the sentences below:

1. Mis abuelos . . . esta casa de madera.
2. Juan y Carlos . . . un coche italiano.
3. Vds. . . . muchos discos buenos.
4. Nuestras esposas . . . muchos vestidos.

5. Los muchachos . . . mucho vino.
6. ¿Cuándo . . . Vds. ese tocadiscos?
7. Mis hijas . . . muchos regalos caros.
8. Los padres de Carlos . . . mi casa.

PATTERN DRILL (B). Say each sentence below. Then repeat it, beginning the sentence with **ayer,** and changing the verb to the preterite:

1. Mis abuelos llegan a la una.
2. Los estudiantes empiezan a llegar.
3. Mis hijos pintan la cocina.
4. ¿Buscan Vds. a Carlos?
5. Vds. no estudian mucho.
6. Las mujeres compran vestidos de seda.
7. Esos hombres empiezan a volver.
8. No esperan a Juan.

Lesson 11

11.1 NUMBERS

The Spanish cardinal numbers from 31 through 39 are:

31	treinta y uno	34	treinta y cuatro	37	treinta y siete
32	treinta y dos	35	treinta y cinco	38	treinta y ocho
33	treinta y tres	36	treinta y seis	39	treinta y nueve

The same three-word pattern is used to indicate numbers from 41 through 49, 51 through 59, etc. The Spanish cardinal numbers from 40 through 100 are, by tens:

40	cuarenta	70	setenta	100	ciento
50	cincuenta	80	ochenta		
60	sesenta	90	noventa		

Before a masculine noun, . . . y uno becomes . . . y un: Compré treinta y un claveles.

Before a feminine noun, . . . y uno becomes . . . y una: Compré sesenta y una rosas.

Before a noun of either gender, ciento becomes cien: Tenemos cien caballos y cien vacas. Unlike English a hundred or one hundred, in Spanish the indefinite article does not precede ciento or cien.

PATTERN DRILL (A). Complete aloud the following sentences:

1. Treinta más diez son . . .
2. Cuarenta más doce son . . .
3. Cincuenta más quince son . . .
4. Sesenta más trece son . . .
5. Setenta más catorce son . . .
6. Ochenta más once son . . .
7. Noventa más diez son . . .
8. Veinte más veinte son . . .

PATTERN DRILL (B). Complete the sentences above, replacing más by menos.

PATTERN DRILL (c). Complete aloud the following sentences:

1. Quince por tres son . . .
2. Quince por cuatro son . . .
3. Veinte por cinco son . . .
4. Treinta por tres son . . .

5. Treinta y cinco por dos son . . .
6. Veinticinco por cuatro son . . .
7. Treinta y tres por tres son . . .
8. Veinte por cuatro son . . .

11.2 AGE

The Spanish word for year is **el año**. The equivalent of the English *to be . . . years old* is **tener . . . años**:

¿Cuántos años tiene Vd.?	How old are you?
Tengo cincuenta y un años.	I'm fifty-one.
¿Tiene María setenta años?	Is Mary seventy years old?

PATTERN DRILL. Say each sentence below. Then repeat it, doubling the original age:

1. Carlos tiene dieciséis años.
2. Mis padres tienen cuarenta y un años.
3. Mi esposa tiene treinta y tres años.
4. ¿Tiene cincuenta años tu abuelo?
5. Ese profesor tiene veintisiete años.
6. ¿Tienes cuarenta y cuatro años?
7. No tengo diecinueve años.
8. Elena tiene treinta y ocho años.

11.3 TIME

Shorter periods than **el año** are **el mes** (month) and **la semana** (week). When these three nouns are preceded by the definite article and followed by the appropriate form of **pasado**, they are equivalent to the English *last*:

Juan llegó el año pasado.	John arrived last year.
Llegamos el mes pasado.	We arrived last month.
Llegué la semana pasada.	I arrived last week.

The same three nouns can be preceded by the appropriate form of **este** to indicate periods of present time:

Ricardo viene este año.	Richard is coming this year.
¿Llega María este mes?	Does Mary arrive this month?
No llegaron esta semana.	They didn't arrive this week.

PATTERN DRILL. Say each sentence below. Then repeat it, changing the verb to the preterite tense, and the period of time to the past:

1. Ricardo no estudia esta semana.   Ricardo no estudió la semana pasada.
2. ¿Trabajan Vds. mucho este mes?
3. No compramos dos coches este año.
4. Juan no llama a Elena esta semana. (*to call*)
5. Mis padres compran la casa este año.
6. ¿Llamas a tu hermano esta semana?
7. Mi esposa compra un vestido de seda este mes.
8. ¿Pintas la cocina esta semana?

11.4 AGO

The equivalents of English *ago* expressions, such as *two weeks ago*, are formed with **hace** followed by the desired amount of time: **hace dos semanas**. In a sentence, such expressions follow a verb in the preterite tense:

Llegué hace dos semanas.	*I arrived two weeks ago.*
Elena llamó hace una hora.	*Helen called an hour ago.*
¿Llamaste hace diez minutos?	*Did you phone ten minutes ago?*
Llegamos hace tres días.	*We arrived three days ago.*

Although this seems quite simple, note, however, that no indefinite article is used in the Spanish equivalents of *a little while ago* and *a long time ago*, or before the adjective **medio** (*half, a half, half a*):

Mi hijo llamó hace poco.	*My son called up a little while ago.*
¿Llamó Vd. hace mucho?	*Did you phone a long time ago?*
Llamé hace media hora.	*I called half an hour ago.*
Llegamos hace una hora y media.	*We arrived an hour and a half ago.*
Llegué hace dos meses y medio.	*I arrived two and a half months ago.*

PATTERN DRILL (A). Say each sentence below. Then repeat it, replacing the original time with **hace media hora**:

1. Llamaron hace cuarenta minutos.   5. Juan llegó hace una semana.
2. Llegamos aquí hace doce años.   6. Llegué hace dos semanas y media.
3. ¿Llamaste hace mucho?   7. Compré el paraguas hace tres días.
4. Hallé a María hace veinte minutos. 8. Llegaron al centro hace una hora.

PATTERN DRILL (B). Repeat each sentence above, replacing the original time with **hace poco.**

11.5 PRETERITE INDICATIVE: INFINITIVES ENDING IN «–ER» AND «–IR»

"Regular" verbs of both the -er and -ir categories follow the same inflectional pattern. In the preterite there are no -er stem changes. The -ir stem changes will be explained in a separate section.

11.5.1   First Person Singular.   To indicate the first person singular, the -er or -ir of the infinitive is replaced by -í: **comí, salí**. *Yesterday I ate lots of ice cream* is **Ayer comí mucho helado.** *I didn't go out last night* is **No salí anoche.** Note that there is no accent mark over the written form of **vi**, *I saw:* **Anoche vi a María.** Why is an accent unnecessary?

PATTERN DRILL (A). Practice aloud using **comí** to form sentences with each of the expressions below:

1. a las dos de la tarde
2. hace una hora
3. ese pollo anoche (*chicken*)
4. tres manzanas hace poco
5. mucho arroz ayer (*rice*)
6. con Elena hace una semana
7. hace media hora
8. mucho pescado esta semana

PATTERN DRILL (B). Say each sentence below. Then repeat it, changing the verb to the preterite, and adding **la semana pasada**:

1. Escribo a mi amigo. (*friend*)
2. Vuelvo al hospital.
3. No veo a Ricardo.
4. Recibo un regalo de mi abuelo.
5. No vendo el coche.
6. Pierdo el reloj. (*to lose*, **perder**)
7. Salgo de esta ciudad.
8. Como en tu casa.

11.5.2   First Person Plural.   To indicate the first person plural, the -er or -ir of the infinitive is replaced by -imos: **comimos, salimos**. *We ate at one o'clock* is **Comimos a la una.** Although the -ir verbs have the identical form in the present indicative, context usually clarifies the meaning. Of course, you can avoid any possibility of confusion by adding words that indicate past time: **Salimos de Madrid anoche,** *We left Madrid last night.*

PATTERN DRILL (A). Practice aloud using **comimos** to form sentences with each of the expressions below:

1. en el centro anoche
2. aquí hace un mes
3. con Juan la semana pasada
4. anoche a las siete menos cuarto
5. hace quince minutos
6. mucho jamón ayer (*ham*)
7. arroz con pollo anoche
8. hace poco

PATTERN DRILL (B). Say each sentence below. Then repeat it, changing the verb to the preterite, and adding **hace una hora y media:**

1. Volvemos a la ciudad.
2. Abrimos las ventanas de la cocina.
3. Perdemos las libretas.
4. Comemos ese helado de fresa.
5. Salimos del teatro.
6. Vemos a Juan y a Carlos.
7. Bebemos mucho vino.
8. Recibimos esta carta importante.

11.5.3 Second Person Singular. To indicate the singular intimate you, the -er or -ir of the infinitive is replaced by -iste: **comiste, saliste.** *When did you eat?* is **¿Cuándo comiste?** *You didn't leave at eleven* is **No saliste a las once.**

PATTERN DRILL (A). Practice aloud using **¿Comiste?** to form questions with each of the expressions below:

1. mucho pollo ayer
2. en aquel restorán caro
3. en casa anoche
4. ese jamón
5. a las ocho menos cuarto
6. mucha ensalada ayer (*salad*)
7. en el centro la semana pasada
8. con tus abuelos anoche

PATTERN DRILL (B). Say each sentence below. Then repeat it, changing the verb to the preterite, and adding **el año pasado:**

1. ¿Escribes a Roberto?
2. No vuelves al Ecuador.
3. Bebes mucho café.
4. No ves muchas películas buenas.
5. ¿Vuelves a la Argentina?
6. Vives en esa casa blanca.
7. ¿Recibes mucho dinero? (*money*)
8. Vendes muchas flores.

11.5.4 Second Person Plural. To indicate the plural intimate you, the -er or -ir of the infinitive is replaced by -isteis: **comisteis, salisteis. Comisteis poco arroz,** *You ate little rice.* **¿Cuándo salisteis de la ciudad?** *When did you leave the city?*

PATTERN DRILL. Say each sentence below. Then repeat it, changing the verb to the preterite, and adding **el mes pasado:**

1. Coméis con vuestros abuelos.
2. No recibís muchas cartas.
3. ¿Bebéis mucha leche?
4. Volvéis del campo.
5. ¿Salís del Uruguay?
6. ¿Veis a vuestros amigos?
7. No vivís en este hotel caro.
8. ¿Vendéis esa casa?

11.5.5 Third Person Singular. To indicate the third person singular, the -er or -ir of the infinitive is replaced by -ió: **comió, salió.** *Where did you eat last night?* is **¿Dónde comió Vd. anoche?** *John left a week ago* is **Juan**

salió hace una semana. In some books you may find an accent mark on vió. In 1952 the Spanish Academy decided that the written accent was no longer necessary.

PATTERN DRILL (A). Practice aloud using comió to complete each of the sentences below:

1. José . . . aquí anoche.
2. La criada no . . . la ensalada.
3. Mi madre . . . con mis abuelos ayer.
4. Vd. . . . en mi casa la semana pasada.
5. Mi hermano . . . mucho jamón ayer.
6. Vd. . . . hace mucho.
7. El muchacho . . . poco arroz.
8. Tu hijo no . . . a las seis.

PATTERN DRILL (B). Say each sentence below. Then repeat it, changing the verb to the preterite, and adding hace cinco minutos:

1. Nuestro padre sale al jardín.
2. El muchacho pierde el dinero.
3. ¿Ve Vd. a Elena?
4. Juan abre esos regalos.
5. Mi hija recibe muchas cartas.
6. La criada vuelve a la tienda.
7. Mi esposa escribe a su padre.
8. María rompe el vaso. (*to break*, romper)

11.5.6 *Third Person Plural.*

To indicate the third person plural, the -er or -ir of the infinitive is replaced by -ieron: comieron, salieron. *What did you eat?* is ¿Qué comieron Vds.? *The girls didn't go out last night* is Las muchachas no salieron anoche.

PATTERN DRILL (A). Practice aloud using comieron to complete each of the sentences below:

1. Mis amigos . . . aquí anoche.
2. Elena y María . . . con Juan hace poco.
3. Vds. no . . . mucho jamón.
4. ¿Dónde . . . Vds. ayer?
5. Tus padres . . . en nuestra casa.
6. Estas muchachas . . . hace una hora.
7. La semana pasada Vds. . . . en casa.
8. Mis hermanos . . . en el centro anoche.

PATTERN DRILL (B). Say each sentence below. Then repeat it, changing the verb to the preterite, and adding **hace poco:**

1. Mis abuelos vuelven a casa.
2. Los muchachos rompen esos platos.
3. ¿Ven Vds. a Ricardo?
4. Esas mujeres salen de la tienda.
5. Mis hijos escriben a su tío.
6. Las criadas abren las ventanas.
7. Vds. reciben nuestra carta.
8. Mis padres venden esta casa.

11.5.7 Orthography. The conventions of written Spanish require that the preterites of the third persons of **leer** be spelled **leyó** and **leyeron.** In addition, accents are necessary over the written forms of **leíste, leímos,** and **leísteis.** Why?

11.5.8 Meaning. Note that in the preterite, **conocer** is the equivalent of *to make the acquaintance of:* **Anoche conocí a los padres de María,** *Last night I met Mary's parents.* **¿Cuándo conociste a tu esposa?** *When did you meet your wife?*

PATTERN DRILL. Say each sentence below. Then repeat it, changing the verb to the pretererite, and adding **anoche:**

1. Juan lee esta lección.
2. ¿Lees el periódico?
3. Leemos una carta interesante.
4. ¿Leen Vds. esas revistas?
5. Conozco a esa mujer bonita.
6. María conoce a mi hermano.
7. ¿Conoce Vd. a ese médico?
8. Conocemos a tus abuelos.

11.6 PRETERITE INDICATIVE: STEM–CHANGING VERBS

In the preterite, stem changes occur only in certain **-ir** verbs. They are the same third-conjugation verbs that undergo stem changes in the present indicative. There are two types of changes.

11.6.1 Preferir. In the third persons singular and plural only, the /-e-/ immediately preceding the final consonant of the stem becomes /-i-/:

Anoche Juan prefirió ir al cine.   **Ayer Vds. prefirieron estudiar.**

The same change occurs in the third persons singular and plural of the preterite of the other **-ir** verbs that undergo stem changes in the present indicative, and whose stem vowel is /-e-/. Reference works usually indicate such verbs in the following way: **preferir (ie, i), servir (i, i), pedir (i, i).**

11.6.2 Dormir. In the third persons singular and plural only, the /-o-/ immediately preceding the final consonants of the stem becomes /-u-/:

¿Dónde durmió Vd. anoche?   **Los hombres durmieron en ese hotel.**

The only other verb with the same stem change in the preterite that you are likely to encounter is **morir (ue, u)**, *to die.*

¿Mueren sus flores?   **Sí, las rosas murieron.**

PATTERN DRILL (A). Say each sentence below. Then repeat it, changing the verb to the preterite, and adding **ayer:**

1. La criada no sirve el café.
2. Mi madre prefiere comer en casa.
3. ¿Dónde duerme Vd.?
4. Tu hermano pide arroz con pollo.
5. Esos hombres piden mucho vino.
6. ¿Qué sirven Vds.?
7. Mi tío muere en el hospital.
8. ¿Duermen Vds. en esta clase?

PATTERN DRILL (B). Say each sentence below. Then repeat it, changing the verb to the present tense:

1. La criada no sirvió pan.
2. ¿Prefirió Vd. esa cerveza?
3. Juan durmió en la sala.
4. Los caballos murieron.
5. Pedí helado de vainilla.
6. ¿Durmieron Vds. en el cine?
7. No serví vino.
8. Preferí volver a casa.

11.7 COGNATES

Spanish nouns ending in **-ancia** and English nouns ending in -*ance* or -*ancy* are often cognates:

la elegancia   *elegance*   **la discrepancia**   *discrepancy*

Similarly, Spanish nouns ending in **-encia** and English nouns ending in -*ence* or -*ency* are often cognates:

la violencia   *violence*   **la clemencia**   *clemency*

PATTERN DRILL. Pronounce carefully each Spanish word below, and then give its English cognate:

1. distancia
2. vigilancia
3. arrogancia
4. repugnancia
5. constancia
6. redundancia
7. agencia
8. urgencia
9. eminencia
10. diferencia
11. diligencia
12. independencia

Lesson 12

12.1 NUMBERS

The Spanish cardinal numbers from 200 through 900 are, by hundreds:

200	doscientos	500	quinientos	800	ochocientos
300	trescientos	600	seiscientos	900	novecientos
400	cuatrocientos	700	setecientos		

These "hundreds" forms end in -as when they refer to feminine nouns: **quinientas vacas.**

Numbers between the hundreds are indicated by using the numbers from **uno** through **noventa y nueve** immediately after the desired "hundreds" form. Unlike the English use of *and* in *a hundred and one, nine hundred and ninety-nine,* etc., in Spanish **y** is not used to connect any of the hundreds to a smaller number:

101	ciento uno	623	seiscientos veintitrés
215	doscientos quince	731	setecientos treinta y uno
516	quinientos dieciséis	999	novecientos noventa y nueve

The agreement of these "hundreds" forms with a feminine noun occurs even when the two are separated by another number:

Aquel libro tiene setecientas veintiuna páginas. (pages)

PATTERN DRILL (A). Complete aloud the following sentences:

1. Doscientos más ciento uno son . . .
2. Trescientos más doscientos son . . .
3. Quinientos más ciento diez son . . .
4. Seiscientos más ciento doce son . . .
5. Ochocientos más ciento veinte son . . .
6. Trescientos veinte más ochenta son . . .
7. Setecientos diez más noventa son . . .
8. Cuatrocientos más trescientos son . . .

PATTERN DRILL (B). Complete aloud the sentences above, replacing **más** by **menos**.

PATTERN DRILL (C). Complete aloud the following sentences:

1. Ciento por siete son . . .
2. Ciento veinticinco por cuatro son . . .
3. Doscientos uno por tres son . . .
4. Cuatrocientos cincuenta por dos son . . .
5. Ochenta por cinco son . . .
6. Setenta por cuatro son . . .
7. Noventa por ocho son . . .
8. Ciento ocho por dos son . . .

12.1.1 Numbers. The Spanish cardinal number following 999 is **mil,** written in Arabic numerals as **1.000.** Mil has neither a feminine nor a plural form, and it is not preceded by the indefinite article:

> **Tengo mil dólares.**   *I have a thousand dollars.*
> **Leí mil páginas.**   *I read one thousand pages.*

Numbers above **mil** are expressed according to the pattern below:

1.001	**mil uno**	2.011	**dos mil once**
1.011	**mil once**	5.726	**cinco mil setecientos veintiséis**
1.111	**mil ciento once**	10.000	**diez mil**

Before **mil, ciento** becomes **cien: cien mil dólares,** *a hundred thousand dollars.*

Unlike English, Spanish does not indicate the years or other numbers above one thousand as multiples of one hundred:

> **mil cuatrocientos noventa y dos**   *fourteen hundred ninety-two*
> **mil ochocientos sesenta y uno**   *eighteen sixty-one*
> **siete mil quinientos**   *seventy-five hundred*
> **nueve mil novecientos**   *ninety-nine hundred*

PATTERN DRILL (A). Complete aloud the following sentences:

1. Ochocientos más setecientos son . . .
2. Quinientos más seiscientos son . . .
3. Novecientos más ochocientos son . . .
4. Cinco mil más seis mil son . . .
5. Setecientos cincuenta por dos son . . .
6. Novecientos por dos son . . .
7. Mil doscientos por tres son . . .
8. Veinte mil por cinco son . . .

PATTERN DRILL (B). Say the sentences below. Can you deduce the meaning of each one from the information given?

1. Colón descubrió el Nuevo Mundo en 1492.
2. Cortés empezó la conquista de México en 1519.
3. Cervantes y Shakespeare murieron en 1616.
4. La Revolución Francesa empezó en 1789.
5. La Guerra Civil Norteamericana empezó en 1861.
6. Las trece colonias proclamaron su independencia en 1776.
7. La Guerra Civil Española terminó en 1939.
8. Este año es . . .

12.1.2 Numbers.

1.000.000 is read as **un millón.**
2.000.000 is read as **dos millones.**

Millón is the only Spanish cardinal number that is not an adjective, but rather a noun. Because of this, **millón** and **millones** are connected to nouns by **de:**

un millón de pesetas   *1,000,000 pesetas* (Spanish monetary unit)
España tiene treinta millones de habitantes. (*inhabitants*)

12.2 DAYS OF THE WEEK

In Spanish, the names of the days of the week are:

el lunes	*Monday*	**el viernes**	*Friday*
el martes	*Tuesday*	**el sábado**	*Saturday*
el miércoles	*Wednesday*	**el domingo**	*Sunday*
el jueves	*Thursday*		

The days of the week are usually preceded by the definite article. However, in reply to **¿Qué día es?** *What day is it?* the article is omitted:

Hoy es lunes.   *Today is Monday*

Unlike English, Spanish does not use any preposition to indicate *on a* particular day (or days):

Llego el viernes.	*I'm arriving on Friday.*
Trabajo los martes.	*I work on Tuesdays.*
Salimos los sábados.	*We go out on Saturdays.*
¿Estudias los domingos?	*Do you study on Sundays?*

Note that only **sábado** and **domingo** add /-s/ to indicate the plural.

PATTERN DRILL (A). Say each sentence below. Then repeat it, changing the time to the following day:

1. Hoy es sábado.
2. Llegué el jueves.
3. Salimos el martes pasado.
4. Vuelvo este domingo.

5. Juan duerme aquí los viernes.
6. ¿Comiste en el centro el lunes?
7. No trabajé el miércoles.
8. Mañana es jueves. (*tomorrow*)

PATTERN DRILL (B). Say each sentence above, changing the time to the preceding day.

12.3 «IR»: PRETERITE TENSE, INDICATIVE MOOD

12.3.1 *First Person Singular.* **Fui al cine anoche** means *I went to the movies last night.* **No fui a la biblioteca ayer** means *I didn't go to the library yesterday.* In some books you may find an accent mark over **fuí.** This written accent is no longer necessary.

PATTERN DRILL (A). Practice aloud using **fui** to form sentences with each of the expressions below:

1. al campo la semana pasada
2. de compras ayer (*shopping*)
3. a la Argentina en 1961
4. a la farmacia ayer (*drugstore*)

5. al centro a la una y media
6. al hospital en coche (*by car*)
7. a un baile anoche
8. a la ciudad en tren (*by train*)

PATTERN DRILL (B). Now use **no fui** with each of the preceding expressions.

12.3.2 *First Person Plural.* **Fuimos de compras ayer** means *We went shopping yesterday.* **No fuimos a esa fiesta** means *We didn't go to that party.*

PATTERN DRILL. Practice aloud using **fuimos** to form sentences with each of the expressions below:

1. a la farmacia a la una menos cuarto
2. a esa librería ayer (*book store*)
3. de compras hace una hora
4. a la playa en tren (*beach*)

5. a Europa en 1957
6. al Brasil en avión (*by plane*)
7. al centro en coche
8. a la panadería ayer (*bakery*)

12.3.3 *Second Person Singular and Plural.*

¿Adónde fuiste anoche?	Where did you go last night?	¿Adónde fuisteis anoche?
Fuiste allí ayer.	You went there yesterday.	Fuisteis allí ayer.

PATTERN DRILL. Practice aloud using ¿**Fuiste?** to form questions with each of the expressions below. Then use ¿**Fuisteis?** in the same way.

1. al baile con Elena
2. a muchas librerías ayer
3. de compras anoche
4. a Europa en avión en 1948

5. allí en tren o en coche (*or*)
6. a la playa el mes pasado
7. a aquella farmacia
8. a la panadería francesa

12.3.4 Third Person Singular. **Isabel fue de compras ayer** means *Elizabeth went shopping yesterday.* ¿**Fue Vd. al centro anoche?** means *Did you go downtown last night?* **La criada no fue a la panadería** means *The maid didn't go to the bakery.* In some books you may find an accent mark over **fué.** This written accent is no longer necessary.

PATTERN DRILL (A). Practice aloud using **Isabel fue** to form sentences with each of the expressions below:

1. al baile con Carlos
2. a la panadería la semana pasada
3. a España en 1955
4. al banco a las diez (*bank*)

5. a la carnicería (*butcher's*)
6. de compras al centro
7. a la tintorería (*dry cleaner's*)
8. a la playa con sus hermanas

PATTERN DRILL (B). Now use ¿**Fue Vd.?** to form questions with each of the expressions above.

12.3.5 Third Person Plural. **Mis padres fueron a la playa ayer** means *My parents went to the beach yesterday.* ¿**Cuándo fueron Vds. a Francia?** means *When did you go to France?* **No fueron a la escuela el viernes** means *They didn't go to school on Friday.*

PATTERN DRILL. Practice aloud using ¿**Fueron Vds.?** to form questions with each of the expressions below:

1. a ese restorán anoche
2. a la playa el domingo
3. a la carnicería ayer
4. al concierto anoche (*concert*)

5. a Puerto Rico en 1940
6. de compras el sábado pasado
7. al concierto el domingo
8. allí en tren o en avión

12.4 «SER»: PRETERITE INDICATIVE

The preterite forms of **ser** and **ir** are identical, because **ir** borrowed the forms of **ser.** Confusion is impossible because of the vastly different contexts in which **ser** and **ir** occur:

Fui al centro.	[ir]	**Fueron a Cuba hace un año.**	[ir]
Fui estudiante.	[ser]	**Fueron pobres hace un año.**	[ser]

PATTERN DRILL (A). Say each sentence below. Then repeat it, changing the verb to the preterite, and ending the sentence with **hace muchos años:**

1. Voy a Inglaterra.
2. Soy soldado.
3. No vamos a la Argentina.
4. Somos estudiantes.

5. ¿Adónde va Juan?
6. María es nuestra criada.
7. José y María van al Canadá.
8. Esos libros son importantes.

PATTERN DRILL (B). Say each sentence below. Then repeat it, changing the verb to the present tense:

1. ¿Fuiste al baile?
2. ¿Fuiste rico el año pasado?
3. No fuimos al centro.
4. José no fue inteligente.

5. ¿Adónde fueron Vds.?
6. ¿Fueron malos aquellos hombres?
7. Hoy fue miércoles.
8. Fui el jueves.

12.5 IRREGULAR PRETERITE STEMS

Approximately a dozen Spanish verbs have irregular stems in the preterite indicative. All these verbs indicate the preterite with the same person and number markers. One such verb is **venir**, whose preterite stem is **vin-**.

12.5.1 *First Person Singular.*   The first person singular is indicated by adding -e to the irregular preterite stem: **vine.**

> **Vine el sábado pasado.**   *I came last Saturday.*
> **No vine el domingo.**   *I didn't come on Sunday.*

PATTERN DRILL. Practice aloud using **vine** to form sentences with each of the expressions below:

1. al Canadá en 1915
2. aquí el lunes
3. del Brasil hace dos años
4. a tu casa el martes

5. a esta ciudad el año pasado
6. con Isabel el lunes pasado
7. a este país en 1931 (*country*)
8. el martes a las cinco de la tarde

12.5.2 *First Person Plural.*   The first person plural is indicated by adding -imos to the irregular preterite stem: **vinimos.**

> **Vinimos aquí hace dos semanas y media.**

PATTERN DRILL. Practice aloud using **vinimos** to form sentences with each of the expressions below:

1. a la una y media de la madrugada
2. el miércoles
3. con Juan el martes pasado

4. a la universidad hace ocho semanas
5. porque queremos estudiar (*because*)
6. a este país con poco dinero
7. aquí el verano pasado (*summer*)
8. a tu casa hace un mes

12.5.3 Second Person Singular and Plural. The second persons singular and plural are indicated by adding -iste and -isteis, respectively, to the irregular preterite stem: **viniste, vinisteis:**

¿Cuándo viniste?   When did you come?   ¿Cuándo vinisteis?

PATTERN DRILL. Say each of the following sentences. Then repeat it, changing the verb to the corresponding preterite form, and ending the sentence with **anoche:**

1. No vienes con Juan.
2. ¿Venís a la fiesta?
3. ¿Vienes a la ciudad en tren?
4. ¿Vienes con mi padre?

5. ¿A qué hora vienes?
6. ¿Por qué vienes a mi casa? (*why?*)
7. Venís a nuestra casa a las ocho.
8. ¿Vienes con tu esposa?

12.5.4 Third Person Singular. The third person singular is indicated by adding -o to the irregular preterite stem: **vino.**

Carlos vino a mi casa el miércoles pasado.
¿Por qué vino Vd. anoche?   *Why did you come last night?*

PATTERN DRILL. Practice aloud using **vino** to complete the sentences below:

1. Mi hermano . . . ayer a las dos.
2. Isabel . . . el jueves.
3. Ese médico . . . aquí en 1937.
4. Vd. no . . . el viernes.

5. Esa mujer . . . a mi casa el martes.
6. Vd. . . . porque quiere trabajar.
7. La criada no . . . el jueves pasado.
8. ¿Cuándo . . . Vd. a este país?

12.5.5 Third Person Plural. The third person plural is indicated by adding -ieron to the irregular preterite stem: **vinieron.**

Esos hombres vinieron el verano pasado.
¿Por qué vinieron Vds. ayer?

PATTERN DRILL. Practice aloud using **vinieron** to complete each sentence below:

1. Mis padres . . . a este país en 1911.
2. Vds. no . . . aquí el verano pasado.

3. Nuestros amigos . . . con sus esposas.
4. Vds. . . . el jueves pasado.
5. Mis hijos . . . el domingo.
6 Tus abuelos . . . en 1867.
7. ¿Por qué . . . Vds. el viernes?
8. Juan y Carlos . . . hace media hora.

12.6 DIRECT OBJECT PRONOUNS

A word used to refer to an expressed or implied noun is called a *pronoun*. In the sentence *Mary came, but we didn't see her,* the pronoun *her* refers to the expressed noun *Mary.* In the sentence *We saw her,* the pronoun *her* implies some feminine, singular noun, such as *Mary,* or *the woman,* or *the girl.* The noun referred to is called the *referend* of the pronoun. In the preceding examples, *her* is directly affected by the action of the verbs, and, therefore, *her* is called a *direct object pronoun.*

All the Spanish direct object pronouns, like their English counterparts, indicate whether the referend is singular or plural, and some of them also indicate the gender of the referend. However, unlike the English direct object pronouns, which always follow the verb with which they are associated, the Spanish direct object pronouns *do not* occupy the same position in every sentence. For the time being, adopt the "rule of thumb" that direct object pronouns immediately precede inflected verbs, and immediately follow infinitives.

12.6.1 *First Person Singular.* Regardless of gender, a singular first-person referend is indicated in Spanish by **me**:

John saw me.	**Juan me vio.**
Did John see me?	**¿Me vio Juan?**
John didn't see me.	**Juan no me vio.**

In sentences such as *John is going to see me,* in which **me** is the direct object of an uninflected verb, **me** immediately follows, and is attached to, that infinitive:

John is going to see me.	**Juan va a verme.**
John isn't going to see me.	**Juan no va a verme.**
Is John going to see me?	**¿Va a verme Juan?**

PATTERN DRILL (**A**). Say each of the following sentences. Then repeat it, beginning the sentence with **anoche,** and changing the verb to the preterite:

1. María me llama.
2. Carlos me ve en el centro.
3. ¿Me buscan Vds.?
4. Mis amigos me llaman a las ocho.

5. Juan me halla en la cocina.
6. Isabel me conoce.

7. ¿Me ves en el jardín?
8. ¿Me esperas a las cinco?

PATTERN DRILL (B). Practice aloud using **me** to complete the sentences below:

1. María . . . busca ahora.
2. Carlos . . . llamó hace una hora.
3. Los muchachos no . . . esperaron ayer.
4. ¿Dónde . . . vio Vd. anoche?
5. ¿A qué hora deseas ver . . .?
6. Mis padres . . . quieren mucho.
7. Elena va a llamar . . . a las cinco.
8. ¿ . . . vieron Vds. el miércoles?

12.6.2   First Person Plural.   Regardless of gender, a plural first-person referend is indicated by **nos:**

John saw us.	**Juan nos vio.**
Did you see us yesterday?	**¿Nos vio Vd. ayer?**
They're going to wait for us.	**Van a esperarnos.**

PATTERN DRILL.   Practice aloud using **nos** to complete the sentences below:

1. Esos hombres no . . . quieren.
2. Roberto . . . llamó el domingo pasado.
3. Vds. no van a hallar . . . en casa.
4. ¿Dónde . . . viste anoche?
5. ¿Por qué . . . llamó Vd.?
6. ¿A qué hora va Vd. a llamar . . .?
7. Nuestros abuelos . . . quieren.
8. ¿ . . . reconoce Vd.? (*to recognize*)

12.6.3   Second Person Singular and Plural.   Regardless of gender, a singular second-person referend is indicated by **te**, and a plural one by **os:**

Te vi ayer.	I saw you yesterday.	**Os vi ayer.**
¿Te reconoce Juan?	Does John recognize you?	**¿Os reconoce Juan?**
Deseo verte a la una.	I want to see you at one.	**Deseo veros a la una.**

PATTERN DRILL.   Practice aloud using **te** to complete the sentences below. Then complete them with **os.**

1. Juan . . . espera en la sala.
2. El médico desea ver . . . hoy.

3. No . . . llamé el jueves pasado.
4. Vamos a esperar . . . a las cinco.

5. Ese profesor . . . busca.   7. María . . . vio en España en 1927.
6. No . . . reconozco en ese coche.   8. Mis padres . . . quieren.

12.6.4 *Third Person Singular.* A masculine, singular third-person referend, whether a person or a thing, is indicated by **lo**:

> **Juan está aquí, pero no lo vemos.**   . . . *but we don't see him.*
> **Deseo ese libro, y voy a comprarlo.**   . . . *and I'm going to buy it.*
> **Cuando Vd. llegó, no lo reconocí.**   . . . *I didn't recognize you.*

Although **lo** is not used in some regions, this question need not concern you now.

A feminine, singular third-person referend, whether a person or a thing, is indicated by **la**:

> **María está aquí, pero no la vemos.**   . . . *but we don't see her.*
> **Deseo esa pluma, y voy a comprarla.**   . . . *and I'm going to buy it.*
> **Cuando Vd. llegó, no la reconocí.**   . . . *I didn't recognize you.*

PATTERN DRILL. Say each sentence below. Then repeat it, replacing the direct object noun with the corresponding form of **lo** or **la**:

1. Compré el coche ayer.   5. Voy a esperar a María a las dos.
2. Vamos a ver a Juan a la una.   6. No busco a mi hermana.
3. Vendimos la casa hace un mes.   7. Vimos la película anoche.
4. Carlos compró esa gabardina aquí.   8. Empiezo a estudiar la lección.

12.6.5 *Third Person Plural.* A masculine, plural third-person referend, whether persons or things, is indicated by **los**, and a feminine referend is indicated by **las**:

> **Los muchachos vinieron ayer, pero no los vi.** . . . *but I didn't see them.*
> **Las mujeres vinieron anoche, pero no las vi.** . . . *but I didn't see them.*
> **Deseo esos pañuelos, y voy a comprarlos.**   . . . *and I'm going to buy them.*
> **Deseo esas corbatas, y voy a comprarlas.**   . . . *and I'm going to buy them.*
> **Cuando Vds. llegaron, no los vi.**   . . . *I didn't see you.*
> **Cuando Vds. llegaron, no las vi.**   . . . *I didn't see you.*

Los is also used to indicate referends of different genders:

> **Juan y María vinieron anoche, pero no los vi.** . . . *but I didn't see them.*

PATTERN DRILL. Say each sentence below. Then repeat it, replacing the direct object noun with the corresponding form of **los** or **las**:

1. Compré los discos la semana pasada.
2. Juan busca a sus hermanas.
3. Perdí la pluma y el reloj.
4. Voy a esperar a Vds. el domingo.
5. Queremos ver a nuestros abuelos.
6. Llamé a Juan y a María ayer.
7. La criada rompió las tazas.
8. No deseo estudiar estas lecciones.

Lesson 13

13.1 IRREGULAR PRETERITE STEMS

The verbs drilled in this section indicate the persons of the preterite with the same markers as **venir** (see 12.5).

13.1.1 Estar. The preterite stem is **estuv-**:

> **Estuve en París el verano pasado.**
> **Juan no estuvo en casa ayer.**
> **¿Dónde estuvieron Vds. anoche?**

PATTERN DRILL (A). Practice aloud using **estuve** to form sentences with each of the phrases below:

1. muy ocupado anoche
2. en ese pueblo ayer (*town*)
3. enfermo la semana pasada
4. allí en enero (*January*)
5. en el campo el jueves pasado
6. aquí el invierno pasado (*winter*)
7. en el centro hace media hora
8. en Madrid en febrero (*February*)

PATTERN DRILL (B). Now use **Carlos estuvo** with each of the phrases above.

PATTERN DRILL (C). Say each sentence below. Then repeat it, changing the verb to the preterite, and adding **anteayer** (*the day before yesterday*):

1. No estoy en casa.
2. ¿Dónde está Vd.?
3. Mis hermanos están en ese pueblo.
4. ¿Por qué está aquí Juan?
5. Estamos muy ocupados.
6. ¿Están Vds. con sus abuelos?
7. Isabel no está en el jardín.
8. ¿Estás muy cansado?

13.1.2 Tener. The preterite stem is **tuv-**:

> **Tuve mucha hambre anoche.**
> **Ayer tuvimos el coche de Carlos.**

In some contexts, the preterite of **tener** is the equivalent of **recibir**. This is similar to the English use of *had* as a synonym of *received*:

Ayer tuve una carta de María. *Yesterday I had a letter from Mary.*
¿Tuvo Vd. el regalo el lunes? *Did you receive the present on Monday?*

Tener que followed by an infinitive is the Spanish equivalent of *to have to.* The use of **tener que** is not, of course, limited to the preterite:

Tengo que estudiar esta página. *I have to study this page.*
¿Tienen Vds. que salir? *Do you have to leave?*
Juan tuvo que trabajar anoche. *John had to work last night.*
Vamos a tener que volver. *We're going to have to return.*

PATTERN DRILL (A). Practice aloud using **tuve que** to form sentences with each of the phrases below:

1. volver a la ciudad anteayer
2. trabajar mucho en marzo (*March*)
3. pintar la sala el mes pasado
4. vender esa casa en abril (*April*)
5. venir aquí en mayo (*May*)
6. vivir allí el invierno pasado
7. estar en el centro a las nueve
8. salir del Perú en junio (*June*)

PATTERN DRILL (B). Now use **¿Tuvieron Vds. que?** to form questions with each of the phrases above.

PATTERN DRILL (C). Say each sentence below. Then repeat it, changing the verb to the preterite, and adding **anteanoche** (*the night before last*):

1. Tengo que comer en el centro.
2. ¿Tiene Vd. una carta de María?
3. La criada tiene que ir al hospital.
4. ¿Tienes una cita con Isabel? (*date*)
5. Tenemos que trabajar mucho.
6. ¿Tienen Vds. mucho frío?
7. Tengo que llamar al médico.
8. Vds. tienen que leer ese libro.

13.1.3 *Querer.* The preterite stem is **quis-**: **Quise pan, pero no lo sirvieron.** Followed by an infinitive, the preterite of **querer** is equivalent to the English *tried to:*

Quise venir anoche. *I tried to come last night.*
Juan quiso volver ayer. *John tried to return yesterday.*

Used negatively, the preterite of **querer** is equivalent to the English *refused:*

No quise comprarlo. *I refused to buy it.*
No quisimos venir a la fiesta. *We refused to come to the party.*
No quisieron llamarme. *They refused to call me.*

PATTERN DRILL (A). Practice aloud using **quise** to form sentences with each of the phrases below:

1. comprarlos ayer
2. ir allí en julio (*July*)
3. llamar a Juan a la una y media
4. llegar a tiempo (*on time*)
5. volver a Cuba el invierno pasado
6. vender el coche en agosto (*August*)
7. estudiar mucho anoche
8. ir a España en septiembre (*September*)

PATTERN DRILL (B). Practice aloud using **ellos no quisieron** to form sentences with each of the phrases below:

1. ir a ese baile anteanoche
2. comer ostras en mayo (*oysters*)
3. vivir en esa casa vieja
4. venir aquí en octubre (*October*)
5. ver esa película italiana
6. ir a la playa en noviembre (*November*)
7. salir de casa a las once
8. ir allí en diciembre (*December*)

13.2 «DAR»: TO GIVE

The verb **dar** is partially irregular in the present indicative, and it has an irregular preterite also.

13.2.1 *Present Indicative.* *I give* is **doy**:

> **Doy el reloj a Carlos.**
> **No doy vino a mis hijos.**

To indicate the other persons in the present, **dar** is inflected as a regular **-ar** verb:

> **¿Das mucha leche a tu hija?**   **No damos helado al perro.**

PATTERN DRILL (A). Practice aloud using **doy** to form sentences with each of the phrases below:

1. la blusa de seda a María
2. los platos sucios a la criada
3. muchos libros a la biblioteca
4. un regalo caro a esa mujer
5. mucha leche al niño (*child*)
6. poco dinero a la universidad
7. un cuadro al museo (*painting*)
8. este vestido verde a Elena

PATTERN DRILL (B). Now use ¿**Da Vd.?** with each of the phrases above.

13.2.2 *Preterite Indicative*. In the preterite indicative tense, **dar** is inflected as if it were an **-ir** verb whose stem is **d-**. However, there are no written accent marks:

Di un regalo a Pedro ayer.	No dimos cerveza a los niños.
¿Diste dinero a la criada?	¿Cuándo disteis los libros a Juan?
José dio los guantes a su madre.	¿Por qué dieron Vds. leche al perro?

In some books you may find an accent mark on **dió**. This written accent is no longer necessary.

PATTERN DRILL. Say each sentence below. Then repeat it, changing the verb to the preterite, and adding **hace un par de días** (*a couple of days ago*):

1. Doy la tinta a Juan. (*ink*)
2. María da la blusa a su hermana.
3. Los hombres dan dos cuadros al museo.
4. Damos los pañuelos a nuestra madre.
5. ¿Dan Vds. esos libros a Pedro?
6. Doy la llave a la criada. (*key*)
7. ¿Das ese dinero a tu hijo?
8. ¿Dais cerveza a la niña?

13.3 INDIRECT OBJECT PRONOUNS

An *indirect object* of a verb is a thing or a person to whom something is given, said, written, or otherwise directed:

I gave the food to the animal.	*I'll write a letter to the woman.*
I told the story to the man.	*We sent a present to our grandfather.*

In English, the most common sign of an "indirect" relationship between a verb and its object is *to*. However, the presence or absence of *to* is not an infallible guide. In English sentences such as *I gave the man the book*, in which the indirect object precedes the direct, there is no *to*. Its omission does not change the "indirect" nature of the relationship between *I gave* and *the man*. In Spanish, an indirect object noun is always preceded by **a**: **Doy el libro al hombre.**

An *indirect object pronoun* is a word that refers to an expressed or implied indirect object noun (the referend). For example, in the sentences *Mary gave the book to him* and *Mary gave him the book*, *him* is an English indirect object pronoun.

All the Spanish indirect object pronouns, like their English counterparts, indicate whether the referend is singular or plural. Although none of them show gender, possible ambiguity is easily avoided. Your main problems with the Spanish indirect object pronouns will be to use them with some verbs whose English equivalents are not accompanied by indirect object pronouns, and to position them in a sentence. The Spanish indirect object pronouns, like the direct ones, immediately precede inflected verbs, and immediately follow infinitives. (Their sequence in sentences with two object pronouns need not concern you until the next lesson.) In the first and second persons singular as well as plural, the Spanish indirect object pronouns have the same forms as the direct object pronouns.

13.3.1   *First Person Singular and Plural.* Regardless of gender, a singular first-person referend is indicated by **me**, and a plural referend is indicated by **nos**:

Juan me dio el paraguas.	*John gave the umbrella to me.*
Elena va a venderme su coche.	*Helen is going to sell me her car.*
Carlos nos escribió ayer.	*Charles wrote to us yesterday.*
Van a mandarnos el regalo.	*They're going to send us the present.*

PATTERN DRILL (A). Practice aloud using **me** to complete each sentence below:

1. Roberto . . . escribió el mes pasado.
2. María no quiso dar . . . la llave.
3. Mis abuelos . . . dieron un cuadro.
4. ¿Vas a mandar . . . muchas cartas?
5. Mi padre . . . da poco dinero.
6. Carlos tiene que escribir . . .
7. ¿. . . mandó Vd. la carta ayer?
8. La criada . . . dio los pañuelos.

PATTERN DRILL (B). Use **nos** to complete each of the sentences above.

13.3.2   *Second Person Singular and Plural.* Regardless of gender, a singular second-person referend is indicated by **te**, and a plural referend is indicated by **os**:

¿Te escribió Juan?	*Did John write to you?*	**¿Os escribió Juan?**
Deseo hablarte.	*I want to speak to you.*	**Deseo hablaros.**

PATTERN DRILL. Practice aloud using **te** to complete each of the sentences below. **Mostrar (ue)** means *to show*.

1. Anoche . . . mandé la carta.
2. Voy a mostrar . . . el libro.
3. ¿Quién . . . mostró la casa? (*who?*)
4. Vamos a mandar . . . ese disco.
5. Roberto va a dar . . . la llave.
6. ¿. . . hablaron esos hombres?
7. Deseo mostrar . . . el coche azul.
8. ¿Quién . . . dio ese dinero?

13.3.3 *Third Person Singular.* Regardless of gender, a singular third-person referend is indicated by le:

Juan vino, pero no le hablé.   . . . but I didn't speak to him.
María viene, pero no voy a hablarle. . . . but I'm not going to speak to
                                                                             her.
Vd. me escribió, pero no le escribí. . . . but I didn't write to you.

In order to avoid ambiguity, or to be emphatic, the meaning of le can be specified by the use of a él, a ella, or a Vd. in addition to le:

Le di la llave a él.   I gave him the key.
Voy a darle la llave a ella.   I'm going to give her the key.
Vamos a mostrarle la casa a Vd.   We're going to show you the house.

PATTERN DRILL (A). Say each sentence below. Then repeat it, replacing the indirect object noun with le:

1. Escribí a mi primo ayer. (*cousin*)   5. Muestro la casa al hombre.
2. Voy a escribir a mi padre.   6. Tengo que escribir a Vd.
3. No doy esta llave a la criada.   7. Dimos un regalo a mi prima.
4. Mando el cuadro a Vd.   8. ¿Por qué dio Vd. el dinero al niño?

PATTERN DRILL (B). Say each sentence above, replacing the indirect object noun with le and clarifying its meaning by the use of a él, a ella, or a Vd., as required.

13.3.4 *Third Person Plural.* Regardless of gender, a plural third-person referend is indicated by les:

Carlos y María vinieron y les di el cuadro.   . . . and I gave them the paint-
                                                                                    ing.
Si Vds. vienen, no voy a hablarles.   . . . If you come, I'm not
                                                                                    going to speak to you.

In order to avoid ambiguity, or to be emphatic, the meaning of les can be specified by the use of a ellos, a ellas, or a Vds. in addition to les:

Les di el cuadro a ellos.   I gave them the painting.
No les di la llave a ellas.   I didn't give them the key.
Voy a darles el libro a Vds.   I'm going to give you the book.
Tengo que escribirles a Vds.   I have to write to you.

PATTERN DRILL (A). Say each sentences below. Then repeat it, replacing the indirect object noun with les:

1. Escribí a mis abuelos anoche.
2. Tengo que mandar regalos a mis primos.

3. Mandé las cartas a las mujeres.
4. ¿Por qué mandó Juan el dinero a Vds.?
5. ¿Escribes a esas muchachas?
6. No damos mucho vino a las criadas.
7. Vamos a mandar el cuadro a Vds.
8. ¿Quién dio ese dinero a Vds.?

PATTERN DRILL (B). Now say each of the preceding sentences again, replacing the indirect object noun with **les** and clarifying its meaning by the use of **a ellos, a ellas,** or **a Vds.,** as required.

13.3.5 Special Uses of the Indirect Object. The verb **pedir** is accompanied by an indirect object pronoun indicating the person of whom something is requested:

Juan me pidió dos dólares.	*John asked me for two dollars.*
Tengo que pedirte el dinero.	*I have to ask you for the money.*

Verbs that imply separation, such as **robar, comprar,** and **quitar** (*to take away*), can have a direct object and an indirect object. The former is the thing being separated: **Robé el dinero,** *I stole the money.* The indirect object is the person from whom a thing is separated. This person is indicated by an indirect object pronoun, or by a noun (or **Vd.** and **Vds.**) preceded by **a:**

Le robé el dinero.	*I stole the money from him.*
Me quitó el cuchillo.	*He took the knife away from me.*
Compré las flores a esa mujer.	*I bought the flowers from that woman.*
No robé el libro a Vd.	*I didn't steal the book from you.*

You will often find Spanish sentences that contain a third-person indirect object noun and also the corresponding indirect object pronoun: **Le compré las flores a esa mujer.** Since the indirect object pronoun occurs before the indirect object noun, the pronoun is said to "anticipate" the noun. Although the pronoun is redundant, this construction is quite common:

Le robé el dinero a Juan.	*I stole the money from John.*
Voy a mandarle el regalo a Vd.	*I'm going to send the present to you.*
Tengo que pedirles un favor a Vds.	*I have to ask you for a favor.*

PATTERN DRILL (A). Practice aloud using **me** to complete each sentence below:

1. Mi hermana . . . quitó el periódico.
2. Roberto . . . pidió el coche ayer.
3. ¿Por qué . . . pides dinero?

4. ¿Vas a quitar . . . la cerveza?
5. Ese hombre . . . robó mucho dinero.
6. María va a pedir . . . las rosas.
7. ¿Quién . . . robó ese caballo?
8. Juan . . . compró la casa.

PATTERN DRILL (B). Say each sentence below. Then repeat it, substituting **le** or **les**, as required, for the indirect object noun:

1. Pedí pan a la criada.
2. Voy a quitar el cuchillo al niño.
3. No pido dinero a mi madre.
4. ¿Quién robó el coche a Vds.?
5. Quiero pedir a Vd. un favor.
6. No voy a pedir el favor a ellos.
7. María quitó la tinta a las niñas.
8. Vamos a comprar los caballos a Juan.

PATTERN DRILL (C). Say each sentence above. Then repeat it, anticipating the indirect object noun with the corresponding redundant indirect object pronoun. The first is: **Le pedí pan a la criada.**

13.4 «DECIR»: TO SAY, TO TELL

In the present indicative, **decir** is partially irregular as well as stem-changing. It also has an irregular preterite stem. **Decir** and a clause (a group of words containing a verb) are always connected by **que: Decir que María está enferma,** *to say that Mary is sick.*

13.4.1 *Present Indicative.* *I say or I tell is* **digo:**

> **Digo que Juan viene.** *I say that John is coming.*
> **No te digo la verdad.** *I'm not telling you the truth.*

In the second and third persons singular and in the third person plural, the /-e-/ of the stem becomes /-i-/:

> **¿Me dices la verdad?** *Are you telling me the truth?*
> **Juan dice que son las tres.** *John says it's three o'clock.*
> **¿Qué dicen Vds.?** *What are you saying?*

The first and second persons plural are "regular":

> **Decimos que no vamos a venir.**   **¿Qué me decís?**

PATTERN DRILL (A). Use **digo** to form sentences with each of the clauses below:

1. que estoy muy ocupado
2. que es la una y media de la madrugada

3. que mi abuelo no está en casa
4. que no vamos a la fiesta
5. que Carlos no va a comprar ese coche
6. que mi casa es roja y blanca
7. que Elena es muy inteligente
8. que voy a llegar tarde (*to be late*)

PATTERN DRILL (B). Answer the following questions affirmatively, using Sí and a complete sentence:

1. ¿Dices que María no vuelve?
2. ¿Dice Pedro que está triste?
3. ¿Dice tu padre que vende la casa?
4. ¿Dicen Vds. que tienen que salir?
5. ¿Dice Vd. que son las dos?
6. ¿Dicen Vds. que van al centro?
7. ¿Dices que quieres a mi hermana?
8. ¿Dice Juan la verdad?

13.4.2 *Preterite Indicative.* The preterite stem of **decir** is **dij-**:

Dije que Juan está aquí.	*I said that John is here.*
Le dijimos la verdad a Vd.	*We told you the truth.*

Note that the third person plural form is **dijeron: Mis padres me dijeron que vamos al campo en junio.**

PATTERN DRILL. Say each sentence below. Then repeat it, changing the form of **decir** to the preterite:

1. Digo que Elena es bonita.
2. ¿Dices que dos más dos son cinco?
3. Carlos le dice la verdad.
4. Vds. no dicen mucho.
5. ¿Dice Vd. *perro o pero*?
6. Digo que tengo que trabajar.
7. Esos hombres me dicen poco.
8. No decimos la verdad.

Lesson 14

14.1 TWO OBJECT PRONOUNS

When both the direct and the indirect objects of an inflected verb are indicated by object pronouns, the indirect object pronoun precedes the direct object pronoun, and both pronouns immediately precede the verb:

Deseo el cuadro, y Juan me lo da.	. . . and John gives it to me.
Pedimos la pluma, y Elena nos la dio.	. . . and Helen gave it to us.
No pediste los libros, pero te los mandé.	. . . but I sent them to you.
¿Deseas esas revistas? Te las mando.	. . . I'm sending them to you.

PATTERN DRILL. Say each sentence below. Then repeat it, replacing the direct object noun with the corresponding direct object pronoun:

1. Pedro me vende el coche.
2. No me mandaste la carta.
3. Juan me presta el libro. (*to lend*)
4. Vd. nos dio las revistas ayer.
5. Mi padre me da el dinero.
6. Te di las manzanas.
7. ¿Te prestó María la pluma?
8. Os damos las llaves.

14.2 TWO OBJECT PRONOUNS WITH AN INFINITIVE

When both the direct and the indirect objects of an infinitive are indicated by object pronouns, the indirect object pronoun precedes the direct object pronoun, and both pronouns immediately follow the verb. In writing, the pronouns are attached to the verb and an accent is placed over the final vowel of the infinitive in order to show that the original stress is maintained despite the addition of two more syllables to the infinitive:

Deseo el libro, y Juan va a dármelo.	. . . and John is going to give it to me.
Deseamos tu manzana, y vas a dárnosla.	. . . and you're going to give it to us.

Deseas mi coche, y voy a prestártelo.	. . . *and I'm going to lend it to you.*
Necesitáis los libros, y quiero mandároslos.	. . . *and I want to send them to you.*

PATTERN DRILL. Say each sentence below. Then repeat it, replacing the direct object noun with the corresponding direct object pronoun:

1. ¿Vas a mandarme la carta?
2. ¿Van Vds. a darnos la llave?
3. Voy a pedirte ese cuadro.
4. Carlos quiere prestarme ese disco.

5. Quiero darte el abrigo.
6. Elena va a prestarme la sartén.
7. No voy a darte las cerezas.
8. ¿Vas a pedirme el dinero?

14.3 TWO OBJECT PRONOUNS IN THE THIRD PERSON

When both the direct and the indirect object pronouns of a verb are in the third person (singular or plural), the indirect object pronoun **le** or **les** is always replaced by **se**:

Mi madre pidió el plato y se lo di.	. . . *and I gave it to her.*
Mi madre pidió la taza y se la di.	. . . *and I gave it to her.*
Carlos pidió los libros y se los dimos.	. . . *and we gave them to him.*
María desea el vino y voy a dárselo.	. . . *and I'm going to give it to her.*
Vd. desea las revistas y quiero dárselas.	. . . *and I want to give them to you.*
Ellos desean el cuadro y vamos a dárselo.	. . . *and we're going to give it to them.*
Mi hijo desea la manzana y voy a dársela.	. . . *and I'm going to give it to him.*

To avoid ambiguity, the meaning of **se** can be clarified by the use of **a él, a ella, a Vd.,** etc.

Juan y Elena desean el cuadro, pero voy a dárselo a Vd.

PATTERN DRILL (A). Say each sentence below. Then repeat it, replacing the indirect object noun with **se**:

1. Lo doy a Juan.
2. Lo pedí a mis abuelos.
3. ¿La mandó Vd. al hombre?
4. ¿No los das a Carlos?

5. Vamos a prestarlo a Elena.
6. Queremos mandarlo a Vds.
7. ¿Van Vds. a darlos a sus hijos?
8. Tengo que prestarlo a la criada.

PATTERN DRILL (B). Say each sentence below. Then repeat it, replacing the direct object noun with the corresponding direct object pronoun:

1. Le pedí el dinero.
2. Les quité los cuchillos.
3. No le di la manzana.
4. Les presté las tazas.

5. Voy a darle la llave.
6. Vamos a pedirles el coche.
7. Tengo que mandarle las cartas.
8. Voy a prestarles los manteles.

PATTERN DRILL (C). Say each sentence below. Then repeat it, replacing both the direct object noun and the indirect object noun with the corresponding direct and indirect object pronouns:

1. No doy las naranjas a Elena.
2. ¿Prestas ese dinero al muchacho?
3. Di los cuadros a Juan y a María.
4. Vamos a prestar las tazas a Vds.

5. Quiero mandar las cartas a Vd.
6. ¿Dio Vd. el reloj a su esposa?
7. No vendo los caballos a esos hombres.
8. No vamos a vender la casa a Vds.

PATTERN DRILL (D). Repeat each sentence above, replacing the object nouns with the corresponding object pronouns, and clarifying the meaning of **se** with **a él, a ella**, etc., as required.

14.4 THE IMPERFECT TENSE

In addition to the preterite, Spanish has a past tense known as the *imperfect indicative*. The primary function of the imperfect is to express an action that was going on during some indefinite past time. English often employs was + -ing for the same purpose: *I was studying*. Another important function of the imperfect is to describe the state of something or someone in the past. English usually does this with its simple past tense: *The house was empty*. The imperfect is also used to indicate a past action that was repeated or customary, and in this function the imperfect is frequently accompanied by reiterative expressions such as **todos los días** (*every day*) or **siempre** (*always*). English often employs *used to* in such contexts: *I used to study every day* (repeated action) or *I always used to study hard* (customary action).

Notice that in all the preceding examples, there is no indication of when in the past the action occurred or the state existed. Nor is there any indications of the duration of the action or the state. Herein lies a basic difference beween the preterite and the imperfect. The preterite is used to indicate when, or for how long, a past action was repeated or went on, or a past state existed. The imperfect, on the other hand, is used to indicate, without reference to time or duration, that in the past an action was going on or was repeated, or that a state existed.

English usage is not always a reliable guide to the difference between the preterite and the imperfect in Spanish. For example, *I used to study every day* can also be expressed with the English simple past as *I studied every day.* However, other words in a Spanish sentence often provide a student with useful clues to identify the appropriate tense. For example, words like **a menudo** (*often*), **de vez en cuando** (*from time to time*), **siempre,** and **todos los días** are often accompanied by the imperfect, provided that a specific time, or time limit, is not also given. On the other hand, words like **ayer** and **el año pasado,** which indicate a specific past time or imply a time limit, are usually accompanied by the preterite: **Fui allí el año pasado,** *I went there last year.* Words that indicate duration, whether **una hora** or **cien años,** also point to the use of the preterite: **Mi abuelo vivió sesenta años en España.**

Verbs that express mental action, such as **querer** or **desear,** usually indicate past action with the imperfect, unless there is an indication of specific time or duration. The hours of the clock are accompanied by the imperfect of **ser.**

Further comparisons between the preterite and the imperfect will be presented after you have learned how the imperfect is formed. In the imperfect tense there are no stem changes, and only three irregular verbs.

14.5 IMPERFECT INDICATIVE: INFINITIVES ENDING IN «–AR»

14.5.1 *First Person Singular.* To indicate the first person singular, the **-ar** of the infinitive is replaced by **-aba**:

Compraba pan todos los días.	*I used to buy bread every day.*
Siempre compraba muchas cerezas.	*I always bought lots of cherries.*
No compraba leche todos los días.	*I didn't buy milk every day.*

To avoid confusion with the third person singular of the imperfect, which is also indicated by **-aba,** it is sometimes necessary to specify *I* by the subject pronoun **yo:**

Yo los buscaba.   *I was looking for them.*

PATTERN DRILL. Say each sentence below. Then repeat it, beginning the sentence with **siempre,** and changing the verb to the imperfect:

1. Estudio mis lecciones.
2. Gasto mucho dinero. (*to spend*)
3. Trabajo en esa tienda.
4. Compro mucho azúcar. (*sugar*)
5. Estoy muy ocupado.
6. Llevo este sombrero. (*to wear*)
7. Llego tarde a la escuela.
8. Llamo a María.

14.5.2 First Person Plural. To indicate the first person plural, the -ar of the infinitive is replaced by -ábamos:

No llegábamos tarde a menudo.   *We weren't late often.*
Comprábamos ese periódico todos los días.
Siempre gastábamos mucho dinero.

PATTERN DRILL. Say each sentence below. Then repeat it, beginning the sentence with **a menudo**, and changing the verb to the imperfect:

1. Estamos en el jardín.
2. Trabajamos los sábados.
3. Deseamos ir a España.
4. Llamamos a María los jueves.
5. Llevamos guantes de lana.
6. Visitamos a mi tío. (*to visit*)
7. Necesitamos azúcar.
8. Llegamos temprano. (*early*)

14.5.3 Second Person Singular and Plural. To indicate the singular intimate you, the -ar of the infinitive is replaced by -abas: **Todos los días deseabas ir a la playa.** *You used to want to go to the beach every day.* **¿Qué buscabas?** *What were you looking for?*

To indicate the plural intimate you, the -ar of the infinitive is replaced by -abais: **Todos los días llegabais tarde.**

PATTERN DRILL. Say each sentence below. Then repeat it, beginning the sentence with **a veces** (*sometimes*), and changing the verb to the imperfect:

1. Llevas ese sombrero rojo.
2. Estás muy ocupado.
3. Estudias poco.
4. Compras mucha mantequilla. (*butter*)
5. Gastas poco dinero.
6. Trabajas los domingos.
7. ¿Compras esa carne?
8. No estudiáis mucho.

14.5.4 Third Person Singular. To indicate the third person singular, the -ar of the infinitive is replaced by -aba:

A veces Vd. gastaba mucho dinero.
Juan estudiaba en Alemania.
¿Estaba enferma tu madre?

PATTERN DRILL. Say each sentence below. Then repeat it, changing the verb to the imperfect:

1. Juan estudia los domingos.
2. ¿Compra Vd. leche todos los días?
3. Carlos busca a María.
4. Isabel siempre llega tarde.
5. A veces Vd. llega temprano.

6. Mi padre no compra cerveza a menudo.
7. Juan nos espera todos los días.
8. ¿Visita Vd. a sus abuelos?

14.5.5 *Third Person Plural.* To indicate the third person plural, the **-ar** of the infinitive is replaced by **-aban**:

A menudo mis padres deseaban volver.   My parents often wanted to return.

¿Deseaban Vds. verme?   Did you want to see me?
Juan y María no llegaban tarde a menudo.   John and Mary weren't often late.

PATTERN DRILL. Say each sentence below. Then repeat it, beginning the sentence with **de vez en cuando,** and changing the verb to the imperfect:

1. Nuestros abuelos nos visitan.
2. Vds. llegan a tiempo.
3. Esos estudiantes trabajan mucho.
4. Mis hijos necesitan zapatos.
5. Esos hombres trabajan los domingos.
6. Mis amigos me llaman.
7. Juan y Pedro nos esperan.
8. Vds. no desean ir a la playa.

14.6 IMPERFECT INDICATIVE: INFINITIVES IN «-ER» AND «-IR»

14.6.1 *First Person Singular.* To indicate the first person singular, the **-er** or **-ir** of the infinitive is replaced by **-ía**:

Siempre comía mucho.   I always ate a lot.
Les escribía todos los días.

To avoid confusion with the third person singular of the imperfect, which is also indicated by **-ía**, it is sometimes necessary to specify *I* by the subject pronoun **yo**: **Yo no quería ir a la playa,** *I didn't want to go to the beach.*

PATTERN DRILL. Say each sentence below. Then repeat it, beginning the sentence with **a menudo,** and changing the verb to the imperfect:

1. Como en aquel restorán.
2. Escribo a mis amigos.
3. Bebo mucho vino.
4. Tengo sueño. (*to be sleepy*)
5. Quiero helado de fresa.
6. Vuelvo a las tres y media.
7. Sirvo mucha fruta. (*fruit*)
8. Duermo en la biblioteca.

14.6.2 *First Person Plural.* To indicate the first person plural, the **-er** or **-ir** of the infinitive is replaced by **-íamos**:

De costumbre les servíamos helado.   We usually served them ice cream.
Recibíamos muchos regalos.   We used to receive a lot of presents.
No queríamos ir al cine.   We didn't want to go to the movies.

PATTERN DRILL. Say each sentence below. Then repeat it, beginning the sentence with **de costumbre,** and changing the verb to the imperfect:

1. Leemos muchos periódicos.
2. Tenemos poca hambre.
3. Volvemos en coche.
4. Bebemos mucha leche.
5. Tenemos razón. (*to be right*)
6. No queremos llegar tarde.
7. Escribimos muchas cartas.
8. Pedimos aceitunas. (*olives*)

14.6.3 *Second Person Singular and Plural.* To indicate the singular intimate you, the **-er** or **-ir** of the infinitive is replaced by **-ías:**

Siempre tenías razón.	*You were always right.*
¿Les escribías?	*Were you writing to them?*

To indicate the plural intimate you, the **-er** or **-ir** of the infinitive is replaced by **-íais:**

¿Comíais allí siempre?	*Did you always eat there?*
¿A qué hora salíais?	*When did you used to leave?*

PATTERN DRILL. Say each sentence below. Then repeat it, beginning the sentence with **muchas veces** (*often*), and changing the verb to the imperfect:

1. Comes muchos plátanos. (*bananas*)
2. ¿Escribes a tu amiga?
3. No tienes razón.
4. No comprendes la lección.
5. ¿Vuelves con Juan?
6. ¿Duermes en la sala?
7. Quieres ir al parque. (*park*)
8. ¿Bebéis vino?

(Note: As you have probably concluded, **no tener razón** is the equivalent of the English *to be wrong,* and **comprender,** *to understand,* is a cognate of the English *comprehend.*)

14.6.4 *Third Person Singular.* To indicate the third person singular, the **-er** or **-ir** of the infinitive is replaced by **-ía:**

¿Tenía Vd. razón?	*Were you right?*
Carlos siempre comprendía las lecciones.	

PATTERN DRILL. Say each sentence below. Then repeat it, changing the verb to the imperfect, and ending the sentence with **todas las noches** (*every night*):

1. Isabel come mucha fruta.
2. Esa muchacha española me escribe.
3. Ese hombre quiere ir al centro.
4. ¿Tiene Vd. que estudiar mucho?
5. ¿Duerme Vd. en ese hotel?
6. ¿Lee Vd. ese periódico?
7. Mi hermano bebe mucha cerveza.
8. Juan vuelve en el coche de Carlos.

14.6.5   Third Person Plural. To indicate the third person plural, the -er or -ir of the infinitive is replaced by **-ían**:

Vds. me escribían muchas veces.	*You used to write to me often.*
Juan y María vivían en aquella casa.	*John and Mary were living in that house.*
Los muchachos no querían beber leche.	*The boys didn't want to drink milk.*

PATTERN DRILL. Say each sentence below. Then repeat it, beginning the sentence with **a menudo,** and changing the verb to the imperfect:

1. Mis hijos reciben muchas cartas.
2. Vds. quieren ir al parque.
3. Elena y María prefieren beber café.
4. Vds. rompen muchos vasos.
5. Esos hombres beben leche.
6. Mis abuelos me escriben.
7. Nuestros amigos nos piden dinero.
8. ¿Vuelven Vds. en ese tranvía? (*trolley*)

14.7   IMPERFECT INDICATIVE: IRREGULAR VERBS

There are only three: **ver, ir,** and **ser.**

14.7.1   Ver. The imperfect of **ver** is formed with the stem **ve-** and the -er/-ir person and number markers:

Veía a Luis todos los días.	*I used to see Louis every day.*
Veíamos a María a veces.	*Sometimes we saw Mary.*
¿Veían Vds. a Carlos a menudo?	*Did you see Charles often?*

PATTERN DRILL. Say each sentence below. Then repeat it, changing the verb to the imperfect:

1. Siempre veo a Luis en el centro.
2. A menudo vemos a la esposa de Juan.
3. Enrique nos ve todos los veranos.
4. ¿Los ven Vds. todos los domingos?
5. Siempre veo películas interesantes.
6. ¿Ves a tus primos muchas veces?
7. Vemos a Carlos los sábados.
8. ¿Las veis todas las semanas?

14.7.2   Ir. The imperfect of **ir** has the following forms:

Singular:	iba	**Iba allí a menudo.**	*I used to go there often.*
	ibas	**¿Adónde ibas?**	*Where were you going?*
	iba	**¿Iba Vd. allí los jueves?**	*Did you go there on Thursdays?*

Plural:	íbamos	Íbamos allí muchas veces.	*We went there often.*
	ibais	¿Por qué ibais a casa?	*Why were you going home?*
	iban	Ellas iban de compras.	*They were going shopping.*

PATTERN DRILL. Say each sentence below. Then repeat it, changing the verb to the imperfect:

1. Voy a la panadería los sábados.
2. Vamos al campo todos los veranos.
3. ¿Vas al centro de vez en cuando?
4. ¿Van Vds. al cine todas las noches?
5. María va a una escuela francesa.
6. Voy a visitarlos los lunes.
7. Vd. va a ese restorán a menudo.
8. Vamos a la playa con nuestros amigos.

14.7.3 Ser. The imperfect of **ser** has the following forms:

Singular:	era	De joven, era soldado.	*As a youth, I was a soldier.*
	eras	¿Eras abogado?	*Were you a lawyer?*
	era	Era la una.	*It was one o'clock.*
		¿Era Vd. rico?	*Were you rich?*
		La casa era de madera.	*The house was wooden.*
Plural:	éramos	Éramos estudiantes.	*We used to be students.*
	erais	¿Erais malos?	*Were you bad?*
	eran	Eran las dos cuando salí.	*It was two o'clock when I left.*
		Los libros eran de Roberto.	*The books were Robert's.*

Note that to tell time in the past, **era** and **eran** are used:

Era la una menos diez cuando llegué.   ¿Eran las ocho cuando Vd. volvió?

PATTERN DRILL. Say each sentence below. Then repeat it, changing the verb to the imperfect in order to describe how something was in the past:

1. Este coche es de mi abuelo.
2. Soy estudiante.
3. Somos muy pobres.
4. Nuestra casa es de ladrillo.
5. ¿Es Vd. hombre de negocios?
6. Mis abuelos son de la Argentina.
7. ¿Quién es su profesor de francés?
8. ¿Son Vds. amigos de Roberto?

Lesson 15

15.1 THE PRETERITE AND THE IMPERFECT

Now that you have mastered the forms of the preterite and the imperfect, the differences between these two aspects of past time can be summarized and contrasted more fully. As you have seen, the preterite is used to indicate when a past action occurred, or for how long a past action went on or a past state existed: **ayer, la semana pasada, hace poco, en 1945.** The imperfect, on the other hand, is used to indicate, without reference to specific time or duration, that in the past an action was going on or a state existed. In short, the preterite expresses what the speaker considers over and done with, no matter how often it occurred or how long it lasted; what is important is that the action or state is considered to have been completed in the past. Thus, **fui al centro** implies arrival, **estuve enfermo** implies an end to the illness, and **tuve que estudiar** implies that "I did study." In contrast, the imperfect simply reports that an action was in progress or that a state was in existence sometime in the past. **Iba al centro, estaba enfermo,** and **tenía que estudiar** say nothing about the outcome of the action or the cessation of the state. Actions repeated in the past can be expressed with either the preterite or the imperfect, depending on the speaker's point of view. The preterite stresses the completion of a series of actions (**Lo vimos todos los días**), whereas the imperfect emphasizes the customary or habitual nature of a series of past actions (**Lo veíamos todos los días**).

Since the preterite implies completion, it is used as a narrative tense; the imperfect, implying lack of completion, is used as a descriptive tense. When someone tells a story, the preterite is used for the essential acts that hold together the thread of the story, and the imperfect is employed for the less important acts that serve as background. You have already seen examples of such usages in the little story about Juan and Carlos in Lesson 14, Lab Drills, Part I:

Juan y Carlos *eran* amigos. Todos los días *iban* a la universidad en el coche de Carlos. Anteayer Carlos le *pidió* cinco dólares a su amigo.

Le *dijo* que *necesitaba* el dinero porque *tenía* una cita con María. Pero Juan también *quería* a María, y *no quiso* prestar el dinero a su amigo. Carlos *tuvo que* pedírselo a su padre. Su padre *no quiso* dárselo porque *dijo* que Carlos no *estudiaba* mucho. Carlos *tuvo que* llamar a María y decirle que *estaba enfermo.*

The essential actions of the story are **pidió, dijo, no quiso,** and **tuvo que.** The background is supplied by **eran, iban, necesitaba, tenía, quería, estudiaba,** and **estaba.**

Here are some examples of contrast between the preterite and the imperfect which may help you to understand the difference between them:

The preterite is used for a completed past act; the imperfect is used for an uncompleted act or an act in progress with no specified beginning or end:

Perdí mi pluma.   Buscaba una pluma de oro.

The preterite is used for a completed series of actions; the imperfect is used to emphasize that a series of actions was customary or habitual:

Fui al campo todos los días.   Iba al campo todos los días.

The preterite is used for a past state within a specific time limit; the imperfect is used for a past state whose duration is not expressed:

Elena vivió en Madrid dos años.   Elena vivía en Madrid.

The preterite is used to summarize the past; the imperfect is used to relive the past:

Cuando estuve enfermo, . . .   Cuando estaba enfermo, . . .

The imperfect is used for an action or state going on in the past that was interrupted by another action; the preterite is used for the interrupting action:

María estaba en casa cuando Juan la llamó.

The imperfect is used to express time of day in the past, and also mental action in the past:

Era la una cuando llegué.   Queríamos ir a México.

When the imperfect of **ir** is followed by **a** and an infinitive, it is the Spanish equivalent of *was going to:*

Juan iba a comprar esa casa.   Dije que iba a mandártelo.

PATTERN DRILL. Complete each sentence below by choosing the correct tense:

1. Ayer yo (*iba, fui*) a la lechería. (*dairy*)
2. Juan dijo que (*iba, fue*) a prestármelo.
3. El abogado (*estaba, estuvo*) muy ocupado cuando llegué.
4. El año pasado (*comprábamos, compramos*) un coche nuevo. (*new*)
5. Cuando salí, (*eran, fueron*) las dos.
6. Comíamos cuando Vd. nos (*llamaba, llamó*).
7. Anoche (*conocía, conocí*) a los padres de Roberto.
8. ¿Por qué no (*venías, viniste*) a mi fiesta ayer?

15.2 IRREGULAR VERBS

The verbs that follow are partially irregular in the present indicative, and they also have irregular preterite stems.

15.2.1 *Poner: to put.* I put is **pongo**:

> **Pongo el vaso en la mesa.** (*on*)
> **No lo pongo en la silla.**

In all the other persons of the present indicative, **poner** is inflected like a regular **-er** verb:

> **¿Pone Vd. la sartén en la cocina?** (*in*)
> **Ponemos la almohada en la silla.** (*pillow*)

The irregular preterite stem of **poner** is **pus-**:

> **Puse la toalla aquí.** (*towel*)
> **¿Dónde los pusieron Vds.?**

PATTERN DRILL. Say each sentence below. Then repeat it, changing the verb to the preterite:

1. Pongo los platos en la mesa.
2. La criada pone el pan en el horno. (*oven*)
3. Mis hermanos ponen las sillas en el comedor.
4. No ponemos esta alfombra en la sala. (*rug*)
5. ¿Pone Vd. ese mantel sucio en la mesa?
6. ¿No pones las almohadas en la cama? (*bed*)
7. Los niños ponen los zapatos en la alfombra.
8. María pone sus libros en la cama.

15.2.2 *Hacer: to make, to do.* I'm making or I'm doing is **hago**:

> **Hago mucho pan.**
> **No lo hago.**

In all the other persons of the present indicative, **hacer** is inflected like a regular -er verb:

Juan hace un viaje.	*John is taking a trip.*
¿Qué hacen Vds. ahora?	*What are you doing now?*

The irregular preterite stem of **hacer** is **hic-**: **Lo hice ayer. ¿Qué hicieron Vds.?** How is the third person singular form [íθo] written? Why?

PATTERN DRILL. Say each sentence below. Then repeat it, changing the verb to the present tense:

1. ¿Qué hiciste?
2. Juan hizo un viaje al norte. (*north*)
3. ¿Hizo Vd. esa falda verde?
4. ¿Cuándo lo hicieron Vds.?
5. Hice una sopa sabrosa. (*delicious*)
6. Hicimos el pan en ese horno.
7. Hice un viaje al sur. (*south*)
8. ¿Por qué lo hicieron Vds.?

15.2.3 *Saber: to know.* **Saber** and **conocer** are not interchangeable. **Conocer** is the equivalent of *to be acquainted with*: **¿Conoces a Juan? Conozco ese museo.** **Saber** indicates *to have factual knowledge about*: **Saber la verdad** and **saber la lección.** Followed by an infinitive, **saber** is the equivalent of *to know how*: **Saber escribir, saber ir al centro en tranvía.**

I know is **sé**:

Sé la hora.	*I know the time.*
No sé si Juan viene.	*I don't know if John's coming.*

In all the other persons of the present indicative, **saber** is inflected as a regular -er verb:

¿Sabe Vd. ir a esa ciudad?	*Do you know how to get to that city?*
No sabemos hablar francés.	*We don't know how to speak French.*

The irregular preterite stem is **sup-**. In the preterite, **saber** is the equivalent of *to find out*:

Lo supe ayer.	*I found it out yesterday.*
Supimos que Juan estaba enfermo.	*We found out that John was sick.*

PATTERN DRILL (A). Practice aloud using **sé** to form sentences with each of the phrases below:

1. leer inglés
2. que te quiero
3. la lección
4. hacer pan

5. cocinar (*to cook*)
6. que Juan va a venir

7. ir allí en coche
8. ese hecho (*fact*)

PATTERN DRILL (B). Complete each of the following sentences with **saber** or **conocer**, as required:

1. Yo (*sé, conozco*) que mis padres me quieren mucho.
2. Ayer Juan y yo (*supimos, conocimos*) que María estaba enferma.
3. En España los niños (*saben, conocen*) hablar español.
4. Anoche Carlos (*supo, conoció*) a ese médico en mi casa.
5. ¿(*Sabe, Conoce*) Vd. si Enrique viene al baile?
6. ¿Cuándo (*supieron, conocieron*) Vds. a mis abuelos?
7. No (*sé, conozco*) si voy a hacer un viaje al sur.
8. ¿(*Sabes, Conoces*) si esa almohada está en mi cuarto?

15.2.4   *Traer: to bring.* I'm bringing is **traigo**:

> **Te traigo un regalo.**
> **No se lo traigo a Juan.**

In all the other persons of the present indicative, **traer** is inflected as a regular -**er** verb: **El niño lo trae. ¿Cuándo me lo traen Vds.?**

The irregular preterite stem of **traer** is **traj-**: **Te lo traje ayer.** Note, however, that the third person plural form is **trajeron.**

PATTERN DRILL. Say each of the following sentences. Then repeat it, changing the verb to the present tense:

1. Traje una manzana al profesor.
2. ¿No trajeron Vds. su coche?
3. Traje ese vino tinto. (*red wine*)
4. ¿Trajiste los vasos a la mesa?
5. ¿Cuántos plátanos trajo Vd.?
6. Las criadas trajeron las llaves.
7. Traje la toalla a la cocina.
8. ¿Trajisteis los periódicos?

15.3 «PODER (UE)»: TO BE ABLE

In the present indicative, the /-o-/ of the stem diphthongizes to /-ue-/ in the usual persons:

> **Puedo ir al cine con Juan.**
> **¿Puedes comprar el coche?**
> **¿No puede Vd. venir a la una?**

> **No podemos ir a esa fiesta.**
> **Sé que podéis hacerlo.**
> **No pueden hallar las almohadas.**

The irregular preterite stem of **poder** is **pud-**: The preterite of **poder** is the equivalent of *to succeed in* when it is used affirmatively, and of *to fail* when it is used negatively:

> **Pude hacerlo.**
> **Juan quiso venir y no pudo.**

> *I succeeded in doing it.*
> *John tried to come and couldn't.*

PATTERN DRILL. Answer the following questions affirmatively, using **Sí** and a complete sentence:

1. ¿Puedes beber mucha cerveza?
2. ¿Pueden Vds. venir a la fiesta?
3. ¿Puede Vd. llamarme el jueves?
4. ¿Puede Juan comprarlo?

5. ¿Pudo Vd. hallar el dinero?
6. ¿Pudiste abrir la puerta?
7. ¿Pudieron Vds. hacer ese viaje?
8. ¿Pudo María vender su casa vieja?

15.4 REFLEXIVE PRONOUNS AND REFLEXIVE VERBS

A *reflexive pronoun* is an object pronoun that refers to the subject of a verb. In the sentence *John cut himself, himself* is an English reflexive pronoun; it is the object of *cut* and it refers to *John*, the subject of the verb.

A *reflexive verb* is a verb accompanied by a reflexive pronoun. A few Spanish verbs are always reflexive. Reference works usually indicate such verbs with **se** attached to their infinitive form: **desayunarse,** *to eat breakfast;* **quejarse de,** *to complain about;* **atreverse a,** *to dare to.* In addition, almost every Spanish verb can be used reflexively when required. Usually there is a difference in meaning between the non-reflexive and the reflexive forms of the same verb. For example, when **llamar,** *to call,* is accompanied by a reflexive pronoun, it is the equivalent of *to be named* (literally, *to call oneself*). Your main problem with Spanish reflexive verbs will be to identify their English equivalents, most of which do not contain reflexive pronouns. For example, what native speaker of English replies to the question *What is your name?* with *I call myself . . .?* Below are several verbs that can be used both non-reflexively and reflexively, along with their English equivalents (their literal meanings are in parentheses):

levantar	*to raise*	**levantarse**	*to get up (raise oneself)*
lavar	*to wash*	**lavarse**	*to wash up (wash oneself)*
bañar	*to bathe*	**bañarse**	*to take a bath (bathe oneself)*
acercar	*to bring near*	**acercarse**	*to approach (bring oneself near)*
despertar (ie)	*to awaken*	**despertarse (ie)**	*to wake up (awaken oneself)*
acostar (ue)	*to put to bed*	**acostarse (ue)**	*to go to bed (put oneself to bed)*

vestir (i, i)	to dress	vestirse (i, i)	to get dressed (dress oneself)
sentar (ie)	to seat	sentarse (ie)	to sit down (seat oneself)
quitar	to take away	quitarse	to take off (take from oneself)
poner	to put	ponerse + noun	to put on (put on oneself)
		ponerse + adjective	to become (put oneself)

The English *-self* words are not a reliable guide to Spanish reflexive verbs because the *-self* words are used not only as reflexive pronouns, but also as intensifying pronouns (*John himself cut it*), and in this latter function they are not equivalent to Spanish reflexive pronouns.

Reflexive pronouns have the same positions in Spanish as the direct and indirect object pronouns—immediately preceding inflected verbs and immediately following infinitives. In these positions, the reflexive pronouns precede all other object pronouns.

The reflexive pronouns referring to the first and second persons, singular as well as plural, have the same forms as the direct and indirect object pronouns that you have studied. The difference between reflexive **me** and non-reflexive **me** is that the former accompanies only a verb indicating the first person singular (**me lavo,** *I'm washing up*), whereas the latter accompanies a verb that indicates any other person (**Juan me lava,** *John is washing me*).

15.4.1 First Person Singular. The first person singular of a reflexive verb is always accompanied by **me**:

Me llamo José.	*My name is Joseph.*
Ayer no me levanté tarde.	*Yesterday I didn't get up late.*
Voy a sentarme en esta silla.	*I'm going to sit down on this chair.*
Tengo que lavarme.	*I have to wash up.*

PATTERN DRILL. Practice aloud using **me** to complete each sentence below:

1. Ayer . . . levanté a las ocho.
2 Voy a acostar . . . a las doce.
3. Le digo que . . . llamo Enrique.
4. Tengo que vestir . . . ahora. (*now*)
5. Anoche . . . acosté a la una.
6. Quiero sentar . . . cerca de María. (*near*)
7. Siempre . . . bañaba los sábados.
8. A veces . . . despierto a las cinco.

15.4.2 First Person Plural. The first person plural of a reflexive verb is always accompanied by **nos**:

Nos llamamos Carlos y María.	Our names are Charles and Mary.
Queremos sentarnos lejos de Juan.	We want to sit far from John.

PATTERN DRILL. Practice aloud using **nos** to complete each sentence below:

1. ¿Por qué . . . levantamos tarde ayer?
2. No queremos acercar . . . a ese perro.
3. No . . . atrevemos a ir al baile.
4. Vamos a sentar . . . lejos de José.
5. Vamos a poner . . . enfermos.
6. Ayer . . . quejamos de la sopa.
7. ¿Cuándo vamos a desayunar . . . ?
8. Tenemos que despertar . . . a las seis.

15.4.3 Second Person Singular and Plural. The singular intimate you of a reflexive verb is always accompanied by **te**, and the plural by **os**:

¿Cómo te llamas?	What's your name?	¿Cómo os llamáis?
¿Te acuestas ahora?	Are you going to bed now?	¿Os acostáis ahora?
¿Vas a quejarte?	Are you going to complain?	¿Vais a quejaros?

PATTERN DRILL. Say each sentence below. Then repeat it, changing the verb to the present tense:

1. ¿Te bañaste esta noche?
2. Tuviste que levantarte temprano.
3. ¿Te pusiste enfermo?
4. ¿Por qué te quejaste?
5. Te acostaste tarde.
6. ¿Te sentaste lejos de tu esposa?
7. Te desayunaste temprano.
8. ¿Te atreviste a acercarte a ese perro?

15.4.4 Third Person Singular and Plural. The third persons of a reflexive verb are always accompanied by **se**:

¿Cómo se llama Vd.?	What's your name?
Mis hermanos se acuestan tarde.	My brothers go to bed late.
¿Por qué van Vds. a quejarse?	Why are you going to complain?
¿Tiene Vd. que levantarse temprano?	Do you have to get up early?

PATTERN DRILL (A). Practice aloud using **se** to complete each sentence below:

1. ¿Cómo . . . llama esa muchacha?
2. María . . . queja mucho de su esposo.
3. Vd. tiene que despertar . . . ahora.
4. Elena . . . pone el sombrero rojo.
5. Mis padres . . . acuestan a las once.

6. Ese niño no quiere lavar . . .
7. ¿Quieren Vds. sentar . . . cerca de Juan?
8. Las mujeres . . . quitaron los guantes.

PATTERN DRILL (B). Practice aloud using the proper form of **levantarse** to complete each sentence below:

1. Juan va a . . . a las siete.
2. Quiero . . . tarde hoy. (*today*)
3. Mi hermano va a . . . a las once.
4. ¿Tiene Vd. que . . . temprano hoy?
5. José y yo vamos a . . . a las seis.
6. Mis hijos no quieren . . . temprano.
7. ¿Vas a . . . ahora mismo? (*right now*)
8. Vds. tienen que . . . a las 8 y 30.

PATTERN DRILL (C). Complete each of the following sentences aloud with the present tense form of **sentarse (ie)** that corresponds to the subject:

1. Me . . . cerca de María.
2. Vds. se . . . en la sala.
3. Juan y yo nos . . . aquí.
4. ¿Te . . . lejos de Carlos?
5. Nos . . . en el comedor.
6. Vd. se . . . con Elena.
7. Las criadas se . . . en la cocina.
8. ¿Por qué te . . . allí?

15.5 POSSESSION

In Spanish, the definite article, rather than the possessive adjective, is used before a part of the body or an article of clothing belonging to the subject of the sentence:

> Juan busca el sombrero.   *John is looking for his hat.*
> Me lavé las manos.   *I washed my hands.*

On the other hand, *John put on my hat* requires a possessive adjective:

> **Juan se puso mi sombrero.**

PATTERN DRILL. Practice aloud using the definite article to complete each sentence below:

1. Me quité . . . abrigo.
2. El niño sabe ponerse . . . zapatos.
3. Me lavé . . . cara. (*face*)
4. Nos ponemos . . . guantes.
5. Busco . . . corbata.
6. Juan se lava . . . cabeza. (*head*)
7. Quiero ponerme . . . sombrero.
8. No me quito . . . chaqueta. (*jacket*)

Lesson 16

16.1 TENSES AND MOODS

The *tense* of a verb is the time that it expresses: past, present, or future. The *mood* of a verb is the point of view from which it expresses an action or a state: as fact or as non-fact (a third Spanish mood need not concern you yet). Up to now, you have studied some tenses of the so-called *indicative* mood—the verb forms used to express actions or states viewed as fact by the speaker. Actions or states viewed by the speaker as non-fact (uncertain, doubtful, possible, desirable, contingent upon something else) are expressed in Spanish with the *subjunctive* mood, which has various tenses. The philosophical distinctions between what is certain and what is uncertain need not bother you. All you have to do is remember that after certain SPANISH *signals*, inflected verbs indicate tense, person, and number with the subjunctive markers.

16.2 SUBJUNCTIVE SIGNALS

Spanish verbs that express desire, such as **desear** and **querer,** are followed by the subjunctive when the subject of these verbs wants SOMEONE ELSE to perform an action. For example, when *I want John to leave,* **deseo** is followed by **que** and a verb indicating the third person singular of the subjunctive of **salir: Deseo que Juan . . .** Similarly, to ask in Spanish if you want *me to return,* **¿Quiere Vd.?** is followed by **que** and a verb indicating the first person singular of the subjunctive of **volver: ¿Quiere Vd. que yo . . . ?** On the other hand, when the subject of **querer** or **desear** wants to perform the action, an infinitive follows: *I want to eat,* **Quiero comer.** *Do you want to leave?* **¿Desea Vd. salir?**

Some of the other Spanish verbs that express desire in various ways are **mandar,** *to order;* **insistir en,** *to insist on;* **dejar,** *to let* or *allow;* and **preferir** (ie, i), *to prefer.* All of them are followed by **que** and the subjunctive when their subjects want SOMEONE ELSE to perform an action. For example:

I order Mary to eat is **Mando que María** and subjunctive of **comer**.
I insist on your leaving is **Insisto en que Vd.** and subjunctive of **salir**.
We don't let them do it is **No dejamos que ellos lo** and subjunctive of **hacer.·**
I prefer that you read it is **Prefiero que tú lo** and subjunctive of **leer**.

Verbs that express doubt or denial are followed by the subjunctive when they refer to the action or state of SOMEONE ELSE. *To doubt* is **dudar**. *I doubt that you will understand* is **Dudo que Vd.** and the subjunctive of **comprender**. *To deny* is **negar** (**ie**). *I deny that John is here* is **Niego que Juan** and the subjunctive of **estar**. Note, however, that since **no dudar** and **no negar** do not indicate doubt or denial, they are not followed by a verb in the subjunctive mood: **No dudo que Vd. lo comprende**.

No estar seguro de, *not to be sure that,* is followed by the subjunctive when its subject is not sure about the action or state of SOMEONE ELSE. *I'm not sure that you* . . . is **No estoy seguro de que Vd.** and a verb in the subjunctive mood. On the other hand, **estar seguro de que** does not signal a subjunctive.

Verbs that express disbelief are followed by the subjunctive when they refer to the action or state of SOMEONE ELSE. Hence, when **creer,** *to believe,* is used negatively or interrogatively, the subjunctive is needed. *I don't believe that you* . . . is **No creo que Vd.** and the subjunctive. *Do you believe that I* . . .*?* is **¿Cree Vd. que yo?** followed by the subjunctive.

Verbs that express one's emotions are followed by the subjunctive when these emotions concern the actions or states of SOMEONE ELSE. **Temer** means *to be afraid.* When I am afraid that you are going to perform or not perform an action, or are in a certain state (such as *ill*), **temo** is followed by **que** and a verb indicating the third person singular of the subjunctive: **Temo que Vd.** . . .

Some of the other Spanish verbs that express emotions are **alegrarse de,** *to be glad;* **sentir** (**ie, i**), *to be sorry;* and **esperar,** *to hope.*

I'm glad that you are here is **Me alegro de que tú** and subjunctive of **estar**.
Are you sorry she's sick? is **¿Sientes que ella?** and subjunctive of **estar**.
I hope you'll come is **Espero que Vds.** and subjunctive of **venir**.

Es necesario, *It is necessary;* **Es lástima,** *It's a pity;* and **Es posible,** *It is possible,* are called *impersonal* expressions because they have no specific subject. When such expressions make general statements, such as *It is necessary to study hard,* they are followed by an infinitive: **Es necesario estudiar mucho.** However, when impersonal expressions of necessity, emotion, possibility, doubt, denial, or uncertainty are used in reference to the action or state of A SPECIFIC PERSON, they are followed by **que** and the subjunctive: *It's necessary for you to return* is **Es necesario que Vd.** and the subjunctive of **volver.** Other impersonal expressions will be introduced in the Pattern Drills that follow.

Additional subjunctive signals will be discussed in subsequent lessons.

16.3 PRESENT TENSE, SUBJUNCTIVE MOOD OF «-AR» VERBS

Regular and stem-changing verbs of the first conjugation indicate the present subjunctive according to the pattern that follows. Stem changes are identical to those of the present indicative.

16.3.1 *First Person Singular.* To indicate the first person singular, the **-ar** of the infinitive is replaced by **-e: compre.** Sometimes it is necessary to use the subject pronoun **yo** in order to avoid possible confusion with the third person singular of the present subjunctive, which has the same marker (see 16.3.4).

John wants me to buy the book.	**Juan quiere que yo compre el libro.**
John doesn't want me to buy the book.	**Juan no quiere que compre el libro.**
Are you afraid that I won't study?	**¿Teme Vd. que yo no estudie?**

PATTERN DRILL. Say each sentence below. Then repeat it, beginning it with **Mis padres desean que yo,** and changing the verb to the present subjunctive:

1. Busco la llave.
2. Estudio mucho.
3. Limpio el coche. (*to clean*)
4. Me acuesto temprano.
5. Empiezo a trabajar.
6. Me lavo ahora.
7. No grito a mi hermana. (*to shout*)
8. No llego tarde a la escuela.

16.3.1.2 *Orthography.* How are [búske], [empiéθe], and [llége] spelled? Why?

16.3.2 *First Person Plural.* To indicate the first person plural, the **-ar** of the infinitive is replaced by **-emos: compremos.**

Do you want us to buy it?	**¿Desea Vd. que lo compremos?**
John hopes we will lend him money.	**Juan espera que le prestemos dinero.**
It's necessary for us to work on Sundays.	**Es necesario que trabajemos los domingos.**

PATTERN DRILL. Say each sentence below. Then repeat it, beginning the sentence with **¿Quiere Vd. que?**, and changing the verb to the subjunctive:

1. Buscamos a María.
2. Nos despertamos temprano.
3. Limpiamos la cocina.
4. Aguardamos a Juan. (*to wait for*)
5. Nos sentamos aquí.
6. Arreglamos los libros. (*to arrange*)
7. Empezamos a hacerlo.
8. Ayudamos a la criada. (*to help*)

16.3.3   Second Person Singular and Plural.   To indicate the singular intimate you, the **-ar** of the infinitive is replaced by **-es: compres.**

I want you to get up early.	**Quiero que te levantes temprano.**
Is John glad that you're buying it?	**¿Se alegra Juan de que lo compres?**

To indicate the plural intimate you, the **-ar** of the infinitive is replaced by **-éis: compréis.**

Is it necessary for you to buy ice cream?	**¿Es necesario que compréis helado?**

PATTERN DRILL. Say each sentence below. Then repeat it, beginning the sentence with **Me alegro de que**, and changing the verb to the subjunctive:

1. Compras ese coche nuevo.
2. Bailas con Juan. (*to dance*)
3. Ayudas a tu madre.
4. Ahorras mucho dinero. (*to save*)
5. Usas esa pluma. (*to use*)
6. Te despiertas a las seis.
7. Descansas esta tarde. (*to rest*)
8. Empiezas a estudiar.

16.3.4   Third Person Singular.   To indicate the third person singular, the **-ar** of the infinitive is replaced by **-e: compre.**

It's probable that he'll buy the house.	**Es probable que él compre la casa.**
I'm glad that you're working now.	**Me alegro de que Vd. trabaje ahora.**

PATTERN DRILL. Say each sentence below. Then repeat it, beginning the sentence with **Siento que** (*I'm sorry that* or *I regret that*), and changing the verb to the subjunctive:

1. Juan no trabaja.
2. Vd. llega tarde.
3. María no baila con Luis.
4. Enrique no gana mucho. (*to earn*)
5. Mis hermanos no descansan.
6. El niño llora. (*to cry, weep*)
7. Vd. usa los tenedores de plata.
8. La tienda no te manda el regalo.

16.3.5   Third Person Plural.   To indicate the third person plural, the **-ar** of the infinitive is replaced by **-en: compren.**

I deny that they're buying it.	**Niego que lo compren.**
It's not necessary for them to work.	**No es necesario que trabajen.**

PATTERN DRILL. Say each sentence below. Then repeat it, beginning the sentence with **Dudo que** (*I doubt that*), and changing the verb to the subjunctive:

1. Los niños se levantan.
2. Juan y Carlos ganan mucho.
3. Me acompañan. (*to accompany*)
4. Vds. ahorran mucho dinero.

5. Mis hijos se acuestan temprano.
6. Ellos fuman mucho. (*to smoke*)
7. Los estudiantes te aguardan.
8. Mis padres compran aquella casa.

16.4 PRESENT SUBJUNCTIVE OF VERBS ENDING IN «–ER» AND «–IR»

Both -er and -ir verbs indicate the subjunctive according to the same pattern. The stem changes are identical to those of the present indicative, except that -ir verbs undergo a further change in the plural of the first and second persons.

16.4.1 *First Person Singular.* To indicate the first person singular, the -er or -ir of the infinitive is replaced by -a: coma, escriba. Sometimes it is necessary to use the subject pronoun yo in order to avoid possible confusion with the third person singular, which has the same marker.

It's necessary for me to eat a lot of meat. **Es necesario que yo coma mucha carne.**

It's doubtful that I'll write to him. **Es dudoso que yo le escriba.**

PATTERN DRILL. Say each sentence below. Then repeat it, beginning the sentence with **Juan teme que yo,** and changing the verb to the subjunctive:

1. Bebo demasiado vino.
2. Duermo hasta las once. (*until*)
3. Vuelvo a casa tarde.
4. No escribo a nuestros amigos.

5. Rompo muchos vasos.
6. Le pido dinero.
7. Como con María este viernes.
8. No aprendo la lección. (*to learn,* -er)

16.4.2 *First Person Plural.* To indicate the first person plural, the -er or -ir of the infinitive is replaced by -amos: comamos, escribamos.

She doesn't let us eat a lot. **Ella no deja que comamos mucho.**
It's impossible for us to write to them. **Es imposible que les escribamos.**

In this person, the /-o-/ and /-e-/ of stem-changing -ir verbs become, respectively, /-u-/ and /-i-/:

Es necesario que durmamos hasta las once.
¿Teme Vd. que no sirvamos cerveza?

PATTERN DRILL. Say each sentence below. Then repeat it, beginning the sentence with **Es necesario que,** and changing the verb to the subjunctive:

1. Vendemos esta casa vieja.
2. Dormimos hasta las ocho.
3. Servimos mucho café.
4. Te pedimos un favor.

5. Devolvemos el libro. (*to give back*)
6. Abrimos las ventanas.
7. Asistimos a la escuela. (*to attend*)
8. No volvemos a casa tarde.

16.4.3   Second Person Singular and Plural.   To indicate the singular intimate you, the -er or -ir of the infinitive is replaced by -as: **comas, escribas.**

I hope you'll write to me.	**Espero que me escribas.**
It's incredible that you are eating now.	**Parece mentira que comas ahora.**

To indicate the plural intimate you, the -er or -ir of the infinitive is replaced by -áis: **comáis, escribáis.**

I'm glad you're attending school.   **Me alegro de que asistáis a la escuela.**

In this person, the /-o-/ and /-e-/ of stem-changing -ir verbs become, respectively, /-u-/ and /-i-/:

> **Espero que durmáis mucho.**
> **Siento que no sirváis vino.**

PATTERN DRILL. Say each sentence below. Then repeat it, beginning the sentence with **Es lástima que** (*It's a pity that*), and changing the verb to the subjunctive:

1. No aprendes a hablar francés.
2. Vendes esos caballos.
3. No comes esta sopa sabrosa.
4. No puedes venir.

5. No asistes a la fiesta.
6. No comprendes la lección.
7. Nos interrumpes. (*to interrupt,* -ir)
8. Vives lejos de la universidad.

16.4.4   Third Person Singular.   To indicate the third person singular, the -er or -ir of the infinitive is replaced by -a: **coma, escriba.**

I don't let my son eat strawberries.	**No dejo que mi hijo coma fresas.**
I'm sorry you don't write to them.	**Siento que Vd. no les escriba.**

PATTERN DRILL. Say each sentence below. Then repeat it, beginning the sentence with **Espero que,** and changing the verb to the subjunctive:

1. Juan lee el periódico.
2. María asiste a la fiesta.
3. Vd. comprende la lección.
4. La criada sirve el café.

5. Vd. no lo esconde. (*to hide,* -er)
6. Ese hombre me devuelve el dinero.
7. Mi hijo duerme hasta las siete.
8. Vd. recibe el regalo.

16.4.5 Third Person Plural. To indicate the third person plural, the **-er** or **-ir** of the infinitive is replaced by **-an: coman, escriban.**

We want the children to eat a lot.	**Queremos que los niños coman mucho.**
Is it possible for you to write to us?	**¿Es posible que Vds. nos escriban?**

PATTERN DRILL. Say each sentence below. Then repeat it, beginning the sentence with **Me alegro de que,** and changing the verb to the subjunctive:

1. Vds. asisten al baile.
2. Mis padres no esconden el vino.
3. Vds. comprenden ese libro.
4. Los muchachos vuelven temprano.
5. Juan y Carlos aprenden a cocinar.
6. Los niños no me interrumpen.
7. Mis amigos sirven mucha cerveza.
8. Isabel y Roberto me escriben.

16.5 PRESENT SUBJUNCTIVE: IRREGULAR VERBS

16.5.1 "Borrowed" Stems. Verbs such as **tener, conocer, ver,** and **salir,** which in the present indicative have an irregular first person singular that ends in **-o** (**tengo, conozco, veo, salgo**), indicate the present subjunctive by adding the **-er/-ir** subjunctive markers to the stems that remain when the aforementioned **-o** is dropped:

tengo:	tenga, tengas, tenga, tengamos, tengáis, tengan
conozco:	conozca, conozcas, conozca, conozcamos, conozcáis, conozcan
veo:	vea, veas, vea, veamos, veáis, vean
salgo:	salga, salgas, salga, salgamos, salgáis, salgan

PATTERN DRILL (A). Say each sentence below. Then repeat it, beginning the sentence with **Es preciso que yo** (It's necessary for me to), and changing the verb to the subjunctive:

1. Vengo a la una y media.
2. Tengo paciencia.
3. Salgo de casa a las nueve.
4. Digo la verdad a mis padres.
5. Me pongo el sombrero.
6. Conozco a esa mujer bonita.
7. Veo al profesor hoy.
8. Lo hago ahora mismo.

PATTERN DRILL (B). Say each sentence below. Then repeat it, beginning the sentence with **Es imposible que,** and changing the verb to the subjunctive:

1. Pones la silla aquí.
2. Juan me dice la verdad.
3. No tenemos razón.
4. Vds. conocen a ese hombre.
5. Te vemos a las doce y media.
6. Vienes con Carlos.
7. Salimos al jardín hoy.
8. Les traemos las botellas. (*bottle*)

16.5.2 *Other Irregular Subjunctives.* The present subjunctives of **ser**, **ir**, and **saber** are formed by adding the **-er/-ir** subjunctive markers to the stems **se-**, **vay-**, and **sep-**:

ser:	sea, seas, sea, seamos, seáis, sean
ir:	vaya, vayas, vaya, vayamos, vayáis, vayan
saber:	sepa, sepas, sepa, sepamos, sepáis, sepan

The present subjunctive of **estar** is irregular only in that the /-e/ of the inflectional endings is stressed, just as the /-a/ of the present indicative:

esté, estés, esté, estemos, estéis, estén

Although **dar** is partially irregular in the present indicative, its present subjunctive is formed regularly: **dé, des, dé, demos, deis, den**. In writing, there is an accent mark over the first and third persons singular in order to distinguish them from the preposition **de**.

PATTERN DRILL. Say each sentence below. Then repeat it, beginning the sentence with **Es dudoso que** (*It's doubtful that*), and changing the verb to the subjunctive:

1. Juan está en la biblioteca.
2. Ella sabe el secreto. (*secret*)
3. Vamos al cine esta noche.
4. Las criadas están en la sala.
5. Voy a hacerlo.
6. Me dan el dinero.
7. Sé la verdad.
8. Ese muchacho es del Brasil.

16.6 SUBJUNCTIVE SIGNALS WITH INDIRECT OBJECTS

Some Spanish verbs that express desire are not only followed by **que** and a verb in the subjunctive mood, but, in addition, they are accompanied by an indirect object. This indirect object is the same person as the subject of the verb in the subjunctive, and it is indicated either by an indirect object pronoun, or else by both a noun (or **Vd.** or **Vds.**) and the corresponding indirect object pronoun.

pedir (i, i) *to ask*	I ask you to return.	**Te pido que vuelvas.**
aconsejar *to advise*	I advise John to come.	**Le aconsejo *a Juan* que venga.**
prohibir *to forbid*	They forbid us to leave.	**Nos prohiben que salgamos.**
permitir *to permit*	Do they permit you to smoke?	**¿Les permiten *a Vds.* que fumen?**
rogar (ue) *to beg*	Mary begs me to eat.	**María *me* ruega que coma.**

Sometimes you will find **mandar** accompanied by an indirect object:

I order John to tell the truth.   **Le mando *a Juan* que diga la verdad.**

PATTERN DRILL (A). Say each sentence below. Then repeat it, beginning the sentence with **Te aconsejo que,** and changing the verb to the subjunctive:

1. Escribes a Juan.
2. Estudias mucho.
3. No bebes mucha cerveza.
4. Sales en seguida. (*at once*)
5. Vuelves mañana.
6. Nos dices la verdad.
7. Lo haces en seguida.
8. Te pones el abrigo.

PATTERN DRILL (B). Complete each sentence below with the required form of the present subjunctive of **volver:**

1. Juan me pide que . . .
2. ¿Le pides a la criada que . . .?
3. Les aconsejamos a Vds. que . . .
4. ¿Por qué no me permite Vd. que . . .?
5. Juan nos ruega que . . . en seguida.
6. ¿Te prohibe Ricardo que . . .?
7. Les mando a los niños que . . .
8. Le prohibimos a Vd. que . . .

PATTERN DRILL (C). Answer each of the following questions affirmatively, using **Sí** and a complete sentence:

1. ¿Le ruegas a Juan que venga?
2. ¿Te pide Roberto que vayas?
3. ¿Nos pide Vd. que salgamos?
4. ¿Me permiten Vds. que lo busque?
5. ¿Le aconsejas a María que estudie?
6. ¿Me pide Vd. que venda mi coche?
7. ¿Nos prohibe Vd. que volvamos?
8. ¿Vas a rogarles que lo traigan?

Lesson 17

17.1 SUBJUNCTIVE SIGNALS: CONJUNCTIONS

The term *conjunction* refers to a word or set of words that joins two clauses. In the sentences *I'm leaving before John returns, We're coming early in case they need us,* and *We'll go provided that Mary is well,* the words *before, in case,* and *provided that* are English conjunctions. The first is called a temporal (or time) conjunction; the other two are called subordinating conjunctions. A clause begun by a conjunction of either type is referred to as a *subordinate* clause; one that is not so begun is called, in contrast, a *main* clause.

The subjunctive is used in a Spanish subordinate clause that expresses non-fact. Some examples of non-fact are actions or states that have not yet occurred at the time of main clause (*I'm leaving **before John returns***), or whose occurrence is not definite (*We're coming early **in case they need us;** We'll go **provided that Mary is well***).

Some Spanish conjunctions, by their very nature, are always followed by non-fact—and the subjunctive. Others, however, will be followed by either the indicative or the subjunctive, according to whether the speaker wishes to indicate certainty or uncertainty.

17.1.1 Non-fact Conjunctions. The Spanish conjunctions listed below (and their synonyms) always introduce non-fact, and therefore are always followed by a verb in the subjunctive mood:

antes de que	*before*	**en caso de que**	*in case*
para que	*so that, in order that*	**con tal (de) que**	*provided that*
sin que	*without*	**a menos que**	*unless*

Salgo antes de que Juan vuelva.	. . . *before John returns.*
Te llamo para que me lo digas.	. . . *so that you'll tell it to me.*
Voy a salir sin que María me vea.	. . . *without Mary's seeing me.*

166

Venimos temprano en caso de que nos necesiten.   . . . *in case they need us.*

Vamos con tal que María esté buena.   . . . *provided that Mary is well.*

No voy a menos que me acompañes.   . . . *unless you accompany me.*

PATTERN DRILL (A). Say each sentence below. Then repeat it, beginning the sentence with **Salgo antes de que,** and changing the verb to the subjunctive:

1. Vds. vuelven.
2. Isabel me ve.
3. Me pides que te lo preste.
4. Ellos me llaman.
5. Vd. empieza a comer.
6. Los niños se despiertan.
7. Juan me lo quita.
8. Vds. lo hacen.

PATTERN DRILL (B). Complete aloud each of the following sentences by changing the infinitive in parentheses to the indicated person of the subjunctive:

1. Te digo el secreto para que tú lo (*decir*) a tu esposa.
2. Ese muchacho bebe vino sin que su madre lo (*ver*).
3. No volvemos a menos que Vds. (*volver*).
4. Te lo mandamos en caso de que tú lo (*necesitar*).
5. No puedo salir de casa sin que el perro me (*acompañar*).
6. Voy a hacerlo a fin de que Vds. no (*tener*) que hacerlo. (*so that*).
7. Te lo presto con tal que me lo (*devolver*) el lunes.
8. ¿Es posible que salgas sin que Carlos te (*pedir*) dinero?

17.1.2 *Other Conjunctions.* Both **aunque** and **aun cuando** are equivalents of the English *although, even though,* and *even if.* **A pesar de que** is equivalent to *in spite of the fact that.* These Spanish conjunctions are followed by the indicative when they introduce an action or a state that the speaker concedes or regards as fact:

Aunque me invitan, no asisto.   *Although they are inviting me,* . . .

No veo a María, aun cuando está aquí.   . . . *although she is here.*

No sales, a pesar de que estás bueno.   . . . *in spite of the fact that you are well.*

On the other hand, these conjunctions are followed by the subjunctive when the speaker wishes to imply uncertainty about an action or a state. (Sometimes English uses *may* in this context.)

Aunque me inviten, no asisto.   *Although they may invite me,* . . .

No veo a María, aun cuando esté aquí.   . . . *even though she may be here.*

No sales, a pesar de que estés bueno.   . . . *in spite of the fact that you may be well.*

The Spanish temporal conjunctions **así que** (*as soon as*), **hasta que** (*until*), and **cuando** (*when*) are followed by the indicative when they introduce an action or a state that has already occurred at the time of the action or state of the main clause, or occurs regularly:

Él me lo dijo así que vine.	*He told it to me as soon as I came.*
No salí hasta que Pedro llegó.	*I didn't leave until Peter arrived.*
Siempre comemos cuando Pablo vuelve.	*We always eat when Paul returns.*

On the other hand, since unaccomplished action is non-fact, **así que, hasta que,** and **cuando** are followed by the subjunctive when they introduce an action or a state that will occur at some indefinite future time:

Él va a decírmelo así que yo venga.	*He'll tell it to me as soon as I come.*
No salgo hasta que Pedro llegue.	*I'm not leaving until Peter arrives.*
Vamos a comer cuando Pablo vuelva.	*We're going to eat when Paul returns.*

PATTERN DRILL. Complete each of the following sentences by changing the infinitive in parentheses to the indicated person of the subjunctive:

1. No se lo vendo, aunque él me (*dar*) mucho dinero.
2. El niño no quiere acostarse, a pesar de que (*estar*) cansado.
3. Pedro trabaja mucho, aun cuando (*ser*) viejo.
4. Te lo doy cuando Carlos me lo (*devolver*).
5. Vamos a llamarte en cuanto Juan (*llegar*). (*as soon as*)
6. No voy a hacerlo hasta que Vds. (*salir*).
7. ¿Vas a comprarlo así que tu padre te (*prestar*) el dinero?
8. Aunque Pablo no (*leer*) muchos libros, sabe mucho.

17.2 DIRECT COMMANDS

Commands are given to people addressed as **Vd.** or **Vds.** by using the third person singular and plural forms, respectively, of the present subjunctive. The use of **Vd.** or **Vds.** after a direct command is optional.

Study.	**Estudie Vd.**	*Don't study.*	**No estudie Vd.**
	Estudien Vds.		**No estudien Vds.**
Write.	**Escriba Vd.**	*Don't write.*	**No escriba Vd.**
	Escriban Vds.		**No escriban Vds.**
Leave.	**Salga Vd.**	*Don't leave.*	**No salga Vd.**
	Salgan Vds.		**No salgan Vds.**

PATTERN DRILL. Say each sentence below. Then repeat it as a direct command:

1. Vd. vuelve a casa.
2. Vds. no comen ahora.
3. Vd. viene hoy.
4. Vds. no compran mucho.

5. Vds. esperan a Carlos.
6. Vd. no sale.
7. Vds. buscan a Juan.
8. Vd. va al centro.

17.2.1 *Direct Commands: Object Pronouns.* Reflexive, indirect, and direct object pronouns immediately follow AFFIRMATIVE commands. An indirect object pronoun precedes a direct object pronoun, and a reflexive pronoun precedes every other object pronoun. In writing, object pronouns are attached to the affirmative commands that they follow, and an accent mark is necessary to show that the original stress of the command is maintained, despite the addition of one or more syllables:

Do it.	**Hágalo Vd.**	**Háganlo Vds.**
Write to me.	**Escríbame Vd.**	**Escríbanme Vds.**
Send it to me.	**Mándemelo Vd.**	**Mándenmelo Vds.**
Get up.	**Levántese Vd.**	**Levántense Vds.**
Put it on.	**Póngaselo Vd.**	**Pónganselo Vds.**

Object pronouns immediately precede NEGATIVE commands in Spanish. The sequence of these pronouns is the same as for affirmative commands—reflexive before indirect before direct.

Don't do it.	**No lo haga Vd.**	**No lo hagan Vds.**
Don't send it to us.	**No nos lo mande Vd.**	**No nos lo manden Vds.**
Don't get up.	**No se levante Vd.**	**No se levanten Vds.**
Don't put it on.	**No se lo ponga Vd.**	**No se lo pongan Vds.**

Commands given to persons addressed with the intimate you will be discussed in a subsequent lesson.

PATTERN DRILL (A). Say each command below. Then repeat it as an affirmative command beginning with **Por favor** (*Please*):

1. No me escriba Vd.
2. No lo haga Vd.
3. No me lo diga Vd.
4. No se sienten Vds. aquí.

5. No se acueste Vd. temprano.
6. No se lo ponga Vd.
7. No me los manden Vds.
8. No se lo den Vds. a Juan.

PATTERN DRILL (B). Say each command below. Then repeat it as a negative command:

1. Dígamelo Vd.
2. Cómprelo Vd.

3. Levántense Vds. temprano.
4. Lávese Vd. la cara.

5. Dénmelos Vds.

6. Quíteselo Vd. a Carlos.

7. Póngaselo Vd.

8. Háganlo Vds. en seguida.

PATTERN DRILL (c). Say each sentence below. Then repeat it as a command:

1. Vd. no compra mucho azúcar.
2. Vd. sale así que yo vuelva.
3. Vds. me las dan.
4. Vd. nos dice la verdad.

5. Vd. se lo pone.
6. Vds. se levantan a las ocho.
7. Vds. no le escriben.
8. Vds. me la devuelven.

17.3 INDIRECT COMMANDS

Indirect commands are commands which, like the English *Let them leave* and *Have him do it*, are transmitted to someone via someone else. In Spanish such commands are given with **que** followed by the third person singular or plural of the present subjunctive, depending on whether the recipient (or subject) of the indirect command is singular or plural. All object pronouns precede indirect commands, and a noun or pronoun indicating the recipient of such a command usually follows it:

> **Que salgan ellos.** *Let them leave.*
> **Que lo haga Juan.** *Have John do it.*

Negative indirect commands are not frequent: **Que no se lo ponga él hasta que lleguemos,** *Don't have him put it on until we arrive* (literally, *Have him not put it on . . .*)

PATTERN DRILL. Say each sentence below. Then repeat it as an indirect command beginning with **Que:**

1. Carlos lo hace.
2. Esos hombres vienen mañana.
3. El niño se acuesta temprano.
4. Isabel te lo dice.

5. La criada lo sirve.
6. Mi primo te lo da.
7. La niña se quita los zapatos.
8. Juan no les dice el secreto.

17.4 LET'S . . .

Spanish has two equivalents of the English *Let's . . .* One of them is the first person plural of the present subjunctive:

> **Empecemos.** *Let's begin.* **No esperemos.** *Let's not wait.*
> **Comamos.** *Let's eat.* **No salgamos.** *Let's not go out.*

When this form of a verb is used affirmatively, object pronouns follow it in the usual order. In writing, an accent mark is needed over the vowel before

-mos in order to show that the original stress is maintained. Object pronouns precede this form of a verb when it is used negatively:

Comprémoslo.   *Let's buy it.*   **No lo compremos.**   *Let's not . . .*
Escribámosle.   *Let's write to him.*   **No le escribamos.**   *Let's not . . .*

To facilitate pronunciation, the final /-s/ of **-mos** is suppressed before the
reflexive pronoun **nos:**

Sentémonos.   *Let's sit down.*   **No nos sentemos.**   *Let's not . . .*
Pongámonoslo.   *Let's put it on.*   **No nos lo pongamos.**   *Let's not . . .*

Only **ir** has an irregular form: **Vamos,** *Let's go* (rather than **vayamos**).
   The other Spanish equivalent of *Let's . . .* is **vamos a** followed by an
infinitive. This is rarely used negatively:

>   **Vamos a hacerlo.**   *Let's do it.*
>   **Vamos a escribirles.**   *Let's write to them.*
>   **Vamos a decírselo.**   *Let's tell it to him.*
>   **Vamos a ponérnoslos.**   *Let's put them on.*

PATTERN DRILL (A).   Say each sentence below. Then repeat it, using the
first person plural of the present subjunctive:

1. Comemos las fresas.   5. Les escribimos en seguida.
2. Salimos a las nueve.   6. La compramos ahora.
3. Lo hacemos esta noche.   7. Nos sentamos en la sala.
4. Nos lavamos las manos.   8. Nos levantamos tarde.

PATTERN DRILL (B).   Repeat each sentence above, replacing the original
verb with **Vamos a** and the corresponding infinitive.

17.5   HACE . . . QUE

To indicate that an action or state began in the past and continues into the
present, English uses the formula *"have* + a past participle + *for* + time":
I have studied for two hours. Spanish expresses the same concept with
"**hace** + time + **que** + a verb in the present tense":

Hace dos horas que estudio.   *I have studied for two hours.*
Hace diez minutos que te esperan.   *They have waited for you for ten
                                           minutes.*

An alternate Spanish formula, placed either before or after the verb in the
present tense, is "**desde hace** + time":

   Desde hace dos horas estudio.   **Te esperan desde hace diez minutos.**

To inquire how long an action or a state has gone on, Spanish uses ¿**Cuánto tempo hace que** . . . ? or ¿**Desde cuándo** . . . ? followed by a verb in the present tense:

¿**Cuánto tiempo hace que Vd. estudia?**   *How long have you studied?*
¿**Desde cuándo me esperan Vds.?**   *How long have you waited for me?*

PATTERN DRILL. Answer each question below with a complete sentence containing **hace dos años que** or **desde hace dos años**, according to the formula used in the question:

1. ¿Cuánto tiempo hace que conoces a María?
2. ¿Cuánto tiempo hace que Vds. viven en esta ciudad?
3. ¿Cuánto tiempo hace que Vd. tiene ese perro?
4. ¿Desde cuándo asisten Vds. a esta universidad?
5. ¿Desde cuándo sabe vestirse el niño?
6. ¿Desde cuándo se levanta Carlos a las seis?
7. ¿Cuánto tiempo hace que Vd. sabe el secreto?
8. ¿Desde cuándo trabaja Juan en aquella tienda?

17.6 HACÍA . . . QUE

To indicate that an action or state began in the past, continued for a period of time, and ended in the past, English uses the formula "*had* + a past participle + *for* + time": *I had studied for two hours.* Spanish expresses the same concept with "**hacía** + time + **que** + a verb in the imperfect tense":

Hacía dos horas que estudiaba.   *I had studied for two hours.*
Hacía diez minutos que te esperaban. *They had waited for you for ten minutes.*

An alternate Spanish formula, placed either before or after the verb in the imperfect tense, is "**desde hacía** + time":

Desde hacía dos horas estudiaba.   Te esperaban desde hacía diez minutos.

To inquire how long an action or state went on in the past before it ended, Spanish uses ¿**Cuánto tiempo hacía que** . . . ? or ¿**Desde cuándo** . . . ? followed by a verb in the imperfect tense:

¿**Cuánto tiempo hacía que Vd. estudiaba?**   *How long had you studied?*
¿**Desde cuándo me esperaban Vds.?**   *How long had you waited for me?*

PATTERN DRILL. Answer each question below with a complete sentence containing **hacía cuatro meses que** or **desde hacía cuatro meses**, according to the formula used in the question:

1. ¿Cuánto tiempo hacía que Vds. vivían allí?
2. ¿Cuánto tiempo hacía que Isabel estaba enferma?
3. ¿Desde cuándo trabajaba allí tu hermano?
4. ¿Desde cuándo los conocías?
5. ¿Cuánto tiempo hacía que Juan tenía ese coche viejo?
6. ¿Desde cuándo estudiaban Vds. cuando vine?
7. ¿Cuánto tiempo hacía que Vd. era soldado?
8. ¿Cuánto tiempo hacía que Vd. asistía a esa escuela?

17.7 DISJUNCTIVE PRONOUNS

The formidable term *disjunctive* refers to pronouns that follow (and are the objects of) prepositions. In the English sentence *Mary is here, but I'm not near her,* the pronoun *her* is the object of the preposition *near.* All the Spanish disjunctive pronouns, like their English counterparts, indicate whether the referend is singular or plural, and some also indicate gender.

17.7.1 *First Person Singular.* The first person singular is indicated by **mí**, regardless of gender:

> **Juan está cerca de mí.**   *John is near me.*
> **Fueron sin mí.**   *They went without me.*

The preposition **con** and the pronoun **mí** form **conmigo: Van conmigo,** *They're going with me.*

PATTERN DRILL. Practice aloud using **mí** to complete each of the sentences below:

1. La silla está cerca de . . .
2. María baila con . . .
3. Están delante de . . . (*in front of*)
4. Vivían lejos de . . .
5. ¿Van Vds. sin . . .?
6. El cuadro está detrás de . . . (*behind*)
7. ¿Quiere Vd. venir con . . .?
8. Dudo que salgan sin . . .

17.7.2 *Second Person Singular.* The second person singular is indicated by **ti**, regardless of gender:

> **No van sin ti.**   *They're not going without you.*
> **El vaso está detrás de ti.**   *The glass is behind you.*

The preposition **con** and the pronoun **ti** form **contigo: Deseo bailar contigo.**

PATTERN DRILL. Practice aloud using **ti** to complete each sentence below:

1. ¿Vive Juan lejos de . . .?
2. Queremos ir con . . .
3. ¿Va María al cine con . . .?
4. El vino estaba delante de . . .

5. ¿Fueron allí sin . . .?
6. Lo puse cerca de . . .
7. Vamos a sentarnos detrás de . . .
8. Vuelvo con . . .

17.7.3 *The Other Persons.* The remaining disjunctive pronouns have the same forms as the subject pronouns, and thus in some cases they do indicate the gender of the referend:

Nosotros estamos aquí, y Juan está con nosotros.	. . . *with us.*
Vosotros vais, pero no voy con vosotros.	. . . *with you.*
Juan está aquí y me siento cerca de él.	. . . *near him.*
Tengo ese sombrero, pero salí sin él.	. . . *without it.*
María viene, pero no vengo con ella.	. . . *with her.*
Si Vd. se sienta aquí, estoy detrás de Vd.	. . . *behind you.*
Mis padres salieron, pero no salí con ellos.	. . . *with them.*
Tengo guantes, pero salí sin ellos.	. . . *without them.*
María y Elena están aquí, pero no bailo con ellas.	. . . *with them.*
Hallé las plumas, pero no vine con ellas.	. . . *with them.*
Si Vds. viven allí, vivo muy lejos de Vds.	. . . *far from you.*

PATTERN DRILL. Complete each sentence below with the disjunctive pronoun suggested by the context:

1. Vi a las muchachas, y me senté detrás de . . .
2. El perro está allí, pero no me acerco a . . .
3. Vamos al campo, pero nuestro hijo no va con . . .
4. Puse los tenedores allí, y las cucharitas cerca de . . .
5. Si no estamos listos, ¿sale Vd. sin . . .?
6. Si Vd. está aquí a las ocho, voy con . . .
7. Sé que Vds. van al concierto, pero no puedo ir con . . .
8. Veo las cucharas, pero los cuchillos están lejos de . . .

17.8 GUSTAR

To express a *liking* for something, Spanish uses the verb **gustar,** *to be pleasing.* The person to whom something is pleasing is indicated by an indirect object pronoun: **me, te, nos,** etc. This pronoun is followed by either

gusta and a singular noun, or else by **gustan** and a plural noun, depending on whether the thing that does the pleasing is singular or plural. Hence, *I like that book* is **Me gusta ese libro**, whereas *I like those books* is **Me gustan esos libros**. Similarly, *I like it* is **Me gusta**, whereas *I like them* is **Me gustan**. *We like* will be either **Nos gusta** or **Nos gustan**; *Do you like?* will be either **¿Le gusta a Vd.?** or **¿Le gustan a Vd.?** and *He doesn't like* will be either **No le gusta a él** or **No le gustan a él.**

The indirect object pronouns are frequently preceded by **a** and the corresponding disjunctive pronoun, either for emphasis or to clarify the meaning of **le** or **les**: **A mí me gusta ese libro, pero a él no le gusta.**

PATTERN DRILL (A). Complete each sentence below with the proper indirect object pronoun:

1. A mí . . . gustan estas uvas.
2. A Juan no . . . gusta esa película.
3. A mi hermano no . . . gustan las fresas.
4. ¿. . . gusta a Vd. esta cerveza?
5. ¿. . . gusta a Vds. este queso?
6. A mí no . . . gusta esta carne.
7. ¿. . . gustan a Vd. estos plátanos?
8. A mis padres no . . . gusta ese vino.

PATTERN DRILL (B). Complete each sentence below with the proper form of the present tense of **gustar**:

1. No nos . . . ese periódico.
2. Me . . . esas manzanas.
3. A Juan le . . . esa muchacha.
4. ¿No le . . . a Vd. esta cerveza?
5. No me . . . ese coche.
6. ¿Les . . . a Vds. este queso?
7. A María no le . . . ese vino.
8. Nos . . . estas fresas.

PATTERN DRILL (C). Answer each of the following questions affirmatively, using **Sí** and a complete sentence:

1. ¿Le gustan a Vd. esas cerezas?
2. ¿Les gustan a Vds. estas rosas?
3. ¿Les gustaba a Vds. esa ciudad?
4. ¿A Juan le gustan esas corbatas?
5. ¿Te gusta este sombrero?
6. ¿Le gustan a Vd. estas muchachas?
7. ¿Les gusta a Vds. estudiar?
8. ¿A María le gustan esos zapatos?

PATTERN DRILL (D). Answer each of the following questions affirmatively, using **Sí** and only the proper indirect object pronoun followed by the proper form of **gustar**. Do not include the noun used in the question. The English equivalents of your replies will be Yes, *I like it* or Yes, *I do;* Yes, *we like them* or Yes, *we do,* etc.

1. ¿Te gusta mi coche?
2. ¿Te gustan las manzanas?
3. ¿Les gustó a Vds. ese restorán?
4. ¿Les gustaban a Vds. esas revistas?
5. ¿Le gusta a Vd. la nieve? (*snow*)
6. ¿Les gustan a Vds. los plátanos?
7. ¿A tus hermanos les gusta ese helado?
8. ¿A Juan le gusta ese vino?

Lesson 18

18.1 THE IMPERFECT SUBJUNCTIVE

A subjunctive signal in the preterite or imperfect tense is not followed by the present subjunctive. Instead, the *imperfect* subjunctive—the past tense of the subjunctive mood—is used:

> **Mandé que Juan** and the imperfect subjunctive
> **Era preciso que yo** and the imperfect subjunctive

18.2 FORMATION OF THE IMPERFECT SUBJUNCTIVE

All Spanish verbs, whether regular, irregular, or stem changing, form the imperfect subjunctive in the same way—by the addition of markers to the stem that remains when **-ron** is removed from the third person plural of the preterite indicative:

> **compraron–compra-   comieron–comie-**

Thus, any irregularity or peculiarity of the third person plural of the preterite is maintained throughout the imperfect subjunctive:

> **durmieron–durmie-   tuvieron–tuvie-   dijeron–dije-**
> **sirvieron–sirvie-   pusieron–pusie-   leyeron–leye-**

All verbs, whether their infinitives end in **-ar, -er,** or **-ir,** use the same person and number markers to indicate the imperfect subjunctive. There are two sets of these markers, one beginning with **-ra** and the other beginning with **-se.** They are interchangeable in all contexts except one—when the **-ra** markers must be used. If the **-ra** markers are used exclusively, the possibility of error is thereby eliminated.

18.2.1 *Third Person Plural.*

The third person plural is indicated by adding **-ran** or **-sen** to the imperfect subjunctive stem: **compraran–comprasen, vendieran–vendiesen, dijeran–dijesen:**

Juan quería que Vds. lo compraran.	*John wanted you to buy it.*
Era necesario que lo vendiesen.	*It was necessary for them to sell it.*
Yo dudaba que Vds. me lo dijesen.	*I doubted that you would tell it to me.*

PATTERN DRILL (A). Say each sentence below. Then repeat it, beginning the sentence with **Era dudoso que**, and changing the verb to the **-se** form of the imperfect subjunctive:

1. Vds. llegaron a tiempo.
2. Juan y Carlos volvieron temprano.
3. Las mujeres me lo devolvieron.
4. Vds. se sentaron cerca de mí.
5. Mis primos me escribieron.
6. Vds. se despertaron a las siete.
7. Las muchachas bailaron con nosotros.
8. Ellos ahorraron mucho dinero.

PATTERN DRILL (B). Say each sentence below. Then repeat it, beginning the sentence with **Me extrañaba que** (*It surprised me that*), and changing the verb to the **-ra** form of the imperfect subjunctive:

1. Vds. me dijeron el secreto.
2. Las muchachas vinieron aquí.
3. Mis padres fueron a ese restorán.
4. Vds. me trajeron el regalo.
5. Vds. sabían hablar francés.
6. Juan y María estaban en casa.
7. Vds. no preferían ir al teatro.
8. Servían vino en la fiesta.

18.2.2 *Third Person Singular.* The third person singular is indicated by adding **-ra** or **-se** to the imperfect subjunctive stem: **comprara–comprase, vendiera–vendiese, supiera–supiese:**

Le pedí a Juan que lo comprara.	*I asked John to buy it.*
Dudábamos que Vd. lo vendiera.	*We doubted that you would sell it.*
Era lástima que Vd. no lo supiese.	*It was a pity that you didn't know it.*

PATTERN DRILL (A). Say each sentence below. Then repeat it, beginning the sentence with **Era difícil que** (*It was unlikely that*), and changing the verb to the **-ra** form of the imperfect subjunctive:

1. Juan lo escondió.
2. El niño lloraba mucho.
3. Vd. se acostó temprano.
4. Carlos bebió ese vino.
5. Mi hermano se levantó a las cinco.
6. Enrique me pidió dinero.
7. María me lo prestó.
8. Vd. aprendía a hacerlo.

PATTERN DRILL (B). Say each sentence below. Then repeat it, beginning the sentence with **Esperábamos que** (*We were hoping that*), and changing the verb to the **-se** form of the imperfect subjunctive:

1. Vd. lo hizo.
2. Juan nos lo dijo.
3. El muchacho quería venir.
4. María trajo el postre. (*dessert*)

5. Vd. no tenía mucha hambre.
6. El profesor no lo supo.
7. Nuestro abuelo estaba bueno.
8. Vd. podía ir al cine con nosotros.

18.2.3 *First Person Singular.* The first person singular is indicated by adding **-ra** or **-se** to the imperfect subjunctive stem: **comprara–comprase, vendiera–vendiese, tuviera–tuviese.** Sometimes it is necessary to use the subject pronoun **yo** in order to avoid possible confusion with the third person singular of the imperfect subjunctive, which uses the same markers.

Juan se alegraba de que yo no lo comprara. *John was glad I didn't buy it.*
Era preciso que yo vendiera mi coche. *It was necessary for me to sell my car.*
Dudaban que yo tuviese razón. *They doubted that I was right.*

PATTERN DRILL (A). Say each sentence below. Then repeat it, beginning the sentence with **Era imposible que yo,** and changing the verb to the **-se** form of the imperfect subjunctive:

1. Bailé con María.
2. Te devolví la llave.
3. Me acosté temprano anoche.
4. Comprendía esa lección.

5. Llamé a Isabel el sábado.
6. Llegué a tiempo.
7. Empecé a estudiar.
8. Fui al centro.

PATTERN DRILL (B). Say each sentence below. Then repeat it, beginning the sentence with **Juan quería que yo,** and changing the verb to the **-ra** form of the imperfect subjunctive:

1. Puse el vaso en la cocina.
2. Lo hice ayer.
3. Dormí en el hotel.
4. Serví las aceitunas.

5. Vine a las tres.
6. Me vestí temprano.
7. Le dije la verdad.
8. Lo traje conmigo.

18.2.4 *First Person Plural.* The first person plural is indicated by adding **-ramos** or **-semos** to the imperfect subjunctive stem while maintaining its original stress: **compráramos–comprásemos, vendiéramos–vendiésemos, hiciéramos–hiciésemos:**

Temían que no lo compráramos. *They were afraid we wouldn't buy it.*
Era imposible que lo vendiésemos. *It was impossible for us to sell it.*
Juan sentía que no lo hiciésemos. *John was sorry that we didn't do it.*

PATTERN DRILL (A). Say each sentence below. Then repeat it, beginning the sentence with **Importaba que** (*It was important that*), and changing the verb to the -ra form of the imperfect subjunctive:

1. Lo hallamos ayer.
2. Escribimos a nuestro tío.
3. Leímos dos lecciones.
4. Nos despertamos a las seis.

5. Te lo devolvimos.
6. Asistimos a la reunión. (*meeting*)
7. Descansamos mucho anoche.
8. Escondimos el dinero.

PATTERN DRILL (B). Say each sentence below. Then repeat it, beginning the sentence with **María se alegraba de que,** and changing the verb to the -se form of the imperfect subjunctive:

1. Vinimos el miércoles.
2. Se lo pedimos a Juan.
3. No se lo dimos a la criada.
4. Lo pusimos en la mesa.

5. Servimos arroz con pollo.
6. Preferimos volver temprano.
7. Trajimos las aceitunas.
8. No sabíamos el secreto.

18.2.5 *Second Person Singular and Plural.* The singular intimate you is indicated by adding -ras or -ses to the imperfect subjunctive stem: **compraras–comprases, vendieras–vendieses, fueras–fueses:**

Temíamos que no compraras leche.	*We were afraid that you weren't buying milk.*
¿Deseaba Carlos que se lo vendieses?	*Did Charles want you to sell it to him?*
¿Era preciso que fueras al centro?	*Was it necessary for you to go downtown?*

The plural intimate you is indicated by adding **-rais** or **-seis** to the imperfect subjunctive stem: **comprarais–compraseis, vinierais–vinieseis:**

¿No os aconsejé que vinierais?	*Didn't I advise you to come?*

PATTERN DRILL (A). Say each sentence below. Then repeat it, beginning the sentence with **¿Era posible que?** and changing the verb to the -ra form of the imperfect subjunctive:

1. Llegaste el martes.
2. Asistías a esas reuniones.
3. Fuiste al cine con ella.
4. Empezaste a leer la novela anoche.

5. Ibas allí todos los días.
6. Te acostaste a las once y cuarto.
7. Ganaste mucho dinero.
8. Comiste ese helado.

PATTERN DRILL (B). Say each sentence below. Then repeat it, beginning the sentence with **Yo dudaba que**, and changing the verb to the **-se** form of the imperfect subjunctive:

1. Me dijiste la verdad.
2. Tenías razón.
3. Fuiste al campo.
4. Nos los diste.

5. Estabas en casa el domingo.
6. La viste en el tranvía.
7. Trajiste el coche nuevo.
8. Preferías vino tinto.

18.3 SEQUENCE OF TENSES

Although a subjunctive signal in the preterite or imperfect tense cannot be followed by a present subjunctive, a subjunctive signal in the present tense can be followed by an imperfect subjunctive when the action or state expressed by the subjunctive verb is wholly past:

I'm glad that you came.	**Me alegro de que vinieras.**
I'm sorry that you were sick.	**Siento que Vd. estuviera enfermo.**
It's incredible that he did it.	**Parece mentira que él lo hiciese.**

PATTERN DRILL. Say each sentence below. Then repeat it, beginning the sentence with **Es extraño que** (*It's strange that*), and changing the verb to the **-ra** form of the imperfect subjunctive:

1. Carlos llegó el martes.
2. Nuestros amigos no vinieron.
3. No te dije el secreto ayer.
4. El niño no tenía sed.

5. Ese hombre no nos escribió.
6. No me esperaste.
7. Vimos a María en la playa.
8. Vds. fueron al cine anoche.

18.4 THE IMPERFECT SUBJUNCTIVE AFTER CONJUNCTIONS

18.4.1 *Non-fact Conjunctions.* When the preterite or the imperfect is used in the main clause of a sentence, a non-fact conjunction is always followed by the imperfect subjunctive:

Volví antes de que ella saliera.	. . . *before she left.*
Te llamé para que me lo dijeras.	. . . *so that you'd tell it to me.*
Queríamos hacerlo sin que María nos viera.	. . . *without Mary's seeing us.*
Vinimos temprano en caso de que nos necesitaran.	. . . *in case they needed us.*
¿Ibas a salir con tal de que volviéramos temprano?	. . . *provided that we returned early?*
No quise ir a menos que me acompañasen.	. . . *unless they accompanied me.*

PATTERN DRILL (A). Say each sentence below. Then repeat it, beginning the sentence with **Salí sin que**, and changing the verb to the -ra form of the imperfect subjunctive:

1. Vd. me vio.
2. Ellos me hablaron.
3. Juan lo supo.
4. Vd. me lo prestó.
5. Vds. me lo dieron.
6. Me pediste dinero.
7. Pablo me lo quitó.
8. Me devolviste el libro.

PATTERN DRILL (B). Complete aloud each of the following sentences by changing the infinitive in parentheses to the indicated person of the imperfect subjunctive (use the -ra forms):

1. Volvimos antes de que ella (*empezar*) a comer.
2. El padre de María le dio diez dólares para que (*comprar*) la falda.
3. Pablo vino a fin de que yo le (*dar*) el cuadro.
4. Escondimos la cerveza en caso de que la criada (*tener*) sed.
5. Ese niño no iba a la escuela a menos que su madre (*ir*) con él.
6. Se lo di a ellos sin que ellos me lo (*pedir*).
7. Me mandaron que no saliera antes de que Vds. (*llegar*).
8. Pedro iba a prestármelo con tal de que Carlos se lo (*devolver*).

18.4.2 *Other Conjunctions*. When the preterite or the imperfect is used in the main clause of a sentence, **aunque, aun cuando**, and **a pesar de que** are followed by the imperfect subjunctive only if the speaker wishes to imply uncertainty about a past action or state. (English uses *may have* in this context).

Carlos no me lo dijo, aunque lo supiera.	. . . *although he may have known it.*
No la vi, aun cuando estuviera allí.	. . . *even though she may have been there.*
Él trabajaba, a pesar de que estuviera enfermo.	. . . *in spite of the fact that he may have been sick.*

When the preterite or the imperfect is used in the main clause of a sentence, the Spanish temporal conjunctions **así que, hasta que**, and **cuando** are followed by the imperfect subjunctive only if they introduce a past action or state that had not occurred at the time of the action or state expressed by the main clause. The difference beween **Dije que iba a salir así que volviste** and **Dije que iba a salir así que volvieras** is that the preterite indicates that I spoke as soon as you returned, whereas the imperfect subjunctive indicates that you had not come back at the time I spoke. (Sometimes English uses *should* in this context).

Yo no quería comer hasta que Vd. viniera.   . . . *until you should come.*
Dije que iba a hacerlo cuando llegaran.   . . . *when they should arrive.*

PATTERN DRILL. Complete aloud each of the following sentences by changing the infinitive in parentheses to the indicated person of the imperfect subjunctive (use the -ra forms):

1. Queríamos hacerlo, aunque no le (*gustar*) a Carlos.
2. Teresa dijo que iba a llamarme así que ella (*volver*).
3. Queríamos salir a las siete, aunque Pablo no (*llegar*) a tiempo.
4. ¿No querías estudiar hasta que tus abuelos (*venir*)?
5. Dije que iba a salir cuando los niños (*tener*) que acostarse.
6. Pedro quería ir al centro, a pesar de que no (*estar*) bueno.
7. Ellos siempre trabajaban mucho, aunque (*ser*) viejos.
8. Les dije que yo quería ir a la playa, aun cuando ellos no (*ir*) conmigo.

18.5 SPECIAL USES OF THE IMPERFECT SUBJUNCTIVE

The conjunction **como si** (*as if*) is always followed by the imperfect subjunctive, regardless of the time indicated in the main clause of the sentence:

Juan habla como si supiese la verdad.   *John speaks as if he knew the truth.*
Juan habló como si supiera la verdad.   *John spoke as if he knew the truth.*

The -ra forms of the imperfect subjunctive of **querer** and **desear** are a polite way of making a request. These subjunctive signals are always followed by the imperfect subjunctive:

Quisiera que Vd. me lo prestase.   *I should like you to lend it to me.*
Deseáramos que Vds. vinieran.   *We should like you to come.*

PATTERN DRILL. Complete aloud each of the following sentences by changing the infinitive in parentheses to the indicated person of the imperfect subjunctive (use the -ra forms):

1. María habla como si (*estar*) enferma.
2. Quisiera que Vds. (*salir*) al jardín conmigo.
3. Gastas dinero como si (*ganar*) mucho.
4. Deseáramos que Vds. nos lo (*dar*) hoy.
5. Juan comía como si (*tener*) mucha hambre.
6. Yo (*querer*) que Vd. me lo mandase.
7. Pablo me habló como si él no (*querer*) vendérmelo.
8. Ese estudiante contesta como si él no (*comprender*) la lección. (*to answer*)

18.6 DEMONSTRATIVE PRONOUNS

A pronoun that points out the noun to which it refers is called a *demonstrative* pronoun. In the sentences *This is a big house* and *I want his books and those,* the words *this* and *those* are English demonstrative pronouns. The Spanish demonstrative pronouns, like their English counterparts, have the same forms as the demonstrative adjectives, except that in writing there is an accent mark over the stressed vowel of each pronoun: **éste, ése, aquél.** Spanish demonstrative pronouns are inflected to show the number and gender of their referends.

Nouns close to the speaker are indicated by **éste, ésta, éstos,** or **éstas:**

Deseo el libro rojo y éste.	*I want the red book and this one.*
Te mando esa revista y ésta.	*I'm sending you that magazine and this one.*
Éstos son guantes de lana.	*These are woolen gloves.*
Deseo uvas, pero no deseo éstas.	*I want grapes, but I don't want these.*

Nouns close to the person spoken to are indicated by **ése, ésa, ésos,** or **ésas:**

Déme Vd. mi sombrero y ése.	*Give me my hat and that one.*
Ésa es una corbata de seda.	*That is a silk tie.*
¿Prefieres mis lápices o ésos?	*Do you prefer my pencils or those?*
¿Deseas estas corbatas o ésas?	*Do you want these ties or those?*

Aquél, aquélla, aquéllos, and **aquéllas** are used to refer to nouns that are not close to either the speaker or the hearer:

Aquél es el coche de Juan.	*That one* [over there] *is John's car.*
Deseo esta pluma y aquélla.	*I want this pen and that one* [over there].
No buscamos aquéllos.	*We're not looking for those* [over there].
¿Desea Vd. esa manzana o aquéllas?	*Do you want that apple or those?*

PATTERN DRILL. Say each sentence below. Then repeat it, replacing the adjective and noun with the corresponding demonstrative pronoun:

1. Voy a mandarte esta revista.
2. No deseamos aquella casa.
3. ¿Vas a devolverme ese libro?
4. Estos libros son interesantes.
5. ¿Quién te dio esas corbatas?
6. ¿Ves aquellos árboles?
7. Te presto este libro.
8. Deseo que me vendas esos caballos.

18.6.1 The Former and the Latter. To indicate the *former* of two items or persons previously mentioned, Spanish uses the forms of **aquél:**

Juan y María son estudiantes, pero
  aquél no estudia.   . . . *the former doesn't study.*
¿Prefieres las uvas o las cerezas?
  —Prefiero aquéllas.   . . . *I prefer the former.*

To indicate the *latter* of two items or persons previously mentioned, Spanish uses the forms of **éste**:

Juan y María son estudiantes, y
  ésta estudia mucho.   . . . *the latter studies hard.*
¿Prefieres las uvas o las cerezas?
  —Prefiero éstas.   . . . *I prefer the latter.*

When both **éste** and **aquél** are mentioned in Spanish, **éste** is dealt with first:

Juan y María son estudiantes: **ésta** estudia mucho, pero **aquél** no estudia.
. . . *the latter studies hard, but the former doesn't study.*

PATTERN DRILL (A). Answer each question below with a complete sentence, choosing the latter of the items mentioned:

1. ¿Prefieres mi coche o el coche de Juan?   —Prefiero éste.
2. ¿Desean Vds. las cucharas o los tenedores?
3. ¿Desea Vd. cerveza o vino?
4. ¿Vas a comer las fresas o el helado?
5. ¿Compra Vd. la corbata o el sombrero?
6. ¿Me mandan Vds. la revista o el periódico?
7. ¿Te pones los guantes o la chaqueta?
8. ¿Prefieren Vds. la gabardina o el abrigo?

PATTERN DRILL (B). Answer each question above with a complete sentence, choosing the former of the items mentioned.

18.6.2 *Neuter Demonstrative Pronouns.* Although there are no neuter demonstrative adjectives in Spanish, there are three neuter demonstrative pronouns: **esto, eso,** and **aquello.** They are used not to refer to something specific, but rather to an unidentified object, or an idea, or a remark:

¿Qué es esto?	*What's this?*	¿Qué es eso? *What's that?*
Eso es imposible.	*That (which you say) is impossible.*	
¿Quién te dijo eso?	*Who told you that?*	
¿Dijo Juan aquello?	*Did John say that?*	
Aquello es muy importante.	*That is very important.*	

Lesson 19

19.1 RELATIVE PRONOUNS

A *relative* pronoun begins an explanatory clause that it links to a noun or pronoun in the preceding clause. The preceding noun or pronoun is called the *antecedent* of the relative pronoun. In the sentences *John wants the books that I bought* and *Where is the man who did it?*, the words *that* and *who* function as English relative pronouns; their respective antecedents are *books* and *man*. Although it is sometimes possible to omit relative pronouns in English (*John wants the books I bought*), they may not be omitted in Spanish.

19.1.1 Que. The most frequently used Spanish relative pronoun is **que**, which is invariable in form. The antecedent of **que** may be singular or plural, a person or a thing. **Que** can be either the subject or the object of the verb following it:

Veo al niño que lo rompió.	*I see the child who broke it.* [subject]
¿Ves los coches que vienen?	*Do you see the cars that are coming?* [subject]
¿Dónde están los hombres que viste?	*Where are the men whom you saw?* [object]
Leí la revista que me diste.	*I read the magazine that you gave me.* [object]

An important restriction upon **que** is that it is used after the prepositions **a, de, en,** and **con** only if the antecedent is a thing:

Leí el libro de que me hablaste.	*I read the book that you spoke to me about.*
Quiero la pluma con que escribes.	*I want the pen with which you're writing.*

PATTERN DRILL. Practice aloud using **que** to complete each sentence below:

1. No conozco al hombre . . . llegó ayer.
2. Éste es el libro de . . . te hablábamos.
3. ¿Perdiste el reloj . . . te dimos?
4. Comimos las aceitunas . . . trajiste.
5. ¿Dónde están los niños . . . vimos?
6. Rompí la botella en . . . estaba el vino.
7. Busco los cuchillos . . . vamos a usar.
8. Éste es el coche en . . . vinimos.

19.1.2 *Quien*. After the prepositions **a, de, en,** and **con,** the relative pronoun **quien** is used if the antecedent is a person. If the antecedent is more than one person, the plural form **quienes** is used:

María es la muchacha a quien escribí.	*Mary is the girl to whom I wrote.*
Conozco al hombre con quien viniste.	*I know the man with whom you came.*
Vi a las mujeres de quienes hablaste.	*I saw the women whom you spoke about.*

PATTERN DRILL. Practice aloud using **quien** or **quienes**, as required, to complete each sentence below:

1. Juan es el hombre de . . . te hablé.
2. Ellos son los niños con . . . vinimos.
3. La mujer con . . . vine es mi esposa.
4. Luis es el abogado a . . . mandé la carta.
5. ¿Vino el hombre de . . . les escribí?
6. Ésos son los hombres a . . . vi ayer.
7. Vi a las niñas de . . . me hablaste.
8. ¿Conoces a la mujer con . . . bailo?

19.1.3 *El cual–el que*. **El cual** and **el que** are the relative pronouns used instead of **que** and **quien** after prepositions of two or more syllables and after **sin**. These compound relative pronouns each have four forms, and, therefore, can indicate the number and the gender of their antecedents:

el cual, la cual, los cuales, las cuales
el que, la que, los que, las que

Juan es el hombre detrás del cual [del que] me senté.	*. . . behind whom I sat.*
Veo a las mujeres cerca de las cuales [las que] estabas.	*. . . whom you were near.*

The forms of **el cual** and **el que** are also used to avoid ambiguity when there is more than one possible antecedent. **Escribí al padre de Juan, que estaba enfermo** indicates that *John* was sick, because **que** refers to the closest antecedent. A more distant antecedent is indicated with **el cual** or **el que.** Thus, **Escribí al padre de Juan, el cual [el que] estaba enfermo** indicates that the *father* was ill. Similarly:

Vi a la madre de María, que me quiere. [Mary loves me]
Vi a la madre de María, la cual me quiere. [Her mother loves me]

PATTERN DRILL (A). Practice aloud using the proper form of **el cual** to complete each sentence below:

1. Aquélla es la casa cerca de . . . vamos a vivir.
2. Vivo con el tío de ella, . . . tiene una casa grande.
3. Ellos son los muchachos al lado de . . . nos sentamos. (*beside*)
4. Vi a la hermana de Juan, . . . estuvo en el centro.
5. Voy allí con el padre de Teresa, . . . viene a las ocho.
6. Pablo y Carlos son los dos muchachos sin . . . no podemos ganar. (*to win*)
7. No podemos hallar los árboles debajo de . . . escondimos el oro. (*under*)
8. Busco a María y a Elena, sin . . . no podemos salir.

PATTERN DRILL (B). Use the proper form of **el que** to complete each sentence above.

19.1.4 Neuter Relative Pronouns. The neuter relatives **lo que** and **lo cual** are used when the antecedent is a previous clause or statement, rather than a noun or pronoun:

Juan no va al baile, lo que [lo cual] me
   extraña.   . . . *which surprises me.*
La niña dice que no fuma, lo que [lo
   cual] es verdad.   . . . *which is true.*

In addition, **lo que** (but not **lo cual**) is the equivalent of the English non-interrogative *what*, or *that which*:

Lo que dices es interesante.   *What you say is interesting.*
Sé lo que Juan desea.   *I know what John wants.*

PATTERN DRILL. Complete the following sentences with the proper neuter relative pronoun:

1. Carlos no quiere . . . tiene.
2. . . . Vd. compra es caro.
3. Dudo que tengas . . . buscamos.
4. ¿Dónde pusiste . . . hallaste?
5. Están enfermos, . . . me extraña.
6. No quise comer . . . me sirvieron.
7. No recibieron . . . les mandé.
8. María no viene, . . . es absurdo.

19.1.5 Whose. The relative pronoun used to indicate possession is **cuyo**, which is inflected to agree in number and gender with THE ITEM POSSESSED, not the possessor:

Hablé a la mujer cuyo esposo murió. . . . the woman whose husband died.

Llamé a Juan, cuya pluma tengo. . . . John, whose pen I have.

Busco a la muchacha cuyos libros . . . the girl whose books I need.
necesito.

Vi a los hombres cuyas hijas están . . . the men whose daughters. . . .
en mi clase.

To inquire about possession, **¿de quién?** or **¿de quiénes?** is used, depending on whether one expects a singular or a plural possessor:

¿De quién son aquellos libros?   Whose books are those?
¿De quiénes es aquella casa?   Whose house is that?

PATTERN DRILL.   Practice aloud using the proper form of **cuyo** to complete each sentence below:

1. Voy a escribir a María, . . . hermano es abogado.
2. ¿Conoces al hombre . . . esposa murió?
3. Vi al muchacho . . . madre es la criada de Vds.
4. Vamos a la casa de Elena, . . . padres son nuestros amigos.
5. Busco a Luis, . . . coche está delante de la casa.
6. Llamé a Enrique, . . . hermanos me lo quitaron.
7. Dudo que venga ese hombre . . . hijas están enfermas.
8. Lo dimos a la criada, . . . hijo tiene dos años.

19.1.6 The One Who. The Spanish equivalents of *the one who, he/she who,* and *the man/woman who* are **quien, el que,** and **la que:**

Roberto es quien sabe eso.   *Robert is the one who knows that.*
Quien busca, halla.   *He who seeks, finds.*
El que estudia poco aprende poco. *He who studies little learns little.*
La que sabe cocinar es Elena.   *The woman who knows how to cook is Helen.*

The plural forms **quienes, los que,** and **las que** are equivalent to the English *those who, they who,* and *the men/women who:*

Quienes gastan mucho tienen poco. *Those who spend a lot have little.*
Los que trabajaban no vinieron.   *The men who were working did not come.*

Elena y María son las que estudian *Helen and Mary are the ones who*
mucho.   *study hard.*

PATTERN DRILL (A). Complete each sentence below with **quien** or **quienes,** as required by context:

1. Mis abuelos son . . . vienen.
2. Juan es . . . lo tiene.
3. Dudo que Vd. sea . . . lo hizo.
4. ¿Es posible que ellas sean . . . salen?
5. . . . no estudia, no aprende.
6. . . . trabajaron ayer lo vieron.
7. No fue Carlos . . . dijo eso.
8. María es . . . sabe cocinar.

PATTERN DRILL (B). Complete each sentence above with the form of **el que** required by the context.

19.2 SUBJUNCTIVE AFTER RELATIVE PRONOUNS

When the antecedent of a relative pronoun is not a specific person or thing, as in *They're looking for a maid who knows how to cook,* a verb in the subjunctive mood follows the relative pronoun:

Buscan una criada que sepa cocinar.

Necesito un hombre que viera el   *I need a man who saw the accident.*
  accidente.

Yo buscaba una tienda que vendiera   *I was looking for a store that sold*
  guantes baratos.   *cheap gloves.*

Similarly, when the antecedent of a relative pronoun is nonexistent, as in *I can't find a single store that sells them,* a verb in the subjunctive mood follows the relative pronoun:

No puedo hallar una sola tienda que los venda.

No es posible hallar un solo hombre que lo viera.

Era imposible encontrar una criada que supiera hacerlo. (to find, **ue**)

(Note that no "personal" **a** precedes an unspecific person. Remember that if the verb in the main clause is in the present tense, any tense of the subjunctive may follow the relative pronoun, but if the verb in the main clause is in the preterite or the imperfect, then the imperfect subjunctive follows the relative pronoun.)

PATTERN DRILL. Complete each of the following sentences with the proper form of the infinitive in parentheses:

1. Ahora buscamos una criada que (*querer*) vivir en nuestra casa.
2. Juan desea un coche que no (*ser*) muy caro.

3. No conozco una biblioteca que (*contener*) esos libros raros. (*to contain*)
4. Deseaban un dependiente que (*trabajar*) los sábados. (*clerk*)
5. No veo una sola toronja que me (*gustar*) en esa tienda.
6. Buscábamos una casa que (*estar*) cerca de la universidad.
7. ¿Conoces un restorán que (*servir*) arroz con pollo?
8. No encontré un solo libro que me (*ayudar*).

19.3 FUTURE INDICATIVE

All Spanish verbs use the same set of person and number markers to form the future tense. These markers are added to the infinitives of all but about a dozen verbs. Some of the verbs that have irregular future stems are:

poner—pondr-	saber—sabr-	hacer—har-
tener	tendr-	poder podr-	decir	dir-
venir	vendr-	querer querr-
salir	saldr-

19.3.1 *First Person Singular.* The first person singular is indicated by adding -é to the infinitive or to the irregular future stem: **compraré, saldré.**

> **Lo compraré mañana.**   *I'll buy it tomorrow.*
> **No saldré hasta la una.**   *I won't leave until one o'clock.*

PATTERN DRILL. Say each sentence below. Then repeat it, replacing **voy a** and the infinitive by the future tense:

1. Voy a ver esa película.
2. Voy a darte el postre.
3. Voy a comerlo mañana.
4. Voy a mandártelo.

5. Voy a venir el viernes.
6. Voy a ponerme la chaqueta.
7. No voy a salir ahora mismo.
8. Voy a quererla.

19.3.2 *First Person Plural.* The first person plural is indicated by adding -emos to the infinitive or to the irregular future stem: **compraremos, podremos.**

> **Lo compraremos este año.**   *We'll buy it this year.*
> **No podremos ir allí.**   *We won't be able to go there.*

PATTERN DRILL. Say each sentence below. Then repeat it, using the future tense instead of the present tense or **vamos a:**

1. Comemos a las siete.
2. Lo estudiamos mañana.
3. Hoy salimos tarde de la escuela
4. Vamos a hacerlo sin ti.

5. Tenemos frío en enero.
6. ¿Dónde vamos a ponerlo?
7. ¿Cuándo vamos a llegar?
8. No te lo mandamos hasta febrero.

19.3.3 Second Person Singular and Plural. To indicate the singular intimate you, -ás is added to the infinitive or to the irregular future stem: **comprarás, dirás.**

¿Cuándo comprarás el coche?	When will you buy the car?
¿Qué les dirás esta tarde?	What will you say to them this afternoon?

To indicate the plural intimate you, -éis is added to the infinitive or to the irregular future stem: **compraréis, tendréis.**

Lo tendréis esta noche.	You'll have it tonight.

PATTERN DRILL. Say each sentence below. Then repeat it, using the future tense:

1. ¿Esperas a María?
2. ¿Vas a cerrarla? (*to close*, **ie**)
3. No lo sabes.
4. ¿Vas a levantarte a las seis?
5. ¿Cuándo vas a empezar?
6. ¿Adónde vas el jueves?
7. ¿Puedes ir al cine conmigo?
8. ¿A qué hora vas a salir de casa?

19.3.4 Third Person Singular. The third person singular is indicated by adding -á to the infinitive or to the irregular future stem: **comprará, hará.**

¿Cuándo comprará Juan la casa?	When will John buy the house?
¿Hará Vd. un viaje este verano?	Will you take a trip this summer?

PATTERN DRILL. Say each sentence below. Then repeat it, using the future tense:

1. María va a decírmelo.
2. ¿Va Vd. a ponerlo aquí?
3. El niño va a romper la botella.
4. Juan se acuesta temprano.
5. Mi abuelo va a darme el reloj.
6. La criada no viene hoy.
7. Carlos va a aprender la lección.
8. ¿Cuándo va Vd. a hacer esto?

19.3.5 Third Person Plural. The third person plural is indicated by adding -án to the infinitive or to the irregular future stem: **comprarán, vendrán.**

Mis padres lo comprarán en 1987.	My parents will buy it in 1987.
¿Cuándo vendrán Vds. al campo?	When will you come to the country?

PATTERN DRILL. Say each sentence below. Then repeat it, using the future tense:

1. ¿Van a venir Juan y Elena?
2. Mis hermanos van a ser abogados.
3. Nuestros amigos van a dárnoslo.
4. Ellos cierran las puertas.
5. ¿Cuándo van Vds. a decírmelo?
6. Los niños no salen hasta las tres.
7. Ellos van a levantarse tarde.
8. ¿Se desayunan Vds. temprano?

19.4 THE CONDITIONAL TENSE

The conditional tense is used to indicate futurity dating from the past: *Yesterday he said that he would come today.* The conditional is formed precisely as the future, by adding markers to an infinitive or to an irregular future stem. A verb that has an irregular future stem has the same irregular stem in the conditional.

The person and number markers of the conditional are:
First person singular: -ía: **compraría, haría.**

Dije que lo compraría hoy. *I said that I would buy it today.*

First person plural: -íamos: **compraríamos, vendríamos.**

Le dijimos que vendríamos hoy. *We told him that we'd come today.*

Second person singular: -ías: **comprarías, saldrías.**

Ayer me dijiste que saldrías hoy.

Second person plural: -íais: **compraríais, sabríais.**

Vuestra madre me dijo que no lo sabríais hasta mañana.

Third person singular: -ía: **compraría, pondría.**

¿Por qué nos dijo Vd. que lo pondría en la mesa?

Third person plural: -ían: **comprarían, tendrían.**

Los muchachos nos dijeron que tendrían hambre a las cinco.

PATTERN DRILL. Complete each of the following sentences by changing the infinitive in parentheses to the indicated person of the conditional:

1. Juan nos escribió que él (*venir*) en junio.
2. No dudábamos que Vd. lo (*hacer*) cuanto antes. (*as soon as possible*)
3. ¿Por qué estabas seguro de que me (*acostar*) temprano?
4. Mis padres me dijeron que yo (*poder*) ir contigo.
5. ¿Dijo María que te (*escribir*) esta semana?
6. Ellos me dijeron que Vd. lo (*querer*) hoy.
7. Carlos no dudaba que Vds. se lo (*mandar*) cuanto antes.
8. María me prometió que lo (*hacer*) mañana. (*to promise*, -er)

19.5 PROBABILITY

In addition to expressing futurity, the future tense is also employed in Spanish to indicate probability in the present:

¿Qué hora es? —Será la una.	*What time is it? It's probably one.*
¿Quién viene? —Será Juan.	*Who's coming? It's probably John.*
Tengo hambre. —¿Qué hora será?	*I'm hungry. I wonder what time it is.*

Similarly, the conditional is used to express probability in the past in Spanish:

¿Qué hora sería cuando llegué?	*I wonder what time it was when I arrived.*
Quien vino sería Juan.	*It was probably John who came.*

19.6 ENGLISH INTERFERENCE

Be careful not to let English mislead you into using the future or the conditional after a subjunctive signal:

I doubt that he will come tomorrow.	**Dudo que él venga mañana.**
I doubted that he would come today.	**Dudaba que él viniera hoy.**

19.7 THE WEATHER

Some aspects of weather are indicated with the third person singular of **hacer:**

¿Qué tiempo hace?	*What's the weather like?*
Hace buen tiempo.	*The weather is good.*
Hace mal tiempo.	*The weather is bad.*

Hace frío.	*It's cold.*	**Hace calor.**	*It's warm.*
Hacía sol.	*It was sunny.*	**Hace luna.**	*The moon is out.*
Hace viento.	*It's windy.*	**Hace fresco.**	*It's cool.*

With the nouns **frío, calor, sol, viento,** and **fresco,** the Spanish equivalent of *very* is **mucho: Hará mucho frío.** With the noun **luna,** the equivalent of *very* is **mucha: Hacía mucha luna,** *The moon was very bright.*

Rain and snow are expressed with the third person singular of **llover (ue)** and **nevar (ie),** respectively:

Hoy llueve mucho.	*Today it's raining hard.*
No nieva aquí en julio.	*It doesn't snow here in July.*

PATTERN DRILL. Answer each of the following questions affirmatively, using **Sí** and a complete sentence:

1. ¿Hace mucho frío hoy?	5. ¿Siente Vd. que llueva hoy?
2. ¿Llovía cuando llegaste?	6. ¿Hizo buen tiempo ayer?
3. ¿Nieva mucho en esta ciudad?	7. ¿Hacía luna cuando saliste?
4. ¿Hará calor mañana?	8. ¿Dijiste que haría sol hoy?

Lesson 20

20.1 PERFECT TENSES

The so-called *perfect* tenses are those Spanish past tenses that consist of **haber** immediately followed by a *past participle*. The latter is invariable, whereas **haber** is inflected to indicate person, tense, and mood. The Spanish perfect tenses correspond in meaning and most uses to the English perfect tenses formed with *to have* and a past participle: *to have studied, to have spoken*. Because of these similarities, English provides a useful "rule of thumb" for Spanish: whenever you would use a perfect tense in English, use the corresponding perfect tense in Spanish, and vice versa. However, remember that the Spanish equivalents of the English "have/had + past participle + for + time" constructions use the special formulae explained in 17.5 and 17.6.

20.2 PAST PARTICIPLES

The past participles of **-ar** verbs are formed by replacing the **-ar** of the infinitive with **-ado**:

> **comprado** *bought*   **estudiado** *studied*   **dado** *given*

The past participles of most **-er** and **-ir** verbs are formed by replacing the **-er** or **-ir** of the infinitive with **-ido**:

> **comido** *eaten*   **vivido** *lived*   **ido** *gone*

The addition of **-ido** to a stem ending in /-a/ or /-e/ does not create a diphthong. This is indicated in writing with an accent mark over the **-i-**:

> **traído** *brought*   **leído** *read*

A few second- and third-conjugation verbs have irregular past participles:

ver	visto	volver	vuelto
decir	dicho	poner	puesto

hacer	hecho	morir	muerto
romper	roto	abrir	abierto
escribir	escrito	cubrir	cubierto (*to cover*)

Of course, verbs such as **devolver, envolver** (*to wrap up*), **suponer** (*to suppose*), **descubrir** (*to discover*), and **describir** (*to describe*) will show the same irregularities: **devuelto, envuelto, supuesto, descubierto, descrito.**

Remember that past participles never agree with the subject of **haber,** and that nothing separates **haber** from the past participle. Object pronouns and **no** precede **haber;** in questions the subject noun or pronoun follows the past participle.

20.3 PRESENT PERFECT INDICATIVE

The present perfect indicative tense is formed with the present indicative of **haber,** and it is the counterpart of the English *I have* + past participle.

20.3.1 First Person Singular. The first person singular is indicated by using **he** before the desired past participle: **he comprado, he comido, he escrito.**

He comprado dos libros hoy.   *I have bought two books today.*
No les he escrito este mes.   *I haven't written to them this month.*

PATTERN DRILL (A). Practice aloud using **he** to complete each sentence below:

1. No . . . comprado esa casa.
2. . . . recibido muchos regalos.
3. Le . . . escrito a Vd.
4. Te lo . . . mandado.
5. Se lo . . . pedido a Juan.
6. No lo . . . hecho.
7. Siempre me . . . acostado tarde.
8. No . . . leído esa novela.

PATTERN DRILL (B). Say each sentence below. Then repeat it, changing the verb to the present perfect tense:

1. No gasto mucho dinero.
2. Como el postre.
3. Te mando el paquete. (*package*)
4. Devolví el libro a la biblioteca.
5. Me pongo los calcetines. (*socks*)
6. No leí esa revista inglesa.
7. Envuelvo el paquete.
8. Estoy enfermo.

20.3.2 First Person Plural. The first person plural is indicated by using **hemos** before the desired past participle: **hemos comprado, hemos comido, hemos vuelto.**

Siempre hemos comido mucha carne.   *We have always eaten a lot of meat.*
Hemos vuelto al campo.   *We have returned to the country.*

PATTERN DRILL. Say each sentence below. Then repeat it, changing the verb to the present perfect tense:

1. Siempre insistimos en esto.
2. Ganamos el partido. (*game*)
3. Descubrimos el secreto.
4. Al fin llegamos. (*finally*)

5. Lo pusimos en la sala.
6. No volvemos a aquel restorán.
7. Al fin recibimos los paquetes.
8. No podemos asistir a los partidos.

20.3.3 Second Person Singular and Plural. The singular intimate you is indicated by using **has** before the desired past participle: **has comprado, has comido, has dicho.**

¿Por qué has comprado eso?	*Why have you bought that?*
¿No nos has dicho la verdad?	*Haven't you told us the truth?*

The plural intimate you is indicated by using **habéis** before the desired past participle:

¿Los habéis envuelto en papel blanco?	*Have you wrapped them up in white paper?*

PATTERN DRILL. Say each sentence below. Then repeat it, changing the verb to the present perfect tense:

1. ¿Escribes a Juan esta semana?
2. Al fin descubriste oro.
3. ¿Compras esa manta? (*blanket*)
4. ¿Por qué te lo quitas?

5. ¿Hiciste lo que queríamos?
6. ¿Lo envuelves en papel rojo?
7. Escondes el tesoro. (*treasure*)
8. ¿Pones la manta en mi cama?

20.3.4 Third Person Singular. The third person singular is indicated by using **ha** before the desired past participle: **ha comprado, ha comido, ha visto.**

Carlos ha comprado mi coche.	*Charles has bought my car.*
¿Ha visto Vd. esta película?	*Have you seen this movie?*

PATTERN DRILL. Say each sentence below. Then repeat it, changing the verb to the present perfect tense:

1. El niño no quiere comer.
2. Mi abuelo murió.
3. El partido es interesante.
4. Siempre hace fresco en abril.

5. ¿Abrió Vd. las ventanas?
6. María me dijo eso.
7. La mujer nos vio.
8. ¿Quién descubrió el tesoro?

20.3.5 Third Person Plural. The third person plural is indicated by using **han** before the desired past participle: **han comprado, han comido, han hecho.**

¿Han comprado Vds. lo que necesitaban?	Have you bought what you needed?
No lo han hecho.	They have not done it.

PATTERN DRILL. Say each sentence below. Then repeat it, changing the verb to the present perfect tense:

1. Esos muchachos comen poco.
2. Juan y Carlos me lo devolvieron.
3. Mis hijos rompen muchos vasos.
4. ¿Hallaron la sábana? (*sheet*)
5. ¿Abren los niños el paquete?
6. Mis amigos no fueron al partido.
7. ¿Tuvieron Vds. que venderla?
8. Vds. no me lo dijeron.

20.4 PLUPERFECT INDICATIVE

The pluperfect indicative tense is formed with the imperfect indicative of **haber,** and it is the counterpart of the English *I had* + past participle. The imperfect indicative of **haber** is "regular":

Me había levantado tarde.	I had gotten up late.
No habíamos dicho eso.	We had not said that.
¿Cuándo habías hecho el viaje?	When had you taken the trip?
¿Habíais visto la película?	Had you seen the movie?
Juan se había vestido cuando salí.	John had dressed when I left.
Estaba seguro de que Vd. lo había hecho.	I was sure that you had done it.
¿Por qué lo habían traído Vds.?	Why had you brought it?

PATTERN DRILL. Say each sentence below. Then repeat it, changing the verb to the pluperfect tense:

1. No he visto aquello.
2. ¿Dónde lo ha escondido Vd.?
3. El niño se ha quitado el zapato.
4. Hemos vuelto en el otoño. (*autumn*)
5. ¿Has ido allí a menudo?
6. No nos han escrito.
7. ¿Por qué lo han hecho Vds.?
8. He abierto las ventanas.

20.5 FUTURE AND CONDITIONAL PERFECT TENSES

The future and conditional perfect tenses are formed with the future and conditional of **haber,** which has the irregular future/conditional stem **habr-: habré** and **habría.** Like their English counterparts, the future and conditional perfects have limited use. The former is the equivalent of *shall/will have* + past participle:

Habré vuelto antes de que salgas.	I'll have returned before you leave.
Creo que Juan lo habrá hecho.	I believe that John will have done it.

The conditional perfect is the equivalent of *should/would have* + past participle:

Habría vuelto, pero no tuve dinero.   *I'd have returned, but . . .*
Creía que Juan lo habría hecho.   *I believed that John would have done it.*

These compound tenses are also used to express probability or supposition:

Juan habrá llegado.   *John has probably arrived.*
¿Habrán salido?   *I wonder if they have left.*

Juan habría llegado.   *John had probably arrived.*
¿Habrían salido ayer?   *I wondered if they had left yesterday.*

PATTERN DRILL (A). Say each sentence below. Then repeat it, changing the verb to the future perfect tense:

1. Juan me ha escrito esta semana.
2. Nos hemos levantado temprano.
3. María lo ha hecho.
4. ¿Dónde lo ha puesto Vd.?
5. He llegado tarde.
6. Vds. no lo han visto.
7. ¿Cuándo lo han mandado?
8. ¿Por qué lo has dicho?

PATTERN DRILL (B). Repeat each sentence above, changing the verb to the conditional perfect tense.

20.6 OTHER USES OF «HABER»

Although **haber** means *to have*, it is not a synonym of **tener.** The uses of **haber** are limited to forming the perfect tenses, and to the following:

20.6.1 *Hay.* The impersonal expression **hay** is the Spanish equivalent of *there is* and *there are:*

Hay una naranja en la mesa.   *There is one orange on the table.*
Hay naranjas en la nevera.   *There are oranges in the refrigerator.*
¿Hay museo que los contenga?   *Is there a museum that contains them?*
No hay tienda que venda eso.   *There is no store that sells that.*

The preterite of **hay** is **hubo,** the imperfect is **había,** the future is **habrá,** and the conditional is **habría.** In no tense does this impersonal expression assume a plural form:

Hubo dos accidentes ayer.   *There were two accidents yesterday.*
Había muchos partidos interesantes.   *There were many interesting games.*
¿Habrá muchos estudiantes allí?   *Will there be many students there?*
Juan dijo que habría tres partidos.   *. . . there would be three games.*

Hay is also used to indicate distance:

¿Cuánto hay de aquí a Madrid?   *How far is it from here to Madrid?*
Hay un kilómetro de aquí a ese pueblo. *It's a kilometer from here to that town.*

20.6.2 *Hay que.* The impersonal expression **hay que** is the equivalent of *it is necessary*, and is always followed by an infinitive:

Hay que buscarlos.   *It is necessary to look for them.*
Había que hacerlo.   *It was necessary to do it.*
¿Habrá que devolverlos?   *Will it be necessary to return them?*
Juan dijo que habría que salir. *. . . it would be necessary to leave.*

When it is necessary for a specific person to perform an action, **hay que** cannot be used. Instead, Spanish uses **es necesario** (or **preciso**) **que** and the subjunctive: **Es necesario que Vd. los busque.**

PATTERN DRILL.   Answer each of the following questions affirmatively, using **Sí** and a complete sentence:

1. ¿Hay muchas mantas en la cama?   5. ¿Hay mucho de Madrid a Sevilla?
2. ¿Habrá dos partidos este sábado?   6. ¿Hay papel rojo en tu cuarto?
3. ¿Hay que suponer eso?   7. ¿Habrá que ir de compras mañana?
4. ¿Había fiestas a menudo?   8. ¿Dijiste que habría clases hoy?

20.6.3 *Haber de.* Followed by an infinitive, **haber de** indicates that something is (or was) expected to happen. It is equivalent to the English *to be to* or *to be expected to:*

He de hacerlo hoy.   *I am to do it today.*
Carlos había de llegar a la una.   *Charles was to arrive at one.*
Habremos de venir mañana.   *We'll be expected to come tomorrow.*
Juan dijo que habríamos de asistir. *. . . we'd be expected to attend.*

PATTERN DRILL.   Say each sentence below. Then repeat it, replacing the verb with the corresponding tense and person of **haber de** + infinitive:

1. El niño se acuesta temprano.   5. ¿Quién lo hace?
2. Lo haré este sábado.   6. Estudiábamos la lección.
3. Vds. venían temprano.   7. ¿Dónde lo pondremos?
4. ¿Cuándo llegan María y Juan?   8. El tren sale en media hora.

20.7 POSSESSIVE PRONOUNS

A pronoun that indicates the possessor of the noun to which it refers is called a *possessive* pronoun. In the sentence *I have John's book and mine,* the word *mine* is an English possessive pronoun; its referend is *book*. Unlike their English counterparts, the Spanish possessive pronouns are inflected to indicate the number and gender of their referends.

20.7.1 *First Person Singular.* The Spanish equivalent of the English pronoun *mine* will be **el mío, la mía, los míos,** or **las mías,** depending on the number and gender of the referend:

¿Necesitas tu lápiz y el mío?	*Do you need your pencil and mine?*
He perdido tu pluma y la mía.	*I've lost your pen and mine.*
Vi a tus abuelos y a los míos.	*I saw your grandparents and mine.*
Rompí esas tazas y las mías.	*I broke those cups and mine.*

PATTERN DRILL. Say each sentence below. Then repeat it, replacing the possessive adjective and noun with the corresponding form of **el mío:**

1. Mi libro está en la mesa.
2. Te prestaré mi revista.
3. ¿Escuchas mis discos? (*to listen to*)
4. ¿Necesitan Vds. mis toallas?
5. ¿Quién tendrá mi corbata?
6. ¿Hallaste mi reloj?
7. ¿Vas a beber mi cerveza también?
8. Te has puesto mis guantes.

20.7.2 *First Person Plural.* The Spanish equivalent of the English pronoun *ours* will be **el nuestro, la nuestra, los nuestros,** or **las nuestras,** depending on the number and gender of the referend:

María prefiere tu disco al nuestro.	*Mary prefers your record to ours.*
Comprarán la casa de Juan y la nuestra.	*They'll buy John's house and ours.*
Juan leyó sus libros y los nuestros.	*John read his books and ours.*
¿Son éstas tus rosas o las nuestras?	*Are these your roses or ours?*

PATTERN DRILL. Say each sentence below. Then repeat it, replacing the possessive adjective and noun with the corresponding form of **el nuestro:**

1. Nuestro hijo trabaja mucho.
2. ¿Por qué rompiste nuestra ventana?
3. Te prestaremos nuestras mantas.
4. ¿Te gustan nuestros vasos?
5. ¿Dónde estarán nuestras toallas?
6. ¿Será éste nuestro cuarto?
7. No vendemos nuestra casa.
8. Nuestros hijos son estudiantes.

20.7.3 *Second Person Singular and Plural.* The forms of the possessive pronoun corresponding to **tú** are **el tuyo, la tuya, los tuyos,** and **las tuyas.** The forms corresponding to **vosotros** are **el vuestro, la vuestra, los vuestros,** and **las vuestras:**

Necesito este libro y el tuyo.	*I need this book and yours.*
Comí mis fresas y las tuyas.	*I ate my strawberries and yours.*
Mis padres están buenos. —¿Y los vuestros?	*. . . and yours?*

PATTERN DRILL. Say each sentence below. Then repeat it, replacing the possessive adjective and noun with the corresponding form of el tuyo:

1. No me puse tu sombrero.
2. Te devolvimos tus libros.
3. ¿Nos prestas tus cucharitas?
4. Escucho tus discos ahora.

5. ¿Dónde estará tu coche?
6. ¿Rompió Juan tus ventanas también?
7. Prefiero tu sopa a aquélla.
8. ¿Limpiaste tus zapatos?

20.7.4 *Third Person Singular and Plural.* The Spanish equivalents of the English possessive pronouns *his, hers, yours,* and *theirs* are expressed by el suyo, la suya, los suyos, or las suyas, depending on the number and gender of the referend (not the possessor):

María me dio ese libro y el suyo. *Mary gave me that book and hers.*
Juan halló mi pluma y la suya. *John found my pen and his.*

Ambiguity can be avoided by replacing suyo with de él, de ella, de Vd., etc.:

Necesito mi libro y el de ella. *I need my book and hers.*
El profesor va a escuchar mi cinta y la de Vd. *. . . my tape and yours.*
Invitaré a mis amigas y a las de Vd. *I'll invite my friends and yours.*

PATTERN DRILL. Say each sentence below. Then repeat it, replacing the possessive adjective and noun with the corresponding form of el suyo:

1. Juan busca su pluma.
2. ¿Ha comido Vd. sus fresas?
3. Teresa quiere sus lápices.
4. ¿Escucha Vd. sus discos a menudo?
5. Carlos gastó su dinero ayer.
6. Esos hombres no bebieron su cerveza.
7. ¿Vendieron Vds. su casa?
8. ¿Halló Vd. sus cucharitas?

20.7.5 *Neuter Possessive Pronouns.* Lo mío, lo nuestro, lo tuyo, lo vuestro, and lo suyo are neuter possessive pronouns. They are the equivalents of *what is mine, what is ours, what is yours,* etc.:

Juan quiere lo mío. *John wants what is mine.*
No te daremos lo nuestro. *We shall not give you what is ours.*
¿Quieren tus amigos lo tuyo? *Do your friends want what is yours?*
No necesito lo de él. *I don't need what is his.*

PATTERN DRILL. Answer each of the following questions affirmatively, using **Sí** and a complete sentence:

1. ¿Quiere Vd. lo mío?
2. ¿Deseas lo mío?
3. ¿Quería Vd. lo nuestro?
4. ¿Querías lo de Juan?

5. ¿Desea Juan lo tuyo?
6. ¿Desean ellos lo de Vd.?
7. ¿Quiere María lo de Vds.?
8. ¿Han gastado Vds. lo suyo?

20.8 POSSESSIVE ADJECTIVES

Spanish has two sets of possessive adjectives. Those that precede nouns are usually called the *unstressed* possessive adjectives. **Mi, tu, su,** etc., are used more often than their *stressed* counterparts, which follow nouns. The stressed possessive adjectives are **mío** and **nuestro** to indicate first-person possessors, **tuyo** and **vuestro** to indicate second-person possessors, and **suyo** to indicate third-person possessors. Each of these adjectives is inflected in the usual ways to agree in number and gender with the nouns they follow.

The stressed possessive adjectives are used in only a few contexts:
(a) When speaking directly to a person: **¿Cómo está Vd.?, amigo mío.**
(b) To indicate possession after **ser:**

El libro es mío.	*The book is mine.*
La casa es nuestra.	*The house is ours.*

(c) When the noun is preceded by another adjective: in this position the stressed possessive adjectives are equivalent to the English *of mine, of ours,* etc.:

Juan es un amigo mío.	*John is a friend of mine.*
Son dos amigas nuestras.	*They are two friends of ours.*
¿Dónde está ese coche tuyo?	*Where is that car of yours?*

PATTERN DRILL. Answer each of the following questions affirmatively, using **Sí** and a complete sentence containing the correct stressed possessive adjective:

1. ¿Es tuyo ese coche azul?
2. ¿Son vuestras estas fresas?
3. ¿Es de Vds. aquella casa?
4. ¿Son de Vd. esos paquetes?

5. ¿Viste a ese hermano tuyo?
6. ¿Vendieron Vds. aquella casa suya?
7. ¿Son de Juan esos zapatos?
8. ¿Vinieron muchos amigos tuyos?

Lesson 21

21.1 PERFECT TENSES: SUBJUNCTIVE MOOD

21.1.1 *Present Perfect Subjunctive.* The present perfect subjunctive consists of the present subjunctive of **haber** followed by a past participle. The present subjunctive of **haber** is formed by adding the -er/-ir subjunctive markers to the stem **hay-: haya, hayas,** etc.:

¿Te alegras de que yo haya llegado?	Are you glad that I have arrived?
Juan siente que no le hayamos escrito.	. . . that we haven't written to him.
Espero que Vd. lo haya hecho.	I hope that you have done it.
Es dudoso que ellos lo hayan visto.	It's doubtful that they've seen it.
Saldré antes de que Vds. lo hayan terminado.	. . . before you've finished it.

PATTERN DRILL (A). Say each sentence below. Then repeat it, beginning the sentence with **Juan se alegra de que,** and changing the verb to the present perfect subjunctive:

1. No he descubierto el secreto.
2. Has llegado a tiempo.
3. Hemos esperado hasta ahora.
4. Vds. se han levantado temprano.
5. Vd. le ha escrito.
6. No ha hecho frío este otoño.
7. Los niños han comido.
8. He aprendido estas lecciones.

PATTERN DRILL (B). Repeat each sentence above, beginning it with **Más vale que** (*It is better that*), and changing the verb to the present perfect subjunctive.

21.1.2 *Pluperfect Subjunctive.* The pluperfect subjunctive consists of the imperfect subjunctive of **haber** followed by a past participle. The imperfect subjunctive of **haber** is formed with the irregular stem **hubie-: hubiera– hubiese**, etc.:

¿Te alegrabas de que yo hubiera llegado?	Were you glad that I had arrived?
Juan sentía que no le hubiéramos escrito.	. . . that we hadn't written to him.
Yo esperaba que Vd. lo hubiese hecho.	I was hoping that you had done it.
Era dudoso que ellos lo hubieran visto.	. . . that they had seen it.
Salí antes de que Vds. lo hubiesen terminado.	. . . before you had finished it.

PATTERN DRILL (A). Say each sentence below. Then repeat it, beginning the sentence with **Luis dudaba que**, and changing the verb to the pluperfect subjunctive (use the **-ra** forms):

1. Me había levantado a las cinco.
2. Lo habías devuelto.
3. Le habíamos dicho la verdad.
4. Vds. habían recibido el paquete.
5. Ese niño había roto la ventana.
6. Vd. había hecho un viaje.
7. La criada lo había puesto allí.
8. Yo había sido estudiante en 1931.

PATTERN DRILL (B). Say each sentence below. Then repeat it, beginning the sentence with **No estoy seguro de que**, and changing the verb to the present subjunctive:

1. Hay mucho helado en la nevera.
2. Hay naranjas en agosto.
3. Habrá dos partidos este sábado.
4. Vds. han de hacer eso.
5. El tren ha de salir a la una.
6. Hay mucho de aquí a ese pueblo.
7. No hay clase el viernes.
8. Has de mandárselo a él.

PATTERN DRILL (C). Repeat each sentence above, beginning it with **Era sorprendente que** (*It was surprising that*), and changing the verb to the imperfect subjunctive.

21.2 SEQUENCE OF TENSES

A subjunctive signal in the present, present perfect, or future tenses may be followed by any tense of the subjunctive mood, depending on the time of the subordinate clause. English tenses are a reliable guide as long as you remember that there is no future or future perfect subjunctive in Spanish:

I am glad that you are going.	Me alegro de que vayas.
. . . . will go.	. . . . . . vayas.
. . . . went.	. . . . . . fueras.
. . . . have gone.	. . . . . hayas ido.
. . . . will have gone.	. . . . . hayas ido.
. . . . had gone.	. . . . . hubieras ido.
. . . . would have gone.	. . . . . . hubieras ido.

I've been glad . . . are going.	Me he alegrado de que vayas.
. . . . went.	. . . . fueras.
etc.	etc.

I'll be glad . . . are going.	Me alegraré de que vayas.
. . . . have gone.	. . . . hayas ido.
etc.	etc.

Since direct commands are given with the present tense of the subjunctive, they can be followed by any tense of the subjunctive mood:

Be glad that I'm going.	Alégrese Vd. de que yo vaya.
. . . . . I went.	. . . . yo fuera.
. . . . . I've gone.	. . . . yo haya ido.
etc.	etc.

However, ONLY the imperfect subjunctive or the pluperfect subjunctive may follow a subjunctive signal in the preterite, imperfect, conditional, or pluperfect tenses. In such cases English is not a reliable guide, except that where English uses a simple tense, Spanish uses the imperfect subjunctive, and where English uses a compound tense, Spanish uses the pluperfect subjunctive:

I was glad that you are going.	Me alegraba de que fueras.
. . . . went.	. . . . fueras.
. . . . were going.	. . . . fueras.
. . . . have gone.	. . . . hubieras ido.
. . . . had gone.	. . . . hubieras ido.

Would you be glad that I am going?	¿Te alegrarías de que fuera?
. . . . I've gone?	¿ . . . . hubiera ido?

I had been glad that you are going.	Me había alegrado de que fueras.
. . . . had gone.	. . . . hubieras ido.

Since the polite request **quisiera** (*I should like*) is in the imperfect tense of the subjunctive, it can be followed only by an imperfect or pluperfect subjunctive:

I should like you to go.	Quisiera que fueras.
. . . . . to have gone.	. . . . . hubieras ido.

PATTERN DRILL (A). Say each sentence below. Then repeat it, beginning the sentence with **Juan siente que,** and changing the verb to the corresponding tense of the subjunctive mood:

1. No lo compro.
2. No lo compraré.
3. No lo compré.
4. No lo compraba.

5. No lo he comprado.
6. No lo había comprado.
7. No lo habré comprado.
8. No lo habría comprado.

PATTERN DRILL (B). Repeat each sentence above, beginning it with **Juan temía que,** and changing the verb to the corresponding tense of the subjunctive.

PATTERN DRILL (C). Say each sentence below. Then repeat it, beginning the sentence with **Es posible que,** and changing the verb to the corresponding tense of the subjunctive. **Acordarse (ue)** means *to remember,* and it is connected to a noun, a pronoun, or a verb by **de.**

1. Él se acuerda de María.
2. Ellos se acuerdan de venir.
3. Me acordaré de aquello.
4. No nos hemos acordado de traerlo.

5. Vds. se habían acordado.
6. No vas a acordarte de aquello.
7. No se acordaron de mandármelo.
8. María duda que me acuerde de eso.

21.3 SUBJUNCTIVE SIGNALS

Under certain conditions, **si** (*if*) will be a signal for either the imperfect subjunctive or the pluperfect subjunctive. Comparisons with English will prove useful in understanding this.

In English, when a sentence has two clauses, one beginning with *if* and the other containing *would* or *would have,* the clause that begins with *if* expresses a condition that is contrary to fact or contrary to the speaker's expectations:

> *If I were you* [but I'm not], *I would leave.*
> *If I had lived in 1492* [but I didn't], *I wouldn't have gone with them.*
> *If it were to rain* [which I think unlikely], *I would need my umbrella.*
> *If I earned $25,000* [but I won't], *I would buy a Cadillac.*

It does not matter whether the *if* clause begins the sentence or not; as long as the other clause contains *would* or *would have,* the *if* clause expresses something contrary to fact or to expectation. The *If . . . , would (would have) . . .* construction has no other function:

> *I would leave if I were you* [but I'm not].
> *I wouldn't have gone with them if I had lived in 1492* [but I didn't].

I would need my umbrella if it were to rain [which I think unlikely].

I would buy a Cadillac if I earned $25,000 [but I won't].

When *would* or *would have* is not present in the clause without the *if*—the so-called *result* clause—then *if* does not express anything contrary to fact or to expectation:

I'll see him if he is here. [This sentence makes no implications about his presence.]

If he came, I didn't see him. [This sentence makes no implications; the result clause merely states a fact.]

If it rains, I'll return. [The speaker offers no opinion about the possibility of rain.]

In Spanish, when a clause beginning with **si** introduces a condition that is contrary to fact or to expectation, **si** is followed by a verb in the imperfect subjunctive or in the pluperfect subjunctive, and the result clause contains a verb in the conditional or in the conditional perfect. English is a reliable guide to the choice of tenses. When English uses simple tenses, so does Spanish: the imperfect subjunctive in the **si** clause, and the conditional in the result clause:

If I were you, I would leave.	**Si yo fuera tú, saldría.**
I would leave if I were you.	**Saldría si yo fuera tú.**
If it rained, I would need it.	**Si lloviera, yo lo necesitaría.**
I would need it if it rained.	**Yo lo necesitaría si lloviera.**

When English uses compound tenses, so does Spanish: the pluperfect subjunctive in the **si** clause, and the conditional perfect in the result clause:

If I had been you, I would have left.	**Si yo hubiera sido tú, habría salido.**
I would have left if I had been you.	**Habría salido si yo hubiera sido tú.**
If I were you, I would have left.	**Si yo fuera tú, habría salido.**
I would have left if I were you.	**Habría salido si yo fuera tú.**

The **si** clause may contain either the **-ra** or the **-se** forms of the imperfect or pluperfect subjunctive:

Si yo fuera tú, . . . or **Si yo fuese tú, . . .**

Si yo hubiera sido tú, . . . or **Si yo hubiese sido tú, . . .**

Si is NEVER followed by a present or present perfect subjunctive, no matter what you may have in English. When **si** does not introduce a condition contrary to fact or to expectation, **si** is followed by a verb in the indicative mood:

If he is here, I'll give it to him.	**Si él está aquí, se lo daré.**
If he came, I didn't see him.	**Si él vino, no lo vi.**
If it rains, I'll need it.	**Si llueve, lo necesitaré.**

PATTERN DRILL (A). Say each sentence below. Then repeat it, beginning it with **Si yo fuera tú,** and changing the verb to the conditional tense:

1. Compraré ese coche.   Si yo fuera tú, compraría ese coche.
2. Haré un viaje a México.
3. Mandaré un reloj de plata a mi madre.
4. No venderé la casa.
5. Iré a la América del Sur. (*South America*)
6. Siempre tendré hambre.
7. No trabajaré en aquella tienda.
8. Les regalaré eso. (*to give as a gift*)

PATTERN DRILL (B). Say each sentence above. Then repeat it, beginning it with **Si yo hubiera sido tú,** and changing the verb to the conditional perfect tense.

PATTERN DRILL (C). Say each sentence below. Then repeat it as though it were contrary to fact or to expectation:

1. Si Vd. me dice la verdad, no la creeré.
2. Si él hace eso de nuevo, no le hablaremos. (*again*)
3. Si me acuerdo de eso, lo traeré conmigo.
4. Si ellos estudian mucho, aprenderán la lección.
5. Si Vds. no se acuestan ahora, no se levantarán a tiempo.
6. Si voy contigo, ¿me lo darás?
7. No les hablaré si vienen.
8. Juan no podrá dormir si hace calor.

21.4 RESULT CLAUSES

The result clause of a condition contrary to fact or to expectation may contain, instead of the conditional or the conditional perfect, the -ra form of the imperfect or pluperfect subjunctive:

> **Si yo fuese tú, saldría   or   saliera.**
> **Si yo hubiera sido tú, habría salido   or   hubiera salido.**

This is the one context in which the -ra and -se forms of the imperfect and pluperfect subjunctives are not interchangeable.

PATTERN DRILL (A). Say each sentence below. Then repeat it, beginning it with **Si fuera posible,** and changing the verb to the -ra form of the imperfect subjunctive:

1. Te lo regalo hoy.   3. Juan se levanta temprano.
2. Lo hago de nuevo.   4. Nos desayunamos a las siete y media.

5. Te escribo todos los días.   7. Lo ponemos en la sala.
6. Veo esa película de nuevo.   8. Ellos no duermen en el hotel.

PATTERN DRILL (B). Repeat each sentence above, beginning it with **Si hubiera sido posible,** and changing the verb to the -ra form of the pluperfect subjunctive.

21.5 NEGATIVE WORDS

The commonest way of making a sentence negative in Spanish is by using **no** before the verb: **No estudio,** *I'm not studying.* Negation can also be expressed with **nunca** (*never*), **nadie** (*no one*), **nada** (*nothing*), and **tampoco** (*neither*). Unlike **no,** these negative words can either precede or follow the verbs they negate. When they precede verbs, they replace **no**: **Nunca estudio.** When they follow verbs, **no** or some other negative word must also precede the verb: **No estudio nunca.** In Spanish, unlike English, a double negative does not make a positive:

Nunca estudio.	**No estudio nunca.**	*I never study.*
Nadie vino.	**No vino nadie.**	*No one came.*
Nada me gusta.	**No me gusta nada.**	*Nothing pleases me.*
Tampoco voy.	**No voy tampoco.**	*Neither am I going.*

Nadie and **nada** are pronouns. They can be either the subject of the verbs they negate, as in the examples above, or the objects of the verbs they negate. When **nadie** is the direct object of a verb, it is preceded by **a:**

A nadie veo.	**No veo a nadie.**	*I don't see anyone.*
Nada tengo.	**No tengo nada.**	*I don't have anything.*

In Spanish, again unlike English, whenever any part of a sentence is negative, the whole sentence becomes negative. Thus, the Spanish equivalent of *I never say anything to anyone* is **Nunca digo nada a nadie** (or **No digo nunca nada a nadie**). Because **sin** implies negation, it is followed by a negative word:

Mi tío vino sin nada.	*My uncle came without anything.*
¿Vas allí sin nadie?	*Are you going there without anyone?*

Ninguno and its feminine form **ninguna** are negative pronouns equivalent to the English *none, no one,* and *neither.* They are used only before **de,** or when referring to a previously mentioned group. In such contexts they replace **nadie** and **nada:**

Ninguno de los muchachos viene.	*None of the boys is coming.*
¿Vinieron las mujeres?—Ninguna vino.	*. . . None came.*

Veo a dos hombres, pero no conozco a ninguno.	. . . *I don't know either.*
Me dieron corbatas, pero ninguna me gusta.	. . . *I don't like any [of them].*

The Spanish equivalent of the English adjective *no* is **ningún** before a masculine singular noun, and **ninguna** before a feminine singular noun:

Ningún hombre haría eso.	*No man would do that.*
No vimos a ninguna mujer allí.	*We didn't see any woman there.*

The negative of **o** (*or*) is **ni**. The Spanish equivalent of *neither . . . nor . . .* is **ni . . . ni . . .**, which is usually accompanied by a plural verb:

Ni Juan ni María vinieron.   No vinieron ni Juan ni María.

Your main problem with negation in Spanish will be interference from your English speech patterns. Remember that in a negative context, the Spanish equivalents of *anyone, anything, ever, either,* and *any of* will be, respectively, **nadie, nada, nunca, tampoco,** and **ninguno de.**

I didn't do anything.	*And John?*	*He didn't either.*
No hice nada.	**—¿Y Juan?**	**—Ni él tampoco.**

The non-negative indefinite words will be considered in a subsequent lesson.

PATTERN DRILL (A). Say each sentence below. Then repeat it, beginning the sentence with **No:**

1. Nadie salió.
2. Nunca vamos al campo.
3. Ninguna de ellas haría eso.
4. Nada quiero.
5. Tampoco voy.
6. Si no tengo dinero, nada compro.
7. Ni Carlos ni Pablo sabían eso.
8. Ningún hombre puede hacerlo.

PATTERN DRILL (B). Say each sentence below. Then repeat it as a negative sentence without using **No:**

1. No vino nadie a la reunión.
2. No llegó a tiempo ninguna de ellas.
3. No quiere hacerlo nadie.
4. ¿No tienes nada?
5. Juan no se acordaba nunca de eso.
6. ¿No van Vds. al baile tampoco?
7. No hablo jamás a nadie. (*never*)
8. No vinieron ni María ni Elena.

21.6 BUT

The usual Spanish equivalent of *but* is **pero: Juan está bueno, pero su hermana está enferma.** However, to contradict a PRECEDING NEGATIVE statement, **sino** is used instead of **pero:**

No somos muchachos, sino hombres.   *We're not boys, but men.*
No es española, sino mexicana.   *She's not Spanish, but Mexican.*

Sino and a verb are connected by **que**:

No estudia, sino que duerme.   *He's not studying, but sleeping.*

PATTERN DRILL.   Practice aloud using **sino** to complete each sentence below:

1. No deseo éste, . . . aquél.
2. No llegué ayer, . . . anteayer.
3. No buscamos a Juan, . . . a Carlos.
4. No me levanto, . . . que me acuesto.
5. No serví cerveza, . . . vino.
6. No pedí pan, . . . mantequilla.
7. No me llamó María, . . . su madre.
8. No fuimos a Madrid, . . . a Sevilla

Lesson 22

22.1 INDEFINITE WORDS

Algo, alguien, and **alguna vez** are used only in non-negative contexts. Their respective English equivalents are *something/anything, someone/anyone,* and *sometime/ever*:

Voy a mandarles algo.	*I'm going to send them something.*
¿Necesita Vd. algo?	*Do you need anything?*
Alguien te llamó.	*Someone called you.*
¿Ha venido alguien?	*Has anyone come?*
¿Has estado allí alguna vez?	*Have you ever been there?*

Alguien is preceded by **a** when it is the direct object of a verb:

Vi a alguien en el jardín.	*I saw someone in the garden.*
¿Esperan Vds. a alguien?	*Are you waiting for anyone?*

Jamás is used in a question when a negative reply is expected:

¿Has estado allí jamás?	*Have you ever been there?*

Alguno is an indefinite pronoun that is inflected to indicate gender and number. The forms of **alguno** are used only before **de** or when referring to a group previously mentioned. The English equivalents of **alguno** are *someone/anyone* and *something/anything*:

Alguno de ellos me lo dio.	*[Some] One of them gave it to me.*
¿Conoces a alguna de mis primas?	*. . . any [one] of my cousins?*
¿Vendiste tus libros? —Algunos.	*. . . Some of them.*
¿Te gustan mis corbatas? —Algunas.	*. . . Some of them.*

Alguno is also used as an adjective. It becomes **algún** before a masculine singular noun. **Algún** and **alguna** are equivalent to *some/any*, whereas **algunos** and **algunas** are equivalent to *several*:

Algún día haremos un viaje.	*Some day we'll take a trip.*
¿Recibiste alguna noticia?	*Did you receive any news?*

Gasté algunos dólares.	*I spent several dollars.*
¿Leíste algunas páginas?	*Did you read several pages?*

Algún and.**algunos** are used less frequently than *some/any* in English. The usual Spanish way of implying an indeterminate quantity is by omission of the definite article (see 5.2.3):

Compré carne.	*I bought some meat.*
¿Quieres manzanas?	*Do you want any apples?*

Alguno and **alguna** are also found in negative sentences after singular nouns, and in this context they are more emphatic than **ninguno:**

No gasté dinero alguno.   *I didn't spend any money at all.*

Cualquiera is a pronoun that is equivalent to the English *anyone at all:*

Cualquiera sabe hacer eso.   *Anyone at all knows how to do that.*

Cualquiera is also used as an adjective. Before a noun **cualquiera** and its uncommon plural form **cualesquiera** lose their final /-a/. They are the equivalent of the English *any . . . whatsoever:*

Venga Vd. cualquier tarde.   *Come any afternoon.*

PATTERN DRILL (A).   Say each sentence below. Then repeat it as an affirmative sentence, replacing the negative words with their non-negative counterparts:

1. Nadie nos llamó hoy.
2. Ninguna de ellas me quiere.
3. Nunca les hablo.
4. No compré·nada en aquella tienda.

5. ¿Nunca les dijiste nada?
6. No vimos a nadie.
7. ¿Nunca has leído eso?
8. Nadie descubrió nuestro secreto.

PATTERN DRILL (B).   Answer each of the following questions negatively, using **No** and a complete negative sentence:

1. ¿Llamó alguien?
2. ¿Compraste algo ayer?
3. ¿Viste a alguien?
4. ¿Vino alguno de tus primos?

5. ¿Has ido al Japón alguna vez?
6. ¿Dijiste algo a alguien?
7. ¿Jamás ves a Juan?
8. ¿Conoces a alguna de ellas?

22.2 PASSIVE SENTENCES

A verb is said to be in the so-called *passive voice* when its subject does not act upon something, but rather is acted upon. For example, *The window was opened by John* is passive, whereas *John opened the window* is active. The person or thing performing the action is known as the *agent*. In

English the passive is always expressed with *to be* followed by a past participle. In Spanish, on the other hand, there are three formulae.

22.2.1 Agent Expressed. When the agent of a passive action is expressed, as in *The window was opened by John*, the Spanish passive construction parallels the English one. The subject of the sentence, if expressed, is followed by the appropriate person, tense, and mood of **ser** and by a past participle inflected to agree in number and gender with the subject. The agent of a physical action is preceded by **por: La ventana fue abierta por Juan.** Similarly:

El postre será servido por la criada.	*The dessert will be served by the maid.*
Los paquetes son envueltos por ella.	*The packages are wrapped by her.*
¿Fueron rotas las tazas por María?	*Were the cups broken by Mary?*
Dudo que esas novelas fueran escritas por él.	*I doubt that those novels were written by him.*

When the passive action is mental rather than physical, **de** precedes the agent:

María es amada de sus primos.	*Mary is loved by her cousins.*
El rey fue temido de sus enemigos.	*The king was feared by his enemies.*

PATTERN DRILL (A). Complete each sentence below with the preterite of **ser**:

1. Las plumas . . . compradas por María.
2. Yo no . . . llamado por ellos.
3. Ese vino . . . bebido por Juan.
4. Los libros . . . escritos por él.
5. El hombre . . . hallado por su enemigo.
6. La lección . . . empezada por mí.
7. Ese platillo . . . roto por mi hijo.
8. Las muchachas . . . vistas por Carlos.

PATTERN DRILL (B). Complete each sentence below with the proper form of the past participle of the infinitive in parentheses:

1. Somos (*amar*) de María.
2. La puerta será (*cerrar*) por Juan.
3. Dudo que Vds. sean (*invitar*) por ella.
4. Las cartas fueron (*escribir*) por mí.
5. El tesoro no fue (*hallar*) por nadie.
6. La cocina será (*pintar*) por mi padre.

7. Las fresas serán (*comer*) por esos niños.

8. Aquellos libros fueron (*vender*) por Carlos.

PATTERN DRILL (c). Say each sentence below. Then repeat it as a passive sentence, making the subject of the original sentence the agent of the passive sentence:

1. Mi padre compró ese coche.

2. Juan escribe muchas cartas.

3. Ese muchacho rompió la ventana.

4. El niño bebió la leche.

5. Compraremos aquella casa.

6. Ellos descubrieron la verdad.

7. ¿Trajo María las aceitunas?

8. Carlos no ama a María.

22.2.2 Passives Without Agents. Your only real difficulty with the passive will arise when the agent of a passive sentence is not expressed. The reason is that in this circumstance Spanish makes a distinction between a so-called *passive of state* and a *passive of action*. The former expresses a state or condition resulting from a prior action, whereas the latter expresses the action itself as taking place. Although English usually does not make this distinction, there is at least one perfect example:

The window was open. (state)   *The window was opened.* (action)

22.2.3 State. To indicate a passive state, Spanish uses **estar** followed by a past participle inflected to agree in number and gender with the subject. Thus, the past participle functions as an adjective:

La ventana estaba abierta.   *The window was open.*

Las ventanas estaban abiertas.   *The windows were open.*

El vaso está roto.   *The glass is broken* [in a broken state].

Al fin la carta está escrita.   _ . . . . is written [that is, finished].

PATTERN DRILL. Complete each sentence below with the proper form of the past participle of the infinitive in parentheses:

1. La tienda está (*cerrar*) ahora.

2. El oro está (*esconder*) en la casa.

3. ¿Están (*escribir*) tus cartas?

4. Dudo que las ventanas estén (*abrir*).

5. La puerta estaba (*cerrar*) cuando llegué.

6. Las ventanas estaban (*romper*) cuando volvimos.

7. Nuestra cocina está (*pintar*).

8. La mesa está (*poner*) ahora. (*to set*)

22.2.4 Action. There are two ways of indicating a passive action without any agent. When the subject of the verb is a *thing*, Spanish uses **se** followed by a third-person singular or plural verb (depending on the subject) followed by the subject:

Se abrió la ventana.	*The window was opened.*
Se abrieron las ventanas.	*The windows were opened.*
Se venden libros aquí.	*Books are sold here.*
Se cierra la tienda a las 5.	*. . . is closed (closes). . . .*
Se abre la biblioteca a las 9.	*The library opens at 9.*

PATTERN DRILL (A). Use **se vende** or **se venden,** as required, to form a sentence with each of the items below. Can you deduce the meanings of the two new nouns:

1. pan en una panadería
2. libros en una librería
3. drogas en una farmacia
4. carne en una carnicería

5. pescado en una pescadería
6. camisas caras en esa tienda
7. zapatos en una zapatería
8. leche en una lechería

PATTERN DRILL (B). Complete each sentence below with the proper form of the present tense of the infinitive in parentheses:

1. Se (*abrir*) la biblioteca a las 9.
2. Se (*cerrar*) esas tiendas tarde.
3. Aquí se (*hablar*) español.
4. No se (*usar*) monedas de oro. (*coins*)

5. ¿Cuándo se (*abrir*) los cines?
6. ¿Se (*necesitar*) naranjas hoy?
7. Se (*vender*) revistas aquí.
8. Se (*perder*) pocas cartas.

22.2.5 **Action.** When the subject of a passive sentence is a *person*, then **se** is followed by a third-person singular verb, and the person acted upon is expressed as the object of that *impersonal* verb. This **se** is equivalent to the English impersonal *one*:

Se llama a Juan.	*John is called.*
Se llamó a esos hombres.	*Those men were called.*
Se halló a la niña.	*The little girl was found.*
Se teme al rey.	*The king is feared* or *One fears the king.*
¿Por qué se me necesita?	*Why am I needed?*
Se nos despertó a las 6.	*We were awakened at 6.*
Dudo que se la quiera.	*I doubt that she is loved.*

In this construction, the masculine direct object pronouns **lo** and **los** are replaced by **le** and **les:**

Se le busca.	*He is sought.*
¿Se les halló?	*Were they found?*

PATTERN DRILL. Complete each sentence below with the third person singular of the present tense of the infinitive in parentheses:

1. Se (*necesitar*) a Juan aquí.
2. Se (*querer*) a la reina. (*queen*)
3. No se (*temer*) a esos muchachos.
4. Se nos (*despertar*) temprano.
5. ¿Por qué no se (*buscar*) a Carlos?
6. Se le (*llamar*) ahora.
7. No se (*necesitar*) a Vd. hoy.
8. ¿Se les (*odiar*) mucho? (*to hate*)

22.2.6 *Action.* When a person is acted upon, an alternate construction involves the use of a third-person plural verb whose object is the person acted upon. This is the equivalent of the English impersonal *they*:

Llaman a Juan.	*John is called* or *They are calling John.*
Lo hallaron.	*He was found* or *They found him.*
Temen al rey.	*The king is feared* or *They fear the king.*
Me despertaron.	*I was awakened* or *They woke me up.*
¿Nos necesitan?	*Are we needed?* or *Do they need us?*
Me dijeron que . . .	*I was told that* or *They told me that. . . .*

PATTERN DRILL (A). Say each sentence below. Then repeat it, replacing the **se** construction with a third-person plural verb:

1. Se buscaba a Carlos.
2. Dudo que se odie a esa mujer.
3. Se halló al ladrón. (*thief*)
4. ¿Por qué se nos busca?
5. Se bañó al niño.
6. Se le despertó a las cinco.
7. Se ha hallado a esos ladrones.
8. ¿Se me llama de nuevo?

PATTERN DRILL (B). Say each sentence below. Then repeat it, replacing the third-person plural verb with the **se** construction:

1. ¿Temen a Juan?
2. Buscaban a las muchachas.
3. ¿Por qué nos necesitan?
4. No las hallaron.
5. Descubrieron a esos hombres.
6. Siento que no la quieran.
7. Me dijeron que María no vendría.
8. No nos despertaron a tiempo.

22.2.7 *Summary.* Although the passive may seem quite complicated, it can be reduced to three simple questions and three "rules of thumb":

(1) *Is the agent expressed?* If the answer is affirmative, use **ser** followed by an inflected past participle and either **por** or **de**: **La ventana fue rota por Juan.** If the answer is negative, ask the second question:

(2) *Does the sentence indicate a passive state or a passive action?* If it is a state, use **estar** and an inflected past participle: **La ventana está rota.** If it is an action, ask the third question:

(3) *Is the subject a thing or a person?* If it is a thing, use **se** followed by a third-person verb that is either singular or plural, depending on the subject:

Se abre la ventana–Se abren las ventanas. If a person is acted upon, use **se** and a third-person singular verb, or else a third-person plural verb without **se.** In either case, the person acted upon is the object of the verb: **Se quiere a Juan–Quieren a Juan.**

22.3 ORDINAL NUMBERS

The Spanish ordinals from *first* through *tenth* are:

primero	cuarto	séptimo	décimo
segundo	quinto	octavo	
tercero	sexto	noveno (or nono)	

The ordinal numbers are inflected, as all adjectives ending in **-o,** to indicate the gender and number of the nouns that they accompany. The ordinals usually precede nouns (as in English):

Los primeros hombres vivieron en cuevas.   *The first men lived in caves.*

No asistí a la primera reunión.   *I didn't attend the first meeting.*

Abra Vd. la tercera ventana.   *Open the third window.*

Perdimos el décimo partido.   *We lost the tenth game.*

Before a masculine singular noun **primero** and **tercero** become **primer** and **tercer:**

¿Quién fue el primer rey de España?   *Who was the first king of Spain?*

El tercer hombre lo hizo.   *The third man did it.*

Like their English counterparts, the Spanish ordinal numbers regularly follow the names of rulers. However, no definite article intervenes in Spanish:

¿Cuántas esposas tuvo Enrique Octavo?   *. . . Henry the Eighth . . . ?*

Isabel Segunda vino al Canadá en 1959.   *Elizabeth the Second . . .*

The Spanish ordinals usually follow the chapters and lessons of a book:

Leí el capítulo tercero.   *I read the third chapter.*

La lección séptima es difícil.   *The seventh lesson is hard.*

In this context, the ordinals can be replaced by the cardinals:

Lean Vds. el capítulo tres.   *Read the third chapter.*

La lección seis es fácil.   *The sixth lesson is easy.*

When both an ordinal and a cardinal number refer to the same noun, as in *I studied the first two lessons,* Spanish word order is the reverse of English: the Spanish cardinal number precedes the Spanish ordinal:

Estudié las dos primeras lecciones.   *. . . the first two lessons.*

The Spanish ordinals, unlike their English counterparts, are not used to express the days of the month, except for **primero**:

Llegué el primero de enero.	*I arrived on January first.*
Volveré el tres de marzo.	*I'll return on the third of March.*

Note that in this context, there is no Spanish equivalent of the English *on*, and that **el** always precedes the number of a day. A day, a month, and a year are connected by **de**:

Vinimos el primero de enero de 1962.   *We came on January 1, 1962.*

Above **décimo**, the ordinal numbers are regularly replaced by the cardinal numbers, which then follow nouns:

Leí el capítulo diecinueve.	*I read the nineteenth chapter.*
¿Cuándo murió Luis Dieciséis?	*When did Louis the Sixteenth die?*
Vivo en la calle cincuenta y dos.	*I live on Fifty-second Street.*

PATTERN DRILL (A).   Read aloud each of the following sentences:

1. Llegaremos el 1 de marzo.
2. Carlos I fue el padre de Felipe II.
3. El capítulo IV es interesante.
4. ¿Quién fue Napoleón III?
5. ¿Leíste la lección VIII?
6. ¿Cuándo murió Luis XV?
7. El año empieza el 1 de enero.
8. ¿Cuándo murió Alfonso X?

PATTERN DRILL (B).   Complete each sentence below with the ordinal number required by context:

1. Enero es el . . . mes del año.
2. Marzo es el . . . mes del año.
3. El hijo de Felipe IV fue Felipe . . .
4. El sábado es el . . . día de la semana.
5. Octobre es el . . . mes.
6. El padre de Isabel II fue Jorge . . .
7. El . . . mes es febrero.
8. Julio es el . . . mes del año.

22.4 CHOICE

Before a noun, Spanish uses **¿qué?** to ask for a choice:

¿Qué libro prefiere Vd.?	*Which book do you prefer?*
¿Qué corbatas compraste?	*Which ties did you buy?*

Before **de** and **ser**, Spanish uses **¿cuál?** and its plural form **¿cuáles?** to ask for a choice:

¿Cuál de los libros prefiere Vd.?   *Which of the books do you*
                                          prefer?
¿Cuáles son las corbatas que compraste? *Which are the ties you bought?*

Before **ser**, **¿qué?** asks for a definition or an explanation, rather than choice:

      ¿Qué es esto?   *What is this?*
      ¿Qué es ese paquete?   *What is that package?*

PATTERN DRILL. Say each sentence below. Then turn it into a question, using **¿qué?** or **¿cuál?** as required by context:

1. Ese muchacho lo rompió.   ¿Qué muchacho lo rompió?
2. Una de las muchachas llamó. ¿Cuál de las muchachas llamó?
3. Aquel libro es mi diccionario.
4. Ésos son los hombres que vinieron.
5. Lees aquellas revistas.
6. Esa ciudad es la capital.
7. Esta ventana fue rota por Juan.
8. Dos de las ventanas están abiertas.

22.5 COGNATES

Spanish adjectives ending in **-oso** and English adjectives ending in -ous are often cognates:

      famoso–*famous*   **curioso**–*curious*

Spanish adjectives ending in **-az** and English adjectives ending in -acious are often cognates:

      sagaz–*sagacious*   **voraz**–*voracious*

PATTERN DRILL. Pronounce carefully each Spanish word below, and then give its English cognate:

1. luminoso	5. furioso	9. audaz
2. numeroso	6. religioso	10. locuaz
3. generoso	7. ambicioso	11. pugnaz
4. poroso	8. contencioso	12. perspicaz

Lesson 23

23.1 IMPERATIVE MOOD

In addition to the indicative and the subjunctive, there is a third Spanish mood called the *imperative*. It is used only to express affirmative commands in the second person. The singular imperative of most Spanish verbs is identical in form to the third person singular of the present indicative. The plural imperative of all verbs is indicated by replacing the final -r of the infinitive by -d. The pronouns **tú** and **vosotros** are usually omitted:

Study.	Estudia.	Estudiad.
Eat.	Come.	Comed.
Sleep.	Duerme.	Dormid.

Only eight verbs have singular imperative forms that are irregular:

Salir	Sal.	Leave.	Hacer	Haz.	Do.
Tener	Ten.	Have.	Decir	Di.	Tell.
Poner	Pon.	Put.	Ser	Sé.	Be.
Venir	Ven.	Come.	Ir	Ve.	Go.

Object pronouns follow the imperative in the usual order: reflexive before indirect before direct. In writing, object pronouns are attached to the imperatives that they follow, and an accent mark is sometimes necessary to show that the original stress of the imperative is maintained, despite the addition of one or more syllables:

Study it.	Estúdialo.	Estudiadlo.
Close it.	Ciérralo.	Cerradlo
Do it.	Hazlo.	Hacedlo.
Tell it to me.	Dímelo.	Decídmelo.

The final /-d/ of the plural imperative is suppressed before the reflexive pronoun **os: Levantaos**, *Get up;* **Poneos los guantes**, *Put on your gloves.* No diphthong is created when the final /-d/ is suppressed after /-i-/, and this is shown in writing by placing an accent mark over the -i-: **Vestíos**, *Get dressed*. There is one exception to all of the foregoing: **irse**, *to go away*. Its plural imperative is "regular": **Idos**.

PATTERN DRILL. Say each sentence below. Then repeat it as an affirmative command:

1. Estudias mucho.
2. Sales a la una y media.
3. Te levantas temprano.
4. Me lo dices.
5. Vienes en seguida.
6. Tienes cuidado. (*to be careful*)
7. Lo haces ahora mismo.
8. Vas de compras mañana.

23.1.1 Negative Second–Person Commands. Negative commands are given to people addressed as **tú** and **vosotros** with the second person singular and plural, respectively, of the present subjunctive. All object pronouns always precede negative commands:

Estudia.	Estudiad.	but	No estudies.	No estudiéis.
Sal.	Salid.	but	No salgas.	No salgáis.
Hazlo.	Hacedlo.	but	No lo hagas.	No lo hagáis.
Dímelo.	Decídmelo.	but	No me lo digas.	No me lo digáis.
Vete.	Idos.	but	No te vayas.	No os vayáis.

PATTERN DRILL (A). Say each command below. Then repeat it as a negative command:

1. Compra ese coche.
2. Come ahora.
3. Sal a las once.
4. Véndelo.
5. Dímelo.
6. Siéntate aquí.
7. Ve con ellos.
8. Póntelo.

PATTERN DRILL (B). Say each command below. Then repeat it, using the intimate you:

1. Váyase Vd. en seguida.
2. No se lo diga Vd. a Juan.
3. Alégrese Vd. de aquello.
4. Póngaselo Vd. ahora.
5. No se quite Vd. la chaqueta.
6. Venga Vd. a las tres.
7. Tenga Vd. cuidado.
8. Levántense Vds. temprano.

23.2 «PARA» AND «POR»

The two Spanish prepositions **para** and **por** can confuse English speakers because in certain contexts both are equivalent to the English preposition *for*. However, they are not interchangeable. Each has certain functions, and each also has various English equivalents.

23.2.1 *Para.* The function of **para** is to indicate:

(a) purpose, use, and destination:

Comemos para vivir.	We eat in order to live.
Compré dos sillas para la sala.	. . . two chairs for the living room.
Necesito una taza para café.	I need a coffee cup.
Salgo para Europa.	I'm leaving for Europe.
Estas cartas son para Vd.	These letters are for you.

(b) a point or limit of future time:

Hazlo para mañana.	Do it for (by) tomorrow.
Lo tendré para el viernes.	I'll have it by (for) Friday.

(c) a comparison in which something is different from what is expected:

Para diciembre hace calor.	For December it's warm.
Juan habla bien para un niño.	John speaks well for a child.

(d) a personal point of view:

Para mí, esto es ridículo.	As far as I'm concerned, this is ridiculous.
Eso no es importante para él.	That's not important for him.

(e) an employer after **trabajar**:

Yo trabajaba para el gobierno.	I used to work for the government.

(f) **Estar para** followed by an infinitive indicates that something is about to happen:

Estoy para salir.	I'm about to leave.
Cuando llamó, estaba para acostarme.	. . . I was about to go to bed.

PATTERN DRILL (A). Practice aloud using **para** to complete each sentence below:

1. ¿Hay algo . . . mí hoy?
2. Eso no es difícil . . . nosotros.
3. No trabajo . . . esa compañía.
4. Buscamos dos botellas . . . vino.
5. Te lo mandaré . . . febrero.
6. Hace mucho frío . . . julio.
7. ¿Cuándo sales . . . el Perú?
8. Llegué cuando estaban . . . comer.

PATTERN DRILL (B). Answer each of the following questions affirmatively, using **Sí** and a complete sentence:

1. ¿Llegarás para el primero del mes?
2. ¿Trabajas para ese hombre?
3. ¿Asistes a la escuela para aprender?
4. ¿Compraste papel para escribir?
5. ¿Es para mí este regalo?
6. ¿Llamaste para decirme eso?
7. ¿Lo harás para el domingo?
8. ¿Tienes algo para mí?

23.2.2   Por.   The function of **por** is to indicate:

(a) cause, reason, motive:

No vinieron por miedo.	They didn't come because of fear.
Por eso no lo vimos.	For that reason (That's why) we didn't see him.
María lo dijo por vanidad.	Mary said it out of (on account of) vanity.
Él luchará por la vida.	He'll fight for his life.
No hice eso por ti.	I didn't do that for your sake.
¿Lo harás por mí?	Will you do it for me? (on my behalf?)
¿Compraste naranjas por toronjas?	. . . for (instead of) . . . ?

(b) the manner or means by which something is done:

Vendremos por vapor.	We'll come by steamship.
Se lo quité por fuerza.	I took it away from him by force.
Lo supe por ellos.	I learned it through them.

(c) the agent of a passive sentence, if the action is physical:

La ventana fue rota por Juan.	The window was broken by John.

(d) the time during which something exists or happens:

Estaré allí por tres días.	I'll be there for three days.
Vivieron aquí por veinte años.	They lived here for 20 years.

(e) the place through which or along which something moves:

El ladrón salió por la ventana.	The thief left through the window.
Íbamos por la calle.	We were going along the street.

(f) vague time or place:

Vendré por enero.	I'll come around January.
Estará por aquí.	It's probably around here.

(g) exchange, price:

Te daré éste por aquél.	I'll give you this one for that one.
Lo compré por un dólar.	I bought it for a dollar.

(h) measurement or rate:

Ese hombre trabaja por hora.	That man works by the hour.
Ganaron veinte pesos por semana.	They earned 20 pesos per week.

(i) the object of an errand after **ir, venir,** and **mandar:**

Ayer fui por pan.	Yesterday I went for bread.
Me mandaron por cerveza.	They sent me for beer.

(j) one's opinion of someone or something:

Te odio por hipócrita.	I hate you as a hypocrite.

(Note that in this context, no indefinite article follows **por.**)

(k) to swear oaths:

¡Por mi vida!	On my life!

(l) **Estar por** followed by an infinitive. When the subject is a person, **estar por** expresses inclination:

Estamos por hacer eso.	We're in favor of doing that.

When the subject is a thing, **estar por** indicates what remains to be done:

Esa carta está por escribir.	That letter is still to be written.

PATTERN DRILL (A). Practice aloud using **por** to complete each sentence below:

1. ¿Saliste . . . la ventana?
2. La criada ha ido . . . leche.
3. Estuve enfermo . . . dos semanas.
4. Lucharon . . . la nación.
5. Nos mandaron . . . el médico.
6. Te lo venderé . . . diez dólares.
7. Dudo que él lo haga . . . Vd.
8. No lo hagas . . . fuerza.

PATTERN DRILL (B). Answer each of the following questions affirmatively, using **Sí** and a complete sentence:

1. ¿Saliste temprano por miedo?
2. ¿Has venido por tu sombrero?
3. ¿Estás por ir a la playa hoy?
4. ¿Me lo venderás por poco dinero?
5. ¿Llegaste por la primavera? (*spring*)
6. ¿Vas a hacerlo por mí?
7. ¿Ganas mucho por hora?
8. ¿Es posible que lo supieras por él?

23.2.3 Summary. As a "rule of thumb," recall that **para** generally indicates *purpose*, whereas *por* generally indicates *cause*. **Para** looks *forward* to the end result, whereas **por** looks *backward* to the reason. The difference between these two Spanish prepositions can be illustrated by two ways of asking *Why are you studying?* **¿Para qué estudias?** asks the purpose, and **¿Por qué estudias?** asks the reason. An answer to the former would be along the lines of **Para ser hombre educado;** an answer to the latter would be something like **Porque me gusta.**

PATTERN DRILL. Complete each of the following sentences aloud with **para** or **por**, as required by context:

1. Tengo un regalo . . . el niño.
2. Lo haré . . . este lunes.
3. No te esperaré . . . tres horas.
4. Hace fresco . . . agosto.
5. La pluma fue rota . . . Juan.
6. Quisiera que fueras . . . leche.
7. No vivimos . . . comer.
8. Lo perdimos . . . aquí.

23.3 SUBJUNCTIVE SIGNALS

Decir and **escribir** are followed by the subjunctive when they transmit commands or requests rather than information:

Te digo que lo hagas.	*I'm telling you to do it.* (command)
Te digo que no lo hiciste bien.	*I'm telling you that you didn't do it well.* (information)
Me escribieron que no viniera.	*They wrote me not to come.* (command)
Me escribieron que no vendrían	*They wrote me that they wouldn't come.* (information)

Ojalá is an expression of emotion equivalent to the English *I wish, I hope,* or *Would that.* It is always the first word in a sentence, and it is sometimes followed by **que. Ojalá** is followed by the present subjunctive if the wish can be fulfilled:

¡Ojalá lleguen pronto!   *I hope they arrive soon!*

If the wish cannot be fulfilled, **ojalá** is followed by the imperfect subjunctive to refer to present time, and by the pluperfect subjunctive to refer to past time:

¡Ojalá que lo tuviera ahora!	*I wish I had it now!*
¡Ojalá que lo hubiéramos hecho!	*Would that we had done it!*

Tal vez, acaso, and **quizás** (or **quizá**) are all equivalents of the English *perhaps.* They are followed by the subjunctive when there is considerable uncertainty in the mind of the speaker:

Tal vez tengas razón.	*Perhaps you are right.*
Acaso Juan haya venido.	*Perhaps John has come.*

PATTERN DRILL. Complete each sentence below with the required form of the present subjunctive of the infinitive in parentheses:

1. ¡Ojalá no (*llover*) hoy!
2. Quizás me (*levantar*) a las seis.
3. ¿Me dices que yo (*hacer*) eso?

4. Tal vez María te lo (*mandar*) mañana.
5. ¿Por qué nos dices que no (*salir*)?
6. Mi padre me escribe que (*estudiar*).
7. ¿Te atreves a decirme que me (*ir*)?
8. ¡Ojalá que no lo (*saber*) mis padres!

23.4 ADVERBS

An *adverb* is a word that provides information about a verb, an adjective, or another adverb. In the sentence *John spoke rapidly*, the adverb *rapidly* provides information about a verb. In *He is very poor*, the adverb *very* provides information about an adjective, whereas in *John spoke very rapidly*, the adverb *very* modifies another adverb.

Just as English contains many adverbs formed by the addition of -ly to adjectives (*rapid–rapidly*), so Spanish contains many adverbs derived from adjectives by the addition of -**mente**. If the adjective is one that shows feminine gender, –**mente** is attached to the feminine singular form. If not, it is attached to the masculine singular form of the adjective. Adverbs formed in this way have two stresses: the original stress of the adjective and also the stress of -**mente**:

rápido	– **rápidamente**	**feliz**	– **felizmente** (*happily*)
completo	– **completamente**	**fácil**	– **fácilmente** (*easily*)
lento	– **lentamente** (*slowly*)	**reciente**	– **recientemente** (*recently*)

When two or more adverbs normally ending in -**mente** follow each other, the -**mente** is dropped from all but the final adverb:

   Lo hice lenta y silenciosamente.   *I did it slowly and silently.*

Although -**mente** is an unmistakable sign of an adverb, not all words that can be used adverbially have this termination. For example:

así	*thus*	**otra vez**	*again*
casi	*almost*	**rara vez**	*seldom*
algo	*somewhat*	**a veces**	*sometimes*
nada	*not at all*	**muchas veces**	*often*
despacio	*slowly*	**varias veces**	*several times*

In a sentence, an adverb usually precedes an adjective, and follows a verb:

Juan es algo viejo.	**Carlos sale muchas veces.**
Gasté casi dos dólares.	**María hablaba despacio.**

However, this word order is not invariable, especially when placing an adverb immediately after a verb would separate the verb from a noun object. In such cases the adverb can precede the verb, or else follow the object: **Rara vez veo a Juan** or **Veo a Juan rara vez** rather than **Veo rara vez a Juan.**

PATTERN DRILL. Answer each of the following questions affirmatively, using **Sí** and a complete sentence:

1. ¿Está muy enfermo Juan?
2. ¿Es algo vieja esta casa?
3. ¿Esperas a Teresa a veces?
4. ¿Van Vds. al cine muchas veces?
5. ¿Vas al campo rara vez?
6. ¿Está casi cerrada la puerta?
7. ¿Hablan muy despacio esos niños?
8. ¿Van Vds. al campo conmigo otra vez?

23.5 COMPARISONS OF EQUALITY

The Spanish equivalent of the English formula for comparison "as + adjective/adverb + as" is "**tan** + adjective/adverb + **como**":

María es tan alta como Juan.	Mary is as tall as John.
Este libro es tan viejo como aquél.	This book is as old as that one.
Estas uvas son tan caras como las cerezas.	. . . as expensive as. . . .
Vd. habla tan rápidamente como yo.	You speak as rapidly as I [do].

The Spanish equivalent of "as much + singular noun + as" is "**tanto (tanta)** + singular noun + **como**":

Comí tanto helado como Vd.	I ate as much ice cream as you [did].
¿Bebes tanta leche como Juan?	Do you drink as much milk as John?

The Spanish equivalent of "as many + plural noun + as" is "**tantos (tantas)** + plural noun + **como**":

Tengo tantos amigos como él.	I have as many friends as he [does].
¿Comiste tantas uvas como yo?	Did you eat as many grapes as I [did]?

The Spanish equivalent of "verb + as much/hard as" is "verb + **tanto como**":

Juan estudia tanto como Carlos.	John studies as much as Charles.
Trabajaré tanto como Vd.	I'll work as hard as you [will].

PATTERN DRILL. Answer each of the following questions aloud with a comparison of equality:

1. María estaba cansada. —¿Y Elena?   Elena estaba tan cansada como María.
2. Juan es alto. —¿Y Carlos?
3. Carlos comió mucho pescado. —¿Y Felipe?
4. Isabel compró muchos libros. —¿Y Elena?
5. Pablo se vistió rápidamente. —¿Y Pedro?
6. Él bebió mucha cerveza.—¿Y Vds.?
7. Carlos nos visitaba. —¿Y Elena?
8. Luis estudia mucho. —¿Y Vd.?

Lesson 24

24.1 UNEQUAL COMPARISON

Adjectives and adverbs have three so-called *degrees* of comparison. The original value of an adjective or an adverb is referred to as the *positive: tall– slowly*. A higher or lower degree of the value is referred to as the *comparative: taller, less tall–more slowly, less slowly*. The highest or lowest degree of the value is referred to as the *superlative: tallest, least tall–most slowly, least slowly*.

24.1.1 *Regular Comparatives*. The comparative degree of most Spanish adjectives and adverbs is indicated by using **más** (*more*) or **menos** (*less*) immediately before the positive form of the adjective or adverb:

alto	*tall*	**lentamente**	*slowly*
más alto	*taller*	**más lentamente**	*more slowly*
menos alto	*less tall*	**menos lentamente**	*less slowly*

María es alta, pero Juan es más alto. Mary is tall, but John is taller.

Leo lentamente; Vd. lee menos lentamente. I read slowly; you read less slowly.

The Spanish equivalent of *than* is **que** in sentences having only one verb:

Juan es más alto que María. *John is taller than Mary.*

Vd. lee menos lentamente que yo. *You read less slowly than I* [do].

PATTERN DRILL. Say each sentence below. Then repeat it, endowing the first person (or thing) with more of the adjective or adverb than the second person (or thing) mentioned:

1. Carlos y María son inteligentes. Carlos es más inteligente que María.
2. Elena y Enrique son bajos. (*short*)
3. Mis padres y mis abuelos son altos.

4. Juan y Pedro corren rápidamente. (*to run*, -er)
5. Mi abuela y mi madre están enfermas.
6. Este libro y aquél son difíciles.
7. Carlos y Roberto son fuertes. (*strong*)
8. Estas corbatas y aquéllas son caras.

24.1.2 Irregular Comparatives. The comparative degree of four adjectives is indicated regularly and also irregularly.

bueno	good	más bueno; mejor	better
malo	bad	más malo; peor	worse
grande	large	más grande; mayor	larger; older
pequeño	small	más pequeño; menor	smaller; younger

Más bueno and **más malo** are used only in reference to personality traits, whereas **mejor** and **peor** are used in reference to everything else:

Juan es más bueno que Pedro.	*John is better than Peter.*
Este hotel es bueno; aquél es mejor.	*This hotel is good; that one is better.*

Más grande and **más pequeño** refer to physical dimensions, whereas **mayor** and **menor** are used in reference to age:

Jorge es más grande, pero no es mayor.	*George is larger, but he isn't older.*
¿Conoces a mi hermano menor?	*Do you know my younger brother?*

The comparative degree of **mucho** and **poco**, which are used as adjectives and as adverbs, is indicated irregularly:

mucho	a lot	más	more
poco	a little	menos	less

Vds. comen más (menos) queso que yo.	*You eat more (less) cheese than I [do].*
Juan tiene más (menos) libros que tú.	*John has more (fewer) books than you.*
Estudiabas más (menos) que nosotros.	*You used to study more (less) than we.*

The comparative degree of two other adverbs is also indicated irregularly:

bien	well	mejor	better
mal	badly	peor	worse

Vds. hablan mejor (peor) que yo.	*You speak better (worse) than I.*

PATTERN DRILL. Say each sentence below. Then repeat it, endowing the first person (or thing) with more of the adjective or adverb than the second person (or thing) mentioned:

1. Esta casa y aquélla son grandes.   Esta casa es más grande que aquélla.
2. Juan y Jorge ganan mucho.
3. María y Elena leen muchas revistas.
4. Este niño y ése hablan bien.
5. Pablo y su hermano comen poco.
6. Carlos y Enrique escriben mal.
7. Esta película y aquélla son malas.
8. Mi hijo y el tuyo comen poca carne.

24.1.3 *Than.*   Before a number, the Spanish equivalent of *than* is **de:**

Nos pidieron más de cien dólares.   *They asked us for more than $100.*
Juan tiene menos de mil libros.   *John has fewer than one thousand books.*

(An exception to the foregoing is the expression **no** + verb + **más que,** which is one Spanish equivalent of *only:* **Juan no tiene más que mil libros,** *John has only a thousand books.*)

When each clause of a comparison has a different verb, and **más** or **menos** is followed by a noun, the clauses are connected by **del que, de la que, de los que,** or **de las que,** depending on the number and gender of the noun:

Nunca gasto más dinero del que gano.   *I never spend more money than I earn.*
Quiero más libros de los que tengo.   *I want more books than I have.*
Compró menos flores de las que necesitaba.   *. . . fewer flowers than he needed.*

When each clause of a comparison has a different verb, and **más** or **menos** is not followed by a noun (but rather by an adjective or an adverb or nothing), the clauses are connected by **de lo que:**

Es menos caro de lo que Vd. cree.   *It's less expensive than you believe.*
Volví más rápidamente de lo que creían.   *. . . more rapidly than they believed.*
Nunca gasto más de lo que gano.   *I never spend more than I earn.*

PATTERN DRILL.   Complete each of the following comparisons aloud with the proper Spanish equivalent of *than:*

1. Me prestaron más . . . mil dólares.
2. Deseo más pan . . . me han servido.
3. ¿Gastaste más dinero . . . tuviste?

4. Están menos enfermos . . . creemos.
5. No te pido más . . . dos dólares.
6. Compré más fresas . . . comimos.
7. Tienes más libros . . . puedes leer.
8. Soy mucho más fuerte . . . Vd. cree.

24.1.4 Superlatives. The highest or lowest degree of comparison of an adjective that follows a noun is indicated by using the definite article or a possessive adjective before the noun, and the comparative of the adjective after the noun:

Juan es el (mi) alumno más alto.   *John is the (my) tallest student.*

The superlative of an adjective that can precede a noun (such as **bueno**) is indicated by using the definite article or a possessive adjective before the comparative form of the adjective:

Juan es el (mi) mejor alumno.   *John is the (my) best student.*

(Sometimes only context distinguishes between the comparative and the superlative, as in **María es mi hermana menor,** in which **menor** can signify *younger* or *youngest*, depending on how many sisters there are.

After a superlative, the Spanish equivalent of *in* is **de:**

Juan es el alumno más alto de la clase.   . . . *the tallest student in the class.*

María es la mejor alumna de la escuela.   . . . *the best student in the school.*

The superlative degree of an adverb is no different in form from the comparative, and only context distinguishes between the two degrees of comparison:

De los dos, Pablo corre más lentamente.   *Of the two, Paul runs more slowly.*

De los tres, Pablo corre más lentamente.   *Of the three, Paul runs most slowly.*

PATTERN DRILL.   Say each sentence below. Then repeat it, using the superlative of the adjective given, and ending the sentence with **de nuestra escuela:**

1. María es una muchacha bonita.
2. Soy un alumno perezoso. (*lazy*)
3. Carlos es un muchacho fuerte.
4. Elena es una buena alumna.
5. Ellos son buenos profesores.
6. Vds. son alumnos perezosos.
7. Enrique es un muchacho inteligente.
8. Ellos son muchachos bajos.

24.1.5 Absolute Superlative. The statement *I'm reading a most difficult book* is called an *absolute* superlative because it expresses the highest degree of an adjective without making comparison to anything else. English also uses *exceedingly* and *extremely* to indicate absolute superlatives: *She is an exceedingly pretty girl; We left extremely early.*

In Spanish the absolute superlative of adjectives, and of adverbs not ending in **-mente**, is indicated by adding **-ísimo** to the positive form: **formal–formalísimo**, *extremely formal*. If the adjective or adverb ends in a vowel, that vowel is dropped before **-ísimo**: **interesante–interesantísimo**, **temprano–tempranísimo**. The stress of the adjective or adverb is transferred to the new suffix: **fácil–facilísimo**:

> **Estas lecciones son dificilísimas.**   *These lessons are extremely difficult.*

The absolute superlative of adverbs ending in **-mente** is indicated by adding **-ísima** before the **-mente**: **lentamente–lentísimamente**:

> **Lo hice lentísimamente.**   *I did it extremely slowly.*

An absolute superlative can also be indicated by using **muy** (*very*) before an adjective or an adverb. However, the use of **-ísimo** is somewhat more forceful:

> **Esta lección es muy difícil.**   *This lesson is very difficult.*
> **Lo hice muy lentamente.**   *I did it very slowly.*

The one exception to the above is **mucho**, whose absolute superlative is always **muchísimo**:

> **Eso nos gusta muchísimo.**   *We like that very much.*
> **Carlos tiene muchísimos libros.**   *Charles has very many books.*

Why will the **-ísimo** superlatives of **rico, amargo** (*bitter*), and **feliz** be written as **riquísimo, amarguísimo,** and **felicísimo?**

PATTERN DRILL. Say each sentence below. Then repeat it, replacing **muy** with **-ísmo**:

1. La lección sexta es muy fácil.
2. Esa novela es muy larga. (*long*)
3. Mi tío era muy rico.
4. Esta iglesia es muy alta. (*church*)
5. Siempre he comido muy poca carne.
6. Lo envolví muy rápidamente.
7. Ese café está muy amargo.
8. Juan es muy perezoso.

24.2 INFINITIVES

In Spanish, the infinitive form of a verb can be used as the subject or the object of another verb. In such cases, the infinitive functions as a noun, and it is sometimes preceded by **el**:

El escribir es muy difícil.   *Writing is very difficult.*
Preferimos estudiar.   *We prefer studying.*

The infinitive can also be the object of a preposition:

Me lo puse antes de salir.   *I put it on before leaving.*
Después de volver, me lo quité.   *After returning, I took it off.*
Al levantarme, los llamé.   *Upon (on) getting up, I called them.*
Nos fuimos sin decir nada.   *We went away without saying anything.*

The infinitive can replace the subjunctive after CERTAIN verbs: **mandar, aconsejar, hacer** (*to cause*), **dejar, permitir, prohibir,** and **impedir (i, i)** (*to prevent*). When the infinitive construction is used, the person or thing that would have been the subject of the verb in the subjunctive mood then becomes the indirect object of **mandar, aconsejar,** etc.:

Mando que Juan salga.   *I order John to leave.*   **Le mando salir a Juan.**
Él hace que yo estudie.   *He makes me study.*   **Él me hace estudiar.**
Te aconsejo que te levantes.   *I advise you to get up.*   **Te aconsejo levantarte.**
No dejan que fumemos.   *They don't let us smoke.*   **No nos dejan fumar.**

PATTERN DRILL. Say each sentence below. Then repeat it, replacing the subjunctive with the infinitive + indirect object construction:

1. Mando que Vd. no haga eso.
2. No dejaron que yo lo comprara.
3. Hacían que dijéramos la verdad.
4. ¿Nos permite Vd. que salgamos?
5. Les aconsejo a Vds. que vendan la casa.
6. Mandaron que nos levantáramos.
7. Juan impidió que yo los viera.
8. ¿Por qué dejas que Luis lo coma?

24.3 PRESENT PARTICIPLES

The present participles of **-ar** verbs are formed by replacing the **-ar** of the infinitive with **-ando**:

comprando   cerrando   contando

The present participles of **-er** and **-ir** verbs are formed by replacing the **-er** or **-ir** of the infinitive with **-iendo**:

comiendo   viviendo

Those -**ir** verbs that undergo a stem change in the third person of the preterite show the same change in their present participles:

durmiendo sirviendo

When -**iendo** is added to a verb whose stem ends in /-a/ or /-e/, it is written as -**yendo,** as is the present participle of **ir:**

trayendo leyendo yendo

Only three verbs have irregular present participles:

decir–diciendo venir–viniendo poder–pudiendo

The present participle is not inflected.

24.3.1 *Uses of the Present Participle.* The present participle is used less frequently in Spanish than in English. It is not used as a noun, nor does it follow prepositions: instead, the infinitive is used (see 24.2). The Spanish present participle is not used as an adjective either. However, in Spanish, as in English, the present participle can be used as an adverb: the Spanish equivalent of the English "*by* + -*ing*" is the present participle without any preposition before it:

Trabajando mucho, lo terminé ayer. *By working hard, I finished it yesterday.*

The present participle regularly follows **seguir (i, i),** *to continue* or *to keep on.* Note that object pronouns follow the present participle in the usual order, and do not affect its original stress:

Sigo trabajando.	*I continue working.*
¿Por qué sigues hablándoles?	*Why do you keep on speaking to them?*
Juan siguió haciéndolo.	*John continued to do it.*
Seguiremos levantándonos temprano.	*We'll continue to get up early.*
No sigan Vds. mandándomelos.	*Don't continue to send them to me.*

The present participle can also follow **estar** to form the so-called *progressive* tenses, which are used in order to emphasize the fact that an action is, or was, in progress:

¿Qué haces?—Estoy estudiando. . . . *I am studying.*
¿Qué hacías?—Estaba estudiando. . . . *I was studying.*

The present participle also follows **ir** to express an action that is, or was, happening gradually: **Vamos aprendiéndolo,** *We're gradually learning it.* Remember, however, that in Spanish the progressive construction is more emphatic and more vivid than the English "to be + -ing": the usual Spanish equivalent of *I am studying* is **Estudio,** and the usual equivalent of *I was studying* is **Estudiaba.**

PATTERN DRILL. Say each sentence below. Then repeat it, replacing the verb with the corresponding person and tense of **seguir** and the present participle:

1. Juan está muy enfermo.
2. Me levanto a las seis.
3. Te aconsejo no hacer eso.
4. Ella me lo decía a menudo.
5. Te visitaremos los viernes.
6. Mi esposa gasta más que yo.
7. ¿Lees esa novela larguísima?
8. ¿Nos escribirás?

24.4 INDEFINITE ARTICLE

In Spanish, the indefinite article is omitted in various contexts where you are accustomed to using it in English. For example, in negative sentences:

No tengo pluma.   *I don't have a pen.*
No hay naranjas.   *There aren't any oranges.*

The indefinite article is also omitted after **ser** when this verb is followed by an unmodified noun indicating occupation, nationality, and religious or political affiliation:

Mi padre es abogado.   *My father is a lawyer.*
Juan es español.   *John is a Spaniard.*
¿Eres conservador?   *Are you a Conservative?*

However, when such nouns are accompanied by an adjective, the indefinite article is used:

Carlos es un pintor famoso.   *Charles is a famous painter.*

The indefinite article is omitted before **cierto** (*a certain*) and **otro** (*another*), as well as after **sin, tal** (*such a*), and the exclamation ¡**qué**! (*what a!*):

Cierto hombre me lo dijo.   *A certain man told it to me.*
¿Buscas otra silla?   *Are you looking for another chair?*
Salí sin sombrero.   *I went out without a hat.*
¿Has visto tal cosa jamás?   *Have you ever seen such a thing?*
¡Qué hombre!   *What a man!*

Note that when an adjective follows a noun in an exclamation, the two are separated by **más** or **tan,** which have no English equivalents in this context:

¡Qué capítulo más largo!	*What a long chapter!*
¡Qué muchachas tan bonitas!	*What pretty girls!*

PATTERN DRILL. Answer each of the following questions affirmatively, using **Sí** and a complete sentence:

1. ¿Viniste sin dinero?
2. ¿Es arquitecto tu padre?
3. ¿Comprarías tal corbata?
4. ¿Es Juan un estudiante perezoso?
5. ¿Necesitan Vds. otra criada?
6. ¿Era tu abuelo un abogado famoso?
7. ¿Sales sin guantes?
8. ¿Te dijo eso cierto hombre?

24.5 DEFINITE ARTICLE

In Spanish, the definite article is used in various contexts where you are accustomed to omitting it in English. For example, it precedes abstract nouns and nouns used in general statements:

La justicia es importante.	*Justice is important.*
El poder corrompe.	*Power corrupts.* (**corromper**)
Los diamantes son caros.	*Diamonds* [in general] *are expensive.*
Las hojas son verdes.	*Leaves* [in general] *are green.*

The definite article also precedes the names of languages, except when the language immediately follows **de, en, hablar, estudiar,** and **aprender:**

El español es una lengua difícil.	*Spanish is a difficult language.*
¿Tienes mi libro de francés?	*Do you have my French book?*
La carta está escrita en inglés.	*The letter is written in English.*
Hablamos italiano en casa.	*We speak Italian at home.*

(If only a subject pronoun separates a language from one of the preceding verbs, the definite article is still omitted: **¿Habla Vd. español?**)

The definite article precedes most titles, except in direct address:

¿Conoces al señor López?	*Do you know Mr. Lopez?*
Vimos al profesor García.	*We saw Professor García.*
Buenos días, señorita Olmedo.	*Good morning, Miss Olmedo.*

One title that is never preceded by a definite article is **don** (feminine **doña**), which is used only before a given name. It used to be a title of nobility, but now it is merely a title of respect. It has no English equivalent:

Vimos a don Jorge.   ¿Conocen Vds. a doña Elena?

PATTERN DRILL. Answer each of the following questions affirmatively, using Sí and a complete sentence:

1. ¿Es difícil el ruso? (*Russian*)
2. ¿Hablan Vds. inglés en casa?
3. ¿Te gustan las naranjas?
4. ¿Quieres visitar al señor García?

5. ¿Sabes decirlo en español?
6. ¿Es barato el pan?
7. ¿Conoces al capitán Gómez?
8. ¿Vieron Vds. a don Antonio?

24.6 IRREGULAR VERBS

The various forms of the two verbs that follow are more easily memorized than categorized.

24.6.1 *Oír: to hear.* Can you explain the accent marks and the spelling changes in the written forms of **oír**?

	PRESENT INDICATIVE		PRETERITE	
First person:	oigo	oímos	oí	oímos
Second person:	oyes	oís	oíste	oísteis
Third person:	oye	oyen	oyó	oyeron

The present subjunctive of **oír** is **oiga, oigas,** etc. The imperfect subjunctive is **oyera–oyese,** etc. The past participle is **oído,** and the present participle is **oyendo.**

PATTERN DRILL. Answer each of the following questions affirmatively, using Sí and a complete sentence:

1. ¿Oyes la música?
2. ¿Oíste ese discurso? (*speech*)
3. ¿Dudabas que yo lo oyera?
4. ¿Es posible que ellos nos oigan?

5. ¿Era imposible que Juan lo oyera?
6. ¿Siempre oyes lo que te digo?
7. ¿Oyeron Vds. el discurso de Carlos?
8. ¿Oye Vd. ese ruido? (*noise*)

24.6.2 *Reír (i, i): to laugh.* **Reír** is also used reflexively with no change in meaning. **Reírse de** is the Spanish equivalent of *to laugh at.* **Reír** has the following forms in the present indicative:

First person:	río	reímos
Second person:	ríes	reís
Third person:	ríe	ríen

The present subjunctive of **reír** is **ría, rías, ría, riamos, riáis, rían.** Note the diphthong of the first person plural and the triphthong of the second person plural.

The preterite indicative of **reír** is doubly irregular in that the -i- of the third person markers is lost:

First person: **reí**   **reímos**
Second person: **reíste**   **reísteis**
Third person: **rió**   **rieron**

The imperfect subjunctive is **riera–riese**, etc. The past participle is **reído**, and the present participle is **riendo**.

PATTERN DRILL. Answer each of the following questions affirmatively, using **Sí** and a complete sentence:

1. ¿Ríe Juan mucho hoy?
2. ¿Se rió Vd. de mí ayer?
3. ¿Dudas que ese hombre ría mucho?
4. ¿Querías que el niño riera?

5. ¿Se ríen Vds. de mi discurso?
6. ¿Era preciso que Vd. se riera de él?
7. ¿Te ríes de tu hermano ahora?
8. ¿Es imposible que Vds. rían?

Lesson 25

25.1 PERFECT INFINITIVE

An inflected verb or a preposition can be followed by the infinitive **haber** and a past participle. This is the Spanish counterpart of the English *to have* + past participle. Since this Spanish construction is so similar to its English equivalent, it will offer you no difficulty the few times you may come across it:

Sentíamos no haber visto eso.   *We were sorry not to have seen that.*
Me alegro de haberlo terminado.   *I am happy to have finished it.*
Salió después de habérmelo dicho.   *He left after having told it to me.*

25.2 DEBER

When the "regular" verb **deber** is not followed by an infinitive, it is the equivalent of the English *to owe:*

    Carlos me debe dos dólares.   *Charles owes me two dollars.*
    ¿Cuánto te debían?   *How much did they owe you?*
    Vd. no nos deberá nada.   *You won't owe us anything.*

Before an infinitive, on the other hand, **deber** is equivalent to the English *must,* either in the sense of obligation or else in the sense of probability, depending on context. **Deber** and an infinitive are sometimes connected by **de** to express probability:

    Debo estudiar más.   *I must (ought to) study harder.*
    Deben (de) ser las tres.   *It must be (probably is) three o'clock.*

Obligation or probability in the past can be indicated with the preterite or imperfect tense of **deber,** or else with the present tense of **deber** and a perfect infinitive. Either construction is equivalent to an English perfect tense because of the nature of the English auxiliaries *must, ought,* and *should:*

Debí estudiar or Debo haber estudiado.   *I should have studied.*
Debía ser la una or Debe haber sido la una.   *It must have been one o'clock.*
It probably was one o'clock.

The difference between **tener que** and **deber** is that the former implies compulsion or necessity, whereas the latter implies duty or moral obligation:

Tengo que devolverlo.   *I have to return it.*
Debo devolverlo.   *I ought to (should) return it.*

Sometimes the imperfect indicative, the conditional, or the imperfect subjunctive in **-ra** of **deber** are used rather than the present indicative to express recommendation, especially in direct address:

Vd. debía (debería, debiera) hacerlo.   *You ought to do it.*
Debías (deberías, debieras) volver.   *You should return.*
Vds. no debían (deberían, debieran) decir eso.   *You shouldn't say that.*

PATTERN DRILL. Complete each of the following sentences with the required person of the present tense of **deber**. Do you know the meaning of each sentence?

1. Ese coche . . . de ser muy caro.
2. Juan no vino; . . . estar malo.
3. Devuélveme el dinero que me . . .
4. Supongo que yo . . . trabajar más.
5. Vds. . . . volver a casa temprano.
6. ¿A qué hora . . . levantarnos?
7. Ellos no . . . dar helado al perro.
8. María . . . haber llegado anoche.

25.3 DESCRIPTIVE ADJECTIVES: POSITION

In Lesson 7 you learned that in Spanish, unlike English, most descriptive adjectives usually follow the nouns to which they refer. Now that you are well accustomed to this difference between the two languages, you are ready for some exceptions.

About a dozen Spanish descriptive adjectives vary in meaning depending on their position. Some of these descriptive adjectives have a literal meaning after nouns, and a more or less figurative meaning before nouns:

pobre: **La mujer pobre no tiene dinero.**   *The poor (penniless) woman . . .*

La pobre mujer está muy mala.   *The poor (pitiable) woman . . .*

nuevo: **Compré un coche nuevo.**   *I bought a new (newly made) car.*

Compré un nuevo coche.   *I bought another car.*

viejo:	Tengo muchos amigos viejos.	I have many old (elderly) friends.
	Tengo muchos viejos amigos.	I have many old (of long standing) friends.

antiguo:	¿Viste aquella casa antigua?	Did you see that old house?
	¿Viste a tu antigua criada?	Did you see your old (former) maid?

grande:	Fue un hombre grande.	He was a large man.
	Fue un gran hombre.	He was a great (distinguished) man.

(Before a singular noun of either gender, **grande** usually becomes **gran**.)

The distinction "figurative–literal" cannot be applied to the different meanings of some other descriptive adjectives which can either precede or follow nouns:

único:	Juan tiene mi corbata única.	John has my unique tie.
	Juan tiene mi única corbata.	John has my only tie.

medio:	Es un hombre medio.	He is an average man.
	Comí media manzana.	I ate half an apple.

mismo:	Juan mismo lo trajo.	John himself brought it.
	El mismo hombre lo trajo.	The same man brought it.

simple:	Luis es un muchacho simple.	Louis is a simple-minded boy.
	Luis es un simple muchacho.	Louis is a mere boy.

cierto:	Busco información cierta.	I'm looking for reliable information.
	Busco cierto libro.	I'm looking for a particular book.

varios:	Se venden libros varios.	Miscellaneous books for sale.
	Compré varios libros.	I bought several books.

PATTERN DRILL. Answer each of the following questions affirmatively, using **Sí** and a complete sentence:

1. ¿Necesita dinero un hombre pobre?
2. ¿Está muy malo ese pobre muchacho?
3. ¿Fue Simón Bolívar un gran hombre?
4. ¿Fue Wáshington un hombre grande?
5. ¿Han muerto tus amigos viejos?
6. ¿Compras un coche nuevo este año?

7. ¿Es Juan tu único hermano?
8. ¿Viste ese partido único?

25.3.1 *Descriptive Adjectives: Position.* You will occasionally find other descriptive adjectives preceding nouns, as in **Esos animales viven en la verde selva,** *Those animals live in the green jungle.*

Following a noun, a descriptive adjective differentiates that noun from others of the same kind. For example, **Vivo en una casa verde.** Green is not a general or normal characteristic of houses, and since **verde** provides information that distinguishes "my" house from other houses, it properly follows **casa.** On the other hand, in **Esos animales viven en la verde selva,** the adjective **verde** expresses a quality that is usually considered characteristic of the jungle. No one ever speaks of a red or a blue jungle. In this context, **verde** can even be omitted without altering the meaning of the sentence. Descriptive adjectives are placed before a noun merely to enhance the value of the noun, and not to differentiate or classify it. You can safely leave this to the poets.

Two descriptive adjectives that often precede nouns are **bueno** (*good*) and **malo** (*bad*). Before a masculine singular noun **bueno** regularly becomes **buen,** and **malo** regularly shortens to **mal:**

Tengo un buen libro.	**Tengo un mal libro.**
Tengo una buena revista.	**Tengo una mala revista.**

The difference between **un buen libro** and **un libro bueno** is not of meaning, but rather of outlook. Before a noun **bueno** and **malo** express personal value judgments. After a noun, on the other hand, they merely classify. Although it is human nature to give opinions, a safe "rule of thumb" is to place **bueno** and **malo** after the nouns that they describe, unless you are answering a question in which they precede.

Since differentiation or classification are the primary functions of most of the descriptive adjectives that you will be using, a good "rule of thumb" is always to place descriptive adjectives indicating color, size, shape, nationality, condition, quality, etc., after the nouns to which they refer.

As you know, when a noun is modified by two adjectives that follow nouns, these adjectives are usually joined by **y: Vivo en una casa roja y blanca.** When a noun is modified by two adjectives that can precede nouns, both these adjectives precede that noun, and they are not joined: **Mi pobre viejo amigo tiene hambre,** *My pitiable friend of long standing is hungry.* This is not very common because of the limited number of adjectives that precede nouns. When a noun is modified by one descriptive adjective that can precede and by another that follows, then that word order is used: **Mi viejo amigo pobre tiene hambre,** *My penniless friend of long standing is hungry.*

25.4 APOCOPATION

Apocopation is the technical term for the shortening of **bueno** and **malo** to **buen** and **mal**. Other adjectives that you have leaned to apocopate before masculine singular nouns are **alguno, ninguno, primero,** and **tercero.** You have also seen the apocopation of **grande** and **cualquiera** before singular nouns of either gender, and that of **ciento** to **cien** before plural nouns of either gender and before numbers that are larger than 100 (**cien mil**).

The only other Spanish adjectives that are apocopated are **postrero** (*last*), which becomes **postrer** before masculine singular nouns, and **Santo** (*Saint*), which becomes **San** before all masculine names except those beginning with /do-/ and /to-/: **San Luis, San Juan,** but **Santo Domingo, Santo Tomás.**

PATTERN DRILL. Answer each of the following questions affirmatively, using **Sí** and a complete sentence:

1. ¿Leíste las cartas de Santa Teresa?
2. ¿Fueron Vds. a San Luis?
3. ¿Me prestas ciento quince dólares?
4. ¿Necesita Vd. cien pesetas?
5. ¿Has estudiado la primera lección?
6. ¿Leyeron Vds. el primer capítulo?
7. ¿Es Madrid una ciudad grande?
8. ¿Fue Bolívar un gran hombre?

25.5 ADJECTIVES USED AS NOUNS AND PRONOUNS

An adjective can be used as a noun or as a pronoun if it is preceded by a definite or indefinite article, a demonstrative adjective, or a number:

El viejo me lo dio.	*The old man gave it to me.* (noun)
Una vieja nos lo dijo.	*An old woman told it to us.* (noun)
Esos viejos lo vieron.	*Those old people saw it.* (noun)
Conocimos a dos españolas.	*We met two Spanish women.* (noun)
Deseo esta corbata y la roja.	*. . . and the red one.* (pronoun)
Deseo estos guantes y esos rojos.	*. . . and those red ones.* (pronoun)
Deseo una rosa blanca y tres rojas.	*. . . and three red ones.* (pronoun)

An adjectival phrase beginning with **de** can also be made into a noun or a pronoun in the same ways:

Compraré esa blusa y la de seda.   *. . . and the silk one.* (pronoun)

The masculine indefinite article assumes the forms **uno** or **una** before an adjective or an adjectival phrase used as a pronoun:

Deso ese lápiz y uno azul.   *. . . and a blue one.*

Compré esta falda y una de lana.   *. . . and a woolen one.*

PATTERN DRILL. Complete each sentence below with the form of the definite article called for by context:

1. ¿Desea Vd. este abrigo o . . . gris?
2. Limpié estos zapatos y . . . negros.
3. ¿Prefieres estas rosas o . . . blancas?
4. Compraré esa corbata y . . . de seda.
5. ¿Quieres estos guantes o . . . de lana?
6. Necesito esa blusa y . . . roja.
7. Siento que . . . viejo muriera.
8. Me gustan esa casa y . . . de ladrillo.

25.6 USES OF THE NEUTER ARTICLE

The neuter article **lo** is used before the masculine singular forms of adjectives in order to make nouns expressing abstract qualities. These **lo** + adjective combinations have various English equivalents:

No puedo hacer lo imposible.	*I can't do the impossible.*
Lo difícil del libro es . . .	*The hard part of the book is . . .*
Lo mejor sería esperar.	*The best thing would be to wait.*
Lo peor fue que . . .	*The worst of it was that . . .*

The neuter article **lo** is also used before inflected adjectives that are followed by **que** and **estar** or **ser.** In this position, **lo** is equivalent to the English *how* of extent or degree:

No sabes lo enferma que está María.	*You don't know how sick Mary is.*
¿Ves lo rojas que son esas rosas?	*Do you see how red those roses are?*

Lo is used before **más** and an adverb followed by **posible.** This construction is equivalent to the English "as + adverb + as possible":

Vine lo más rápidamente posible.	*I came as rapidly as possible.*
Vuelvan lo más temprano posible.	*Return as early as possible.*

The same construction is used when **que** and **poder** follow an adverb:

Vine lo más temprano que pude.	*I came as early as I could.*

Lo de is equivalent to the English *that business of* or *that matter of:*

Lo de ayer fue estúpido.	*That business of yesterday was stupid.*
Lo de la criada es importante.	*That matter of the maid is important.*

PATTERN DRILL. Complete each sentence below with **lo.** Do you know the meaning of each sentence?

1. . . . mejor sería hacerlo ahora.
2. . . . más difícil es llegar a tiempo.
3. . . . único que necesito es pan.
4. . . . de anoche no fue importante.

5. Me levanté . . . más tarde posible. 7. . . . más importante es hallarla.
6. No sabes . . . tristes que estamos. 8. Estudien Vds. . . . del subjuntivo.

25.7 OBJECT PRONOUNS

A direct or an indirect object noun may precede its verb for emphasis. When this happens, the corresponding object pronoun is also used:

Ese libro lo compré en Madrid.	*I bought that book in Madrid.*
A Juan lo vi en la cocina.	*I saw John in the kitchen.*
A María le di las naranjas.	*I gave the oranges to Mary.*
A esos niños les gusta el helado.	*Those boys like ice cream.*

The direct object pronoun **lo** is regularly used with **saber, decir,** and **preguntar** (*to ask*) when these verbs have no other direct object or are not followed by a clause. Often this **lo** has no English equivalent:

Sí, sabemos la verdad.	but:	**Sí, lo sabemos.**	*Yes, we know.*
Juan me dijo que vendría.	but:	**Juan me lo dijo.**	*John told me.*
Les preguntaré el secreto.	but:	**Se lo preguntaré a ellos.**	*I'll ask them.*

PATTERN DRILL. Complete each sentence below with the proper object pronoun:

1. Esos vasos . . . rompió la criada.
2. A esos niños . . . dimos mucha leche.
3. A tu esposa . . . vimos ayer.
4. ¿Cuándo te . . . dijeron?
5. Aquella película . . . vi en 1957.
6. A él no . . . prestaremos nada.
7. Esas flores me . . . dio Roberto.
8. ¿Por qué me . . . preguntas?

25.8 RECIPROCITY

The Spanish equivalent of "we + verb + each other" is **nos** used with a first-person plural verb form. The Spanish equivalent of "they + verb + each other" is **se** used with a third-person plural verb form:

Nos odiamos.	*We hate each other.*
Juan y María se quieren.	*John and Mary love each other.*

Sometimes reciprocal **se** and **nos** are accompanied by **uno a otro, una a otra, el uno al otro, la una a la otra, unos a otros,** etc.:

Nos escribíamos el uno al otro. *We used to write to each other.*

This construction is unavoidable when reflexive verbs are used reciprocally:

Las niñas se visten una a otra.	*The little girls dress each other.*
Nos despertamos el uno al otro.	*We woke each other up.*

Compare the sentences above with:

Las niñas se visten.	*The little girls get dressed* [severally].
Nos despertamos.	*We woke up* [severally].

PATTERN DRILL. Answer each of the following questions affirmatively, using **Sí** and a complete sentence:

1. ¿Se vieron Vds. anoche?
2. ¿Se quieren Vd. y Juan?
3. ¿Van a verse Vd. y Carlos?
4. ¿Se escribían Vd. y María?

5. ¿Se hablan Teresa y Juan?
6. ¿Van a escribirse esas mujeres?
7. ¿Se odian Pedro y Jorge?
8. ¿Se querían mucho tus abuelos?

25.9 NOUNS

Spanish nouns of Greek origin ending in **-ma, -pa,** and **-ta** are usually masculine: **el idioma,** *language;* **el mapa,** *map;* **el poeta,** *poet.*

When a *singular* feminine noun beginning with stressed /a-/ must be preceded by the definite article, the special feminine definite article **el** is used:

El agua está fría.	*The water is cold.*
¿Rompiste el hacha nueva?	*Did you break the new axe?*
El águila y la serpiente	*The Eagle and the Serpent* (a Mexican novel)

25.10 EUPHONY

The conjunction /i/, written **y,** is replaced by /e/, written **e,** before a word beginning with /i-/:

Hablamos español e inglés.	*We speak Spanish and English.*
Fernando e Isabel lo firmaron.	*Ferdinand and Isabella signed it.*
González e Hijos.	*González and Sons.*

The conjunction /o/, written **o,** is replaced by /u/, written **u,** before a word beginning with /o-/:

Mándeme siete u ocho.	*Send me seven or eight.*
¿Eres mujer u hombre?	*Are you a woman or a man?*

PATTERN DRILL.   Answer each of the following questions affirmatively, using
Sí and a complete sentence:

1. ¿Vinieron Roberto e Isabel?   5. ¿Son Vds. arquitectos e ingenieros?
2. ¿Estaba fría el agua?   6. ¿Ves el águila?
3. ¿Compraste ese mapa viejo?   7. ¿Tienes el hacha nueva?
4. ¿Comprendes muchos idiomas?   8. ¿Estudia Vd. español e historia?

25.11 IDIOMS

For practical purposes, an *idiom* may be defined as a combination of
Spanish words whose English equivalent cannot be readily deduced from
the meanings of the individual words. For example, when the present tense
of **acabar** (*to finish*) is followed by **de** (*of*) and an infinitive, the resultant
combination is equivalent to the English "*to have just +* past participle":

> **Acabo de comer.**   *I have just eaten.*
> **¿Acabas de levantarte?**   *Have you just gotten up?*
> **Acaban de volver.**   *They have just returned.*

The imperfect tense of **acabar** followed by **de** and an infinitive is equivalent
to the English "*had just +* past participle":

> **Cuando llegué, Juan acababa de salir.**   *. . . John had just left.*
> **Acabábamos de venderlo.**   *We had just sold it.*

When **volver** (*to return*) is followed by **a** (*to*) and an infinitive, the
resultant idiom means "to perform the action [of the infinitive] again":

> **Vuelvo a hacerlo.**   *I'm doing it again.*
> **Jorge volvió a salir.**   *George went out again.*
> **No vuelvas a escribirles.**   *Don't write to them again.*

Not all Spanish idioms contain a verb. **Ya no,** which precedes verbs, is
equivalent to the English *no longer* (or *not . . . anymore*):

> **Ya no vivo allí.**   *I no longer live there.*
> **Pablo ya no trabaja aquí.**   *Paul doesn't work here anymore.*

PATTERN DRILL (A).   Answer each of the following questions with the
present tense of **acabar de** and the infinitive of the verb used in the
question:

1. ¿Cuándo saliste?   Acabo de salir.
2. ¿Cuándo te levantaste?
3. ¿Cuándo lo compró Vd.?
4. ¿Cuándo me lo mandaste?
5. ¿Cuándo llegó Juan?

6. ¿Cuándo se despertaron Vds.?
7. ¿Cuándo te lo preguntó María?
8. ¿Cuándo lo trajeron Vds.?

PATTERN DRILL (B). Say each sentence below. Then repeat it, using the corresponding person and tense of **volver a** rather than **de nuevo:**

1. Juan me habla de nuevo.   Juan vuelve a hablarme.
2. Ellos se quejan de nuevo.
3. Me acuesto de nuevo.
4. El niño se lo quita de nuevo.
5. Jorge me lo manda de nuevo.
6. Los llamaré de nuevo.
7. ¿Salieron Vds. de nuevo?
8. ¿Me lo dirás de nuevo?

PATTERN DRILL (C). Answer each of the following questions negatively, using **No** and a sentence in which **ya no** precedes the verb:

1. ¿Está Vd. ocupado?
2. ¿Te gusta la cerveza?
3. ¿Come Vd. mucho pan?
4. ¿Se bañan Vds. los sábados?
5. ¿Tienen Vds. hambre?
6. ¿Está enferma Isabel?
7. ¿Sales con Elena?
8. ¿Vives en una ciudad grande?

Appendix

A.1 PRETERITE PERFECT

The preterite perfect tense, formed with the preterite indicative of **haber** and a past participle, is another Spanish equivalent of the English *I had +* past participle. It is found only in literature, where it is used only after temporal conjunctions such as **cuando, luego que** (*as soon as*), **apenas** (*hardly, scarcely*), and **no bien** (*no sooner*) in order to express an action that occurred immediately before another past action. In conversation the preterite perfect is usually replaced by the preterite or by the pluperfect. **Haber** has the irregular preterite stem **hub-**:

Cuando hube comido, salí.	*When I had eaten, I left.*
Llegaron luego que hubimos vuelto.	*They arrived as soon as we had returned.*
Apenas Vd. hubo salido cuando él llamó.	*Hardly had you left when he called.*
No bien hubieron venido cuando empezó a llover.	*No sooner had they come . . .*

PATTERN DRILL. Complete each sentence below with the required person of the preterite perfect of the infinitive in parentheses:

1. No bien yo (*hacer*) eso cuando mi padre volvió a casa.
2. Tan pronto como te (*acostar*), Carlos llamó. (*as soon as*)
3. Cuando Vd. (*terminar*), ellos salieron del cuarto.
4. Así que mi madre me lo (*decir*), salí de casa.
5. Fuimos a la playa luego que mis primos (*llegar*).
6. Después que nos (*levantar*), lo hicimos. (*after*)
7. Apenas se (*abrir*) el banco cuando los ladrones llegaron.
8. En cuanto Vds. (*salir*), Juan los llamó. (*as soon as*)

A.2 OBJECT PRONOUNS: POSITION

Up to now you have placed direct and indirect object pronouns after infinitives and present participles. A pronoun that is the object of an infinitive or of a present participle may also precede the inflected auxiliary verb:

Va a dármelo or **Me lo va a dar.**   *He is going to give it to me.*
Sigo estudiándolo or **Lo sigo estudiando.**   *I continue to study it.*

In literature you will occasionally find object pronouns following an inflected verb that begins a sentence: **Díjonos que vendría,** *He told us that he would come.* It is not necessary for you to imitate this.

A.3 OBJECT PRONOUNS: «LEÍSMO»

In some parts of the Spanish-speaking world, the direct object pronouns **lo** and **los** are not used. Instead, they are replaced by **le** and **les**:

¿Juan? —No le vi.   *John? I didn't see him.*
Les llamé ayer.   *I called them yesterday.*

Some "authorities" recommend as a safe medium the use of **le** and **les** when the direct object is a masculine person, and the use of **lo** and **los** when the direct object is a masculine thing. However, this distinction is by no means universal. Since the Spaniards themselves cannot agree, you may use either **le** and **les** or **lo** and **los** as masculine direct object pronouns.

Sample Oral
Examination

The questions in Parts I–X are worth one point each. The questions in Part XI are worth two points each (one for the content and one for the Spanish).

PART I. GENERAL KNOWLEDGE

Answer each of the following questions to the best of your ability in Spanish. Use a complete sentence whenever possible.

1. ¿Cómo se llama Vd.?
2. ¿Cuántos años tiene Vd.?
3. ¿Se venden libros en una carnicería?
4. ¿Cuántos son trescientos más doscientos?
5. ¿En qué año descubrió Colón el Nuevo Mundo?
6. ¿Qué tiempo hace hoy?
7. ¿Qué día de la semana será mañana?
8. ¿En qué país está Vd. ahora mismo?
9. ¿Cuántos días hay en este mes?
10. ¿A qué hora se levantó Vd. esta mañana?
11. ¿Fue Vd. al cine anoche?
12. ¿Qué hora es?
13. ¿Cuántos son ciento por diez?
14. ¿Le gustan a Vd. las naranjas?
15. ¿Cuántos minutos hay en una hora?

PART II. REPETITION DRILL

Repeat each word or group of words that you hear.

1. Juan es mexicano.
2. ¿Están Vds. ocupados?
3. Bebo mucho vino.

4. Roberto quiere mi perro.
5. ¿Qué hace ella?
6. En el invierno.
7. En Europa.
8. Veinte más treinta.
9. Vinimos la semana pasada.
10. Tres fresas grandes.

PART III. QUESTION & ANSWER DRILL

Answer each question affirmatively, using **Sí** and a complete sentence. Listen to this practice question and answer.

Question: **¿Tienes mi libro?**   Answer: **Sí, tengo tu libro.**

1. ¿Tienes mis plumas?
2. ¿Tiene Vd. mi lápiz?
3. ¿Tiene Vd. nuestras libretas?
4. ¿Tiene Juan el coche de Vd.?
5. ¿Vive María en la casa de Vds.?

PART IV. TRANSFORMATION DRILL

Repeat each sentence as a command. Listen to this practice sentence.

Cue: **Vd. come.**   Response: **Coma Vd.**

1. Vd. viene.
2. Vds. estudian.
3. Vd. me escribe.
4. Vd. me lo da.
5. Vd. no me lo dice.

PART V. TRANSFORMATION DRILL

Repeat each sentence, changing the verb to the present tense, indicative mood. Listen to this practice sentence.

Cue: **Comí poco.**   Response: **Como poco.**

1. Lo haré.
2. Volví tarde.
3. He visto a Juan.
4. Carlos tendrá hambre.
5. Me reí.
6. Fuimos al centro.

7. La conocí.
8. Me acosté.
9. Eran las tres.
10. Me lo puse.

PART VI. QUESTION & ANSWER
REPLACEMENT DRILL

Answer each question affirmatively, using **Sí** and a sentence containing the object pronouns that correspond to the nouns used in the question. Listen carefully to this practice sentence.

Question: **¿Compras el libro?**   Answer: **Sí, lo compro.**

1. ¿Ves a las muchachas?
2. ¿Escribes a Juan?
3. ¿Te pones los guantes?
4. ¿Das el libro a Carlos?
5. ¿Da Vd. las fresas a Pablo?
6. ¿Me prestas el dinero?
7. ¿Nos presta Vd. los libros?
8. ¿Vas a darme el queso?
9. ¿Va Vd. a darme las flores?
10. ¿Quieres que te mande el libro?

PART VII. QUESTION & ANSWER DRILL

Answer each question negatively, using **No** and a complete negative sentence. Listen carefully to this practice question and answer.

Question: **¿Lo tienes?**   Answer: **No, no lo tengo.**

1. ¿Ven Vds. a alguien?
2. ¿Viene alguien?
3. ¿Necesita Vd. algo?
4. ¿Dudas que Juan lo sepa?
5. ¿Van Vds. también?
6. ¿Va Juan con Vd.?
7. ¿Saldrías si hiciera frío?
8. ¿Fue rota la ventana por Juan?
9. ¿Son ellas buenas amigas tuyas?
10. ¿Vino alguna de esas muchachas?

PART VIII. EXPANSION DRILL

Repeat each sentence, beginning it with **Siento que.** There is no model sentence.

1. María no viene.
2. Juan lo hace.
3. Vds. han vuelto.
4. Vd. sale ahora.
5. Ella lo sabe.

PART IX. EXPANSION DRILL

Repeat each sentence, beginning it with **Es imposible que.** There is no model sentence.

1. Juan lo tiene.
2. Dormimos mucho.
3. Vds. van al cine.
4. Servimos cerveza.
5. Lo traemos.

PART X. EXPANSION DRILL

Repeat each sentence, beginning it with **Era preciso que.** There is no model sentence.

1. Lo hacemos.
2. Pongo la mesa.
3. Vamos al centro.
4. Te lo digo.
5. Vds. lo devuelven.

PART XI. COMPREHENSION DRILL

Listen carefully to the following story. You will hear it twice, and then you will be asked some questions.

Juan vivía en el sur de España. Era pobre, y no tenía más que un caballo. Este animal era blanco y viejo, y no podía trabajar mucho. Por eso Juan quería venderlo y comprar un caballo más fuerte. Un día Juan salió de casa muy temprano y fue a un pueblo cerca de su casa. En el mercado vendió su caballo por mil pesetas. Después de buscar mucho, vio un caballo negro que le gustaba. El hombre que lo vendía pedía dos mil pesetas. Le dijo a Juan que ese caballo era joven y fuerte, y que también sabía leer. Juan dudaba que eso fuera verdad, y antes de comprar el caballo negro, le mostró un periódico. El caballo miró el periódico como si lo leyera, pero no dijo nada. Juan empezó a reírse. El vendedor le dijo que aunque el caballo sabía leer muy bien, no sabía hablar. Al fin, Juan lo compró. El caballo fue directamente a la casa de Juan sin que éste tuviera que decirle nada. Eso le extrañó mucho, y al llegar a casa, dijo a su esposa que había comprado un caballo maravilloso. Cuando Juan y su esposa hablaban, empezó a llover mucho. La esposa se acercó a la ventana porque quería ver ese animal tan caro e inteligente. Después de un par de minutos, gritó a su esposo: —Mira, Juan, ese caballo no es negro, sino blanco. Cuando Juan salió a mirar el caballo, vio que era el mismo animal que él había vendido esa mañana: alguien lo había pintado de negro. La esposa, furiosa, le preguntó: —Estúpido, ¿cómo es posible que hayas vivido diez años con ese caballo y no lo reconocieras?

Each question will be asked twice, and then there will be a pause for your answer.

1. ¿Dónde vivía Juan?
2. ¿Cuántos caballos tenía?
3. ¿Por qué deseaba Juan vender su caballo blanco?
4. ¿Cuánto recibió por su animal?
5. ¿De qué color era el caballo que le gustaba?
6. ¿Qué dudaba Juan?
7. ¿Qué hizo el caballo cuando Juan le mostró el periódico?
8. ¿Adónde fue la esposa de Juan cuando empezó a llover?
9. ¿Qué descubrió Juan cuando salió a mirar su nuevo caballo blanco?
10. ¿Cuántos años hacía que Juan tenía el caballo blanco?

Index

API